the
Likely
Lads
?

The cover picture shows James Bolam as Terry and Rodney Bewes as Bob. (*Radio Times*)

'BBC character comedy at its unbeaten best'
Peter Black on the programme in the *Daily Mail*.

What ever happened to the Likely Lads ?

by Dick Clements and Ian La Frenais
adapted from the T.V. Series
by Patrick Tilley

British Broadcasting Corporation

Published by the British Broadcasting Corporation,
35 Marylebone High Street, London W1M 4AA
ISBN 0 563 12569 1
First published 1974
Reprinted 1975

Printed in England by Hunt Barnard Printing Ltd,
Aylesbury, Bucks

Contents

I

Strangers on a Train

Bob Ferris twisted the lens of the slide projector into focus on the wall of Thelma's mother's living-room, sat back on the arm of her settee and clicked in the first colour slide.

'Picture One. Our plot.'

Thelma sat beside him in the darkness. She gave his free hand a cozy squeeze and let out a long happy sigh.

For good measure, Bob pressed the automatic focus control and blurred the pictures in and out of focus in an effort to improve on his original setting. Having exhibited his mastery of Japanese electronics, he reset the lens by hand and sighed in his turn at the coloured image on the wall.

Picture One was a stunningly uninteresting view of a windswept north-eastern plot of land marked out with pegs and string.

'What's that in the sky?' asked Thelma.

'They're your mother's flying geese,' said Bob. 'I forgot to take them down off the wall.'

Thelma gave his hand another warm squeeze to indicate that it was time for the next slide.

Picture Two was the same plot of land, but with the addition of a large pile of bricks and a concrete mixer. Bob was perched proudly on top of the bricks like Hilary on top of Everest.

Picture Three was yet another view of the building site. In the pouring rain. The foundations and main drains had been put in. Thelma stood in the embryo hallway in a yellow raincoat and an outsize pair of wellington boots.

Bob broke into a laugh.

'Where on earth did you get those wellies?'

'Off the man in the site office. Don't you remember? The little one with the limp.'

'Oh, yes,' said Bob, not able to remember any little man at all, with or without a limp. He clicked in the next slide.

Picture Four was yet another picture of the building site. This time their dream house had grown a full foot and a half out of the ground.

The appearance of so many bricks earned Bob another warm squeeze.

'Oh, Bob, look . . . the damp course . . . '

'How could I ever forget.'

Picture Five showed the outside walls complete to the eaves. The bare rafters of the roof are now in place.

'Ahhhh . . . ' said Thelma. 'The roof.'

Any additional comment seemed superfluous, so Bob pressed the slide button. They both gazed at Picture Six.

'Of my house,' said Bob. There they both were, arm in arm, on the threshold of their brand-new house, both dying for a pee but unable to go because a workman had cracked the lavatory pan.

'My house,' said Bob. 'I can't get used to saying that. "Have you seen my house? Why don't you all come round to *my* house? We can always meet at my house. As a matter of fact, I'm thinking of selling my house." '

'Oh, come on,' said Thelma. 'We haven't moved in yet. Anyway, it's *our* house.'

The rebuke was delivered sweetly, but there was enough sharpness underneath the sugar to prompt Bob back into line.

'Of course, love. *Our* house. Chez nous.'

Thelma cuddled against him in a warm moment of togetherness. 'Oh, Bob, I can't wait to move in. Are there any more of the house?'

'No, that's the last one, love. The rest are just a mixture of the old "Down Memory Lane" stuff.'

Thelma looked up at Bob. The round lines of his

face were lit by the reflected redbrick glow of the colour slide.

'Are you happy? I mean, are you really *happy*, happy?'

'Fantastically happy.'

Thelma looked reassured. 'So am I. I know it's silly but sometimes it worries me that I'm so happy. I keep expecting something to come along and spoil it.'

Bob inserted a new colour slide into the projector.

'Daft thing. What could possibly do that?'

Thelma's reply came out as a muted scream of horror. Bob looked at the picture on the wall.

Terry Collier leered out at them from behind a raised mug of ale, fag-end behind the ear, pie-eyed plastered. Bob remembered the picture. It had been taken on a works outing. Looking at it now, it was quite a gem. The quintessential Terry. Unrepentantly arrogant, incredibly vulgar.

Thelma jumped up from the settee and switched on the ceiling light. She gave Bob a tight-lipped stare. 'You did that on purpose.'

'Of course I didn't, darling. I didn't know it was there. I was just going through the pile.'

Thelma folded her arms petulantly. 'Some jokes I can understand – like electrocuting people – or putting a pirhana in their bath, but – ' Thelma nodded towards Terry. 'Suddenly producing him just like that – that's not funny at all.'

Bob looked at the offending picture. In the glare of the mock-Spanish wrought-iron ceiling cluster, Terry's six-foot-high face had faded into a thin, ghostly image on the cream pebble-grained Lincrusta. Bob switched off the projector. Terry vanished. Bob waved reassuringly at the empty wall, but Thelma refused to be mollified.

'Oh, come on love, take it easy. It was an accident. I just picked one out. Like a lucky dip – or an unlucky dip in this case. It could have been anything. My first bicycle, your sister's wedding, us caravanning in East

Lincs. It just happened to be the Creature from the Black Lagoon.'

Thelma softened. Bob put his arm around her.

'I'm sorry. It was just the shock of . . . ' She sighed. 'He's always been there you know, Bob. A nagging doubt. Haunting me.'

Bob kissed the tip of her nose. She had a nice nose. He kissed it again. 'Love . . . dearest . . . it isn't as if he's even a friend of mine any more. I mean he hasn't spoken to me, hasn't written to me in over four years. Not a whisper. Even when he came home two Christmases ago, he didn't look me up. Even though my mother sent him a racing calendar . . . well, I mean, let's face it, I don't know him any more. He's a complete stranger.'

Now it was Thelma who kissed him on the nose. The reconciliation was complete. Bob grabbed the opportunity of a quick neck-to-knee hug, but any further intentions he might have had were frozen by a resolute look from Thelma. Bob let go and watched Thelma rearrange the pleats in her skirt.

'I know what's wrong with you. You're upset 'cos I'm going to London.'

'No I'm not.'

'Yes – of course you are. But I'm going there on business, not for a last big fling. I'm not going to get far on a cheap-day return.'

Thelma laughed. 'No, love, you're not.' She looked apologetically at Bob. 'I'm sorry . . . it was just seeing *that*!' She waved at the empty wall.

'How about a cup of tea?' suggested Bob.

'And some cheese and biscuits?'

'Smashing.'

Total forgiveness.

Thelma went into the kitchen. Bob picked up the next slide, put in the projector and switched off the room lights. The colour picture glowed out of the wall. It was of Bob and Terry in their earlier, happier days. They both looked pleasantly plastered – as did the two

Butlin Redcoat girls sandwiched between them . . .

Bob let his mind drift back to the events that led up to the picture – and what happened afterwards. He slumped back on the settee and let a happy wave of nostalgia break over him.

Terry Collier gazed out across the Kent countryside as the train chundered along towards London. A small, woolly baby boy was perched on his knee.

His spirits, which had soared at the sight of a stretch of hop fields, sagged as the train carried him past a cluster of converted oast houses and a gravel courtyard complete with an XJ6, Range Rover and a buff, smoked-glass Mini-Cooper. Yes, it was all right for some . . .

Five minutes later, the fields gave way to a long line of cement works and gravel pits. So much for England's green and pleasant land. Way up ahead, the outer suburbs of the New Jerusalem showed up as a smudgy red-grey line on the overcast horizon. Another forty-five minutes or so and they'd be at Victoria.

Terry turned away from the window as he became aware of the small girl tugging at his sleeve. She was three years old, and sister to the boy on his lap. She had chocolate smeared round her mouth, and she'd been tugging at his sleeve most of the way from Dover.

Terry gave her a baleful glance. The girl hid her face behind a fluffy, flop-eared rabbit.

'My rabbit is hungry. He wants some chocolate.'

Terry poked a reproving finger into the rabbit's tum.

'Rabbits don't eat chocolate. They eat carrots and lettuce and stuff like that. They're vegetarians.'

'My rabbit isn't.'

Terry grabbed the rabbit by the ears and pulled it clear of the girl's face.

'Look. I think rabbit wants a little lie-down. I don't think he's feeling too well, what with the train ride and all the chocolate he's had already.'

Terry yanked the rabbit out of the girl's hands and stowed it out of reach on the luggage rack.

'I think he'll feel much better after he's had a little sleep up here.'

He sat down again and settled the boy back on his lap. The little girl looked up at the rabbit then looked at Terry. 'He says he doesn't want to sleep. He wants some more chocolate.'

Terry stuck out a warning finger. 'No he doesn't. You are wrong, and I am right. Bunny is up there in his bunk pitting furiously and dreaming of Bunny girls. He does not wish to be disturbed until we get to London.'

Terry pointed to the silent one-year-old on his knee. 'What's his name?'

'Wayne.'

'Should we let him sleep, Wayne?' asked Terry. He jogged his knee up and down and Wayne's head wobbled back and forth. 'There you are,' said Terry. 'Your brother agrees with me.'

The compartment door slid open and a young woman came in. A nice little plump size fourteen blonde in a size twelve dress. She smiled at Terry and took the baby from him.

'Ta, it's ever so nice of you. Have they been playing you up much?'

'No, not at all. I've got a way with kids.'

'Mum,' said the little girl. 'Can I have my rabbit?'

Her mother had already sat down opposite Terry. She looked across at him. 'Would you mind?'

Terry retrieved the rabbit from the luggage rack and handed it back to the little girl. She turned to her mother.

'My rabbit wants some more chocolate.'

'I've already told you, Sharon. Mummy doesn't have any more chocolate. Rabbit will have to wait till we get home.'

Sharon turned and stared fixedly at Terry.

He stared back, looked at her mother to weigh up his chances, then fished the rest of the chocolate bar out of his pocket.

'You shouldn't encourage her, really you shouldn't,' said her mother, giving Terry an encouraging look of her own. She put baby Wayne on the seat beside her and smoothed the creases out of her dress.

I'll have this cracked by Catford, thought Terry.

The woman studied the kitbag and suitcase on the rack above his head. Terry had taken care to plaster it with exotic European luggage labels. Her eyes met his. No doubt about it. He was definitely on.

'You've been around then.'

'Here and there,' said Terry.

'In the Services, are you?'

'Was. Back on terminal leave. Finished. Been everywhere. Seen the lot. Done it all.'

'That must have been nice.'

'Yep. Five years.'

No doubt about that sly smile, Terry lad. Feet under the table here.

'Did you enjoy it?'

'Yeah, apart from this.' Terry patted his right thigh.

'Oh, what happened?'

'I never talk about it.'

'I'm sorry, I didn't – '

'Please,' said Terry. 'You weren't to know.' He carefully rubbed the outside of his right thigh again. He didn't want to give her the wrong impression.

'Do you live in London?'

'No,' said Terry. 'Just passing through. Getting the train up North tonight.'

That means no time for bread and breakfast, love. Just afternoon tea and a quick kip . . .

'Got a few hours to kill then . . . '

'Yeah, suppose so, yes.'

Terry could always tell the ones that weren't getting enough. It stood out a mile. I'll lay even money, he thought, her old man's either doing porridge or he's a long-distance lorry driver. Ten year's hard or halfway to Budapest with a forty-ton artic.

'Well you're more than welcome to come home with me if you like.'

Terry could see it all. Draped nylon curtains, pink

satin eiderdown. Neat black underwear. Definitely not held together with safety pins. Not this one.

'Get your feet up for the rest of the day if you want.'

And the rest, boyo. As old Charlie used to say – 'A slice off a cut loaf is never missed.'

'Great,' said Terry. 'But are you sure it'll be all right?'

'Yes, of course it will. My husband's meeting me at the station. He loves gassing about the Army and that kind of thing.'

'Daddy was in the Commandos,' said Sharon from behind the rabbit.

Terry's hateful stare bounced off harmlessly. She may have only been three years old, but she knew what the score was.

Game, set and match.

Terry spent the afternoon traipsing round the strip clubs in Soho checking on the state of the art. Compared to some of the stuff he'd clocked in Hamburg most of the shows were as racy as a vicar's tea party. Still there was one place where a couple of blondes and a coloured girl had ended up in an interesting triangular relationship. Yes, there had been no lack of inter-racial harmony there. And in another, there had been an animal act where a crafty boa-constrictor almost got his other end away. Still, the British were noted for their love of animals. All in all quite an uplifting afternoon.

Terry took the tube to Kings Cross station. There was an hour to kill before his train, so he hovered round the bookstall eyeing the permissive paperbacks. He bought a copy of *Titbits, Reveille, The European Cup Souvenir Book* and the latest copy of *Health & Efficiency*. It had come a long way from those shaven full frontals that had been passed along the back row of Park Road Junior school.

There being no talent visible on the platform, he went into the buffet and had a cup of coffee and a near fatal encounter with a British Rail sandwich.

The train was due out at 8.20 p.m. Terry laid out his

luggage and magazines on the seats to make it look as if it was all booked and settled down by the window. He left one seat empty. In films, this was always occupied by a tall brunette that got on breathlessly at the last minute. So far it had never happened to him, but there was always a first time. Then it would be blinds down for three hundred miles with a quick breather at Grantham and Doncaster. Night trains were one of his favourite fantasies. It didn't have to be a brunette. Marlene Dietrich in a dark wig would do.

Several single girls passed by the window and down the corridor. Two actually paused but thought better of it. Just as well, thought Terry. Neither were what you'd call crumpet. More your mouldy old type of muffin.

The guard's whistle blew and the train lurched forward with a great clatter as the carriage buffers collided with each other all the way down the train. Terry was still in solitary possession of the compartment. Marlene had missed it again. And so had Anne Miller, Rhonda Flemming, Lauren Bacall and Cyd Charisse. And none of them would be likely to get on at Grantham.

Terry picked up his copy of *Reveille* and addressed the nipple-less nude on the cover. 'So it's just you and me, darling.'

A man paused in the corridor outside. He carried a briefcase, overnight bag, and a large purple package that totally obscured his face. After several attempts, he hooked a finger into the handle, eased it open and slid it back with his foot.

Terry watched him idly out of the corner of his eye and stuck his feet on the seat opposite.

'Excuse me,' said the man.

As he spoke, the light went out, plunging the train into total darkness.

Not a glimmer of light anywhere.

'Arghh, sod it,' said Terry.

'Are there any spare seats?'

'One,' said Terry. He put his feet back on the floor just in time for the invisible man to step heavily on one of them.

'Sorry, was that your foot?'

'Don't worry,' said Terry. 'I've got another.'

There was a great deal of uncoordinated fumbling and rearrangement as the man stowed away his luggage and finally flopped back opposite Terry with a great sigh.

What a burk, thought Terry. The whole bloody carriage to sit in and he goes and sits dead opposite. Now neither of us can put our bloody feet up.

'Must be a power cut.'

'Typical,' said Terry.

'And here we are in the seventies. The jet age. High Speed gas and all that. "Inter-City makes the going great." I can't believe it.'

'Typical,' said Terry again. He didn't want to encourage this bloke to go on yakking.

'That'll mean no heat as well. Is there any heat on your side?'

Before Terry could move, the invisible man had got up to see for himself. He cannoned heavily into Terry.

'Oops, sorry, was that your – ?'

'No,' said Terry. 'It was my knee.'

'Ah.'

Dennis the Menace sat down again. 'The heat is off, by the way.'

'Good. How far are you going?'

'Newcastle.'

'Well, sit still will you,' said Terry. 'Otherwise I'll be black and blue by the time we get there.'

'You live up that way?'

'Yeah. Haven't been back for ages. Just come out of the Army.'

'Oh, aye. Enjoy it?'

'Got a lot out of it,' said Terry. 'Got a lot out of it.'

'I nearly went in once.'

'Could have done a lot worse.'

'Actually it was rather a funny story,' said the invisible man. 'You see, I had this mate. Well, my best mate. You know, really close. Anyhow, a few years back I decided to go into the Services. You know, get away for a bit, see something of the world. So I signed on. Well, when I went away this mate of mine couldn't take it. Absolutely went to pieces. Couldn't function without me. I suppose it was like losing your right arm. So he signs on too. Just to be with me. Only you'll never guess what happened – I have to laugh whenever I think of it – '

And laugh he did. Like a seal with hiccoughs. Terry waited patiently while his invisible story-teller recovered.

'You see, as soon as he gets in, *I* get discharged with flat feet. So I'm free and he's lumbered for three years. I'll never forget it. As he came marching in with this new intake, I was walking out. You should have seen the look on his face. I didn't stop laughing for weeks.'

There was a pause for another giggle.

'No, but I mean it's a sad story in some ways, 'cos he's never spoken to me since. But when you're telling the story, like when you tell someone else, you can't help seeing the funny side. I mean, you've got to laugh, haven't you?'

The man started to laugh again then lapsed into silence as no reaction came out of the dark.

Terry counted up to ten very slowly then said, 'You bastard . . . '

No sooner were the words out than the train lights switched back on, revealing Bob Ferris on the seat opposite him. Bob sat there like a stuck pig, his pop-eyes glued on Terry, his mouth making wobbly O-shapes, but unable to produce a sound.

Terry, however, was not at a loss for words.

'You bastard. You've got to laugh, haven't you? You've got to see the funny side of it. You've got to laugh at the fact that your *best* mate missed the most important years of his life. It is a JOKE. While you were at home enjoying the Permissive Society, I was in every God-forsaken corner of the globe sweating my bollocks off. Oh, yes, you've got to laugh at that.'

'I'm very sorry, Terry,' said Bob contritely.

'*Sorry*?!! What does that mean?! That's what you said a few miles back when you trod on my foot.'

Terry mimicked Bob's strangled apology. 'I'm sorry' . . . I suppose you think that's enough to wipe the slate clean?'

Bob had now got most of his voice back. 'We tried to buy you out. Honestly, Terry, I swear to you. As soon as I got back I organised a whip-round at work. But we just couldn't raise enough funds.'

'What d'you mean,' said Terry indignantly. 'What about my going away whip-round? There was no shortage of funds for that!'

'Yes, I know,' said Bob uncomfortably. 'But we just couldn't seem to be able to raise the same amount of support for you, well . . . for coming back.'

Terry eyed him sourly. 'I suppose you had a good laugh at that as well.'

'I didn't mean it was funny ha-ha,' said Bob hesitantly. 'I meant that it was . . . well, ironical if you like.'

Terry slumped back into the corner of the window seat. 'Yes, it's ironical all right. Ironical that when this country goes through a social transformation, I'm not here to see it. It's ironical that when everyone here's having the best time they've ever had since the Roaring Twenties, *I'm* living in a Nissen hut in BAOR 14.'

Terry paused and let out a long sigh through closed teeth. 'I missed it all. Swinging Britain was just hearsay to me. Something I read about in the overseas edition of the *Daily Mail.* The death of censorship. The new morality. *Oh Calcutta.* Topless waitress – .' He looked at Bob. 'See-through knickers.'

'They never caught on,' said Bob. 'Topless waitresses, I mean.'

'Thank you,' said Terry. 'One small crumb of comfort. I'd have liked, at least, to have *seen* them not catching on.' He waved a hand helplessly. 'The Permissive Society . . . I missed it all. Here I am and what's left? Malcolm Muggeridge, Lord Longford and the Jesus Revolution!'

'It wasn't all that much. You know how people exaggerate.'

'I still bet it was better than München-Gladbach,' said Terry, gloomily.

'Where?'

'Exactly,' said Terry. 'Good question. München-Gladbach.'

'Where's that?'

'That is the West Hartlepool of West Germany. Do you get the picture?'

'Oh,' said Bob, hardly able to imagine such an appalling prospect.

'Exactly.' Terry folded his arms, crossed a leg and gazed out of the window again. The gloom was pierced by the red glow of an iron-smelting works.

Bob searched for something to say that might make up for München-Gladbach. 'Look, Terry, what happened happened. I didn't engineer it. I didn't *want* it to happen. It wasn't part of some grand plan. It wasn't a conspiracy. It was Kismet. Fate. Like Doris Day's song – "Que sera sera!" '

Terry kept his eyes on a line of iron-ore wagons unreeling past the window. 'I can't stand Doris Day.'

It was clear a more emotional ploy was called for. Bob sat back in his corner with limp resignation. 'All right, Terry, why should you believe me. Just let me ask you one last question. Could I have *forged* flat feet?'

Terry reluctantly tore his gaze away from the endless line of iron-ore trucks and looked at Bob.

'Ask yourself that,' said Bob. 'Would I, in all seriousness, want my own two feet to be flat? I mean, would I deliberately parade my affliction in front of the authorities and expose myself to public ridicule?'

Terry looked grudgingly impressed. 'I suppose not.'

'Well, there you are then,' said Bob. 'And don't forget while you were whisked off by the Army, I had to go back and brave all the bad jokes about flat feet. I mean you may have been suffering, but so was my self-respect.'

'Yes,' said Terry. 'Must have been rotten, that.' His voice didn't quite carry the necessary degree of conviction.

'And it was not as though you were forgotten,' said

Bob. 'Me and the lads at the factory spent two months and fifty plain postcards trying to get you a request on Family Favourites.'

'That's news to me. I never heard it.'

'Well, don't blame me, Terry. Take it up with Michael Aspel.'

'What was the request?'

'It was Doris Day,' said Bob. 'Singing "Que Sera Sera".'

'I can't stand Doris Day!'

'How was I to know that? You could once. I remember how upset you were when Rock Hudson got her in bed in *Pillow Talk.*'

'That was bloody ages ago.'

'Well, how could I know what your musical tastes were? I mean, not having heard from you, for all I know you might have been anywhere from The Pink Floyd to the Foden Motor Works Brass Band!'

Bob paused. There was no response from Terry. He was looking out of the window. From the darkness outside, his reflected face looked back at Bob.

'Anyway,' said Bob to Terry's glum reflection. 'You look well enough.'

'I am,' said Terry. 'Fighting fit. Apart from this.' He patted his right thigh.

'What happened?'

'I never talk about it.'

'Oh . . . ' said Bob, averting his gaze from the concealed wound. Knowing Terry, the possibilities could range from an enemy bayonet to falling on a bottle opener. He looked up to find Terry studying him.

'How have you been?' Terry's voice had lost its edge.

'Fine, said Bob. 'Can't complain.'

'Good. Glad to hear it.'

'Had me appendix out a couple of years ago.'

'Oh . . . can be dangerous that.'

There was an embarrassed silence while they looked at each other. Bob stuck out his hand impulsively. 'No hard feelings?'

Terry hesitated for a moment, then gripped Bob's hand. 'No. No hard feelings.'

Bob held onto Terry's hand and smiled sheepishly. Terry's face cracked, then they both smiled broadly.

'Welcome back,' said Bob.

'Glad to be back,' said Terry.

'Good lad.' Bob laid his left hand on top of the handshake. His mouth crumpled up as tears started in his eyes. Terry looked embarrassed.

'Oh, come on, mate. No need for that.'

'Sorry,' sniffed Bob. 'I'm all right. I'm all right. Always was a bit emotional.'

'Here.' Terry held out a crumpled handkerchief.

Bob buried his nose in it for a couple of great honking blows, then folded it over carefully. As he wiped away the tears a hardened ball of chewing gum almost lost him the sight of one eye. Bob peeled the gum from the handkerchief.

'Is this yours?'

'Oh, cheers,' said Terry. 'I thought I'd thrown that away.' He popped it into his mouth and began to chew. 'Helps keep your mouth fresh.'

Bob felt the bile rise to his.

That, plus a need to stretch their legs, and an urge to celebrate the return of the prodigal led the lads to the swaying British Rail buffet bar midway down the train. Apart from the steward, the only other occupants were two tired commercial travellers who'd run out of jokes. Since one of them, from what the lads had overheard, travelled in rubber goods and the other in ladies underwear they probably didn't have too much to laugh about.

Bob and Terry leaned against the bar and watched the steward puncture their sixth pair of Newcastle Brown.

'I saw your Mother the other week,' said Bob. 'She looked very well.'

'Oh, aye?' Terry lifted his refilled glass. 'Cheers.'

'Cheers,' said Bob. He sipped his ale. 'Not to speak to, like. Just through the car window.'

'Throug h the *what* window?'

'The car window.'

'What car window?'

'*My* car window.'

Terry lowered the glass from his lips. 'You mean to say that you've got a car?'

'Well, I haven't just got the window.'

'But you can't drive.'

'Of course I can drive,' said Bob. 'I've been driving for ages. This is my second car, this is.'

Terry had to lower the glass again from his still dry lips. 'What happened to the first?'

Bob gave an airy shrug. 'Too small.'

'I see . . . ' Terry studied the head on his glass of ale, then took a long pull. He appeared to have difficulty in swallowing it.

Bob watched him as he turned the glass around in his hands and examined the remaining contents.

'Yes . . . well . . . of course,' said Terry. 'Obviously one of the first things *I'll* have to do is get a car.'

'Oh, have you got a licence then?'

'Well, er – not exactly,' said Terry. 'The Army one won't count, will it? I mean driving tanks and things . . . it's not the same.'

Bob nodded tactfully and decided not to ask Terry when he transferred from the Royal Electrical and Mechanical Engineers to the Tank Corps.

'Let's see,' he said. 'You've been away *five* years, haven't you?'

'Have I?'

'I thought you only signed on for three.'

'Did I?'

'So that means you must have signed on for an extra two.'

'Well, if you put it that way, I suppose I must have.'

'So it couldn't have been all *that* bad. I mean, you must have enjoyed it.'

'I might have, I suppose,' said Terry. He drained his glass and placed it on the counter with a shrug. 'Looking back, in retrospect, overall, by and large, it was a rewarding experience.'

'Same again,' said Bob to the steward.

'There were enough good things to compensate for the bad.' Terry grimaced, and rubbed his thigh.

'Would you rather we sat down?' asked Bob.

'I don't think that would be a bad idea,' said Terry.

'You go on then,' said Bob. 'I'll carry the glasses.'

Terry limped over to a table. Apart from the mysterious wound, his right leg now seemed to have shrunk three inches. Bob joined him with two glasses and two more refills.

'Mind you,' said Terry, drowning the pain in beer. 'It did give me a chance to see the world. Aye . . . some fantastic places.'

'Like München-Gladbach.'

'That was only part of it, mate.' Terry gave a knowing wink. 'Wasn't in Germany all the time. I moved around. Seen it all. Places the ordinary bloke would never go to.'

'Like where, for instance?'

'Like Malta, for one. Now there's a place. I could tell you some.'

Bob laughed. 'Malta? Why, I've been there. Last year. For two weeks. Quite enjoyed it.'

'Oh,' said Terry. 'Yes, well, Malta isn't really that much cop. A lot of people get there now.'

'Where else did you go?'

Terry paused for effect, then said casually. 'Spent a lot of time in Cyprus.'

'Not Famagusta.'

Terry's mouth tightened. 'Yes.'

'In those kind of medieval barracks near the port?'

'Yes, why?'

'We were in that new luxury hotel just beyond there. Seventh floor with a balcony. We could look right down on your quadrangle.'

'Parade ground,' said Terry, tightening his grip on his glass of ale.

'I'm surprised they didn't include you in the brochures.

"On a clear day, you can see Corporal Collier." ' Bob chuckled. 'Looked a desperate place that. By God, it did.'

'Yes, well, I only worked there. Every weekend I was off all over the place.' Terry leaned towards Bob. 'I once spent a whole week's leave in Tunis.'

'I don't believe it.'

'It's true,' said Terry.

'That's incredible,' said Bob. 'I was there this year. Smashing hotel – two pools, French cuisine – '

'And then I was posted to the Gobi desert,' said Terry. 'How surprising we didn't run across each other there!'

Bob parried the spiteful glance with a bland smile. 'No, really, people keep saying it, but it's true just the same, it really is a small world, isn't it? I mean, when you think while I've been sitting in my luxury hotels, on my balconies sipping martinis . . . there you've been, just an olive stone's throw away. In some dusty barracks swilling NAAFI beer.'

'Swilling NAAFI beer . . . ' Terry's voice was heavy with sarcasm. 'You're living in the dark ages, man. The Army's not like that today. It's all technical and sophisticated. It's water skiing with nurses in Hong Kong and growing your hair longer.'

'Please fill in the coupon for your free colour brochure. I bet they don't mention München-Gladbach in that.' Bob was beginning to enjoy himself.

'Stop taking the piss,' said Terry. 'All I'm saying is that I don't regret it. I learned a hell of a lot, mate.'

'Well, I'm glad,' said Bob. 'It makes me feel a whole lot better about everything. It's nice to know you owe it all to my flat feet.'

'Let's drink to them,' said Terry with a look that should have curdled Bob's beer.

'My flat feet,' said Bob. He clinked Terry's glass and raised his own with a happy smile. If the beer was curdled, he certainly didn't let on.

Terry signalled for four more cans of beer. 'So, what's been happening while I've been away?'

Bob pondered for a moment. 'Don't know where to

begin. I told you about my appendix. Yes, of course . . .' He lapsed into silence.

'Obviously a fantastic amount has happened,' said Terry.

'A fantastic amount,' agreed Bob. 'Let's see now. Let me think . . . we've got BBC 2.'

'We had that before I went away.'

'Did we? My God – how time flies. Let's think. What's happened? Oh, yes, I know – Cloughy's retired and bought a newsagents.'

'Has he?'

'Newsagent and confectioners along the Coast Road.'

'Oh, good.'

'I was in there last week to buy a birthday card for Mrs Morris.'

There was a lengthy silence as Bob tried to drag up some more interesting items from the past.

'That's it, is it?' asked Terry. 'How fascinating. The recorded highlights of what I've missed in the last five years. You've had your appendix out, Cloughy's opened a shop, and Mrs Morris has had a birthday.'

'Oh, come on,' said Bob. 'Obviously more things than that have happened.'

'Oh, yes?'

'I just can't pick out things at random like that. Just wait till you see the changes there's been up there. If you'd kept in touch . . . ' Bob tailed off.

Terry arranged the cans of beer in a neat diamond pattern. 'I meant to, Bob. When I came back that first Christmas I fully intended to call round and make it up. Wipe the slate clean. Then me Mum told me you'd got engaged to Thelma Chambers . . . so, well – I never got round to it.'

'You never liked Thelma, did you?'

'Of course I did! That's got nothing to do with it. It was just suddenly realising that nothing was going to be the same. Realising that you can't turn the clock back. Maybe even jealousy if you like. Just brought me down that's all. Nothing personal to do with Thelma. I admire her. Always have.'

'I wish you'd come round,' said Bob. 'We broke it off after that.'

Terry brightened visibly. 'Did you?'

'Yeah.'

'Well, I can't say I'm sorry. I'll be perfectly honest with you, Bob, that really is a load off my mind. I mean, after all, you are my mate, and if you want to get married, fine, go ahead and get married, but not to anybody like Thelma Chambers. Hell's teeth, even you deserve to do better than that.'

Terry prattled on without noticing that Bob's face had gone as hard and grey as constipated cement.

'Honestly, I mean this,' he continued. 'I just couldn't see what you saw in her. Talk about toffee nosed. She was so stuck up she thought her arse was a scent factory!'

Bob put down his glass of ale and stood up, trembling. Terry looked at him surprised.

'What's up?'

'I happen to be marrying Thelma Chambers in three weeks' time.'

Terry's mouth dropped open like a stranded goldfish. 'But you said . . . '

'We made it up again.'

'But –'

Bob cut him off with a dignified wave of the hand. 'Don't bother to apologise.'

'But – '

'What does "I'm sorry" mean? After all, you can't turn the clock back.'

'But – '

'Can't expect to pick up things where you left off.' Bob counted out enough change to pay for Terry's round of beer. 'It's obvious that you and I have very little in common now.' A slight laugh. 'In fact, it amazes me that we ever did. It only remains for me to wish you the very best of luck and please give my regards to your father and mother.'

Bob turned on his heel and walked out of the buffet

car. Very slowly, Terry closed his mouth, sighed, then swallowed the last of the beer.

The steward cleared away Bob's glass, the cans and the cash on the table. Terry picked up his own glass and walked over to the bar.

'Same again?' asked the steward.

'Aye – no, hang on – make it a large Scotch.' Terry watched the steward draw off two measures of Bells from the optic.

'That'll be fifty pence. Ice?'

'No thanks.' Terry paid the steward. 'What's the next stop – Doncaster?'

'That's right.'

'Will I be able to get a train back to London at this time of night?'

'Should think so, sir.'

Terry half raised his glass of whisky in a toast to life in general. 'Never go back.'

The steward looked at him. Feeling that his remark required amplification, Terry waved at the door through which Bob had made his haughty exit.

'I sacrificed the five best years of my life for that fella. And now he tells me he's getting married.'

The steward laid a limp-wristed hand on top of Terry's. 'Never mind, sailor,' he said. 'Lots of other pebbles on the beach.'

Doncaster Station at ten thirty in the evening cannot be described as one of the brighter spots of the western world. Even by the people who live there. The few figures on the platform were waiting to escape on the incoming train.

As the train glided slowly past the platform Terry noticed two disconsolate porters with a large trolley. They were probably there to unload food parcels. The train stopped with a faint squeal of brakes and the carriage buffers cannoned off each other. Terry took a deep breath, took his luggage and his courage in both hands and stepped down on to the platform.

Bob, who had fallen asleep in the compartment, woke with a start to see Terry walking away from the train. He leapt up with a strangled curse, grabbed his coat, bag and gift-wrapped parcel, and just managed to get off the train as the guard blew his whistle.

As someone shouted, Terry turned around. Bob was hurrying along the platform trying to put on his top coat without letting go of his bag or parcel. He was wriggling about like a man trying to get out of a chained sack.

'Thank you very much,' said Bob. 'You were just going to let me sleep on, I suppose.' He now had the gift-wrapped parcel between his knees. 'I suppose that was your childish way of getting your own back.'

'Beg pardon?'

Behind them, the train began to pull out. Bob now had one arm in and one arm caught in the lining.

'You were just going to let me wake up in Edinburgh. I know we've exchanged a few harsh words, but a tap on the window wouldn't have hurt.'

'I didn't think there was any point in waking you to tell you I was getting off at Doncaster,' said Terry mildly.

'Where?!'

'Doncaster,' said Terry. He pointed to the platform sign above his head.

Bob whirled round in time to see the red tail lights of the train half-way up the platform and on their way to Newcastle. David Bedford might just have made it, but not with a gift-wrapped parcel and one arm stuck in the lining of his coat. He rounded on Terry.

'What the hell did you get off at Doncaster for?!'

Terry gave him a pitying look then turned on his heel and walked away.

It was bad enough having to phone Thelma to tell her he was at Doncaster. Having to reverse the charges made it that little bit worse. And having to tell her that it was because he'd met Terry Collier made it just awful. Unspeakable. The verbal equivalent to indecent exposure.

'I knew it,' said Thelma. 'I knew that slide was no

accident. It was an act of God. An omen. And now you're trapped with him in Doncaster. Well, this is it, isn't it? This is the point of no return. The moment of truth. I hope you realise, Bob, the next half-hour could be a landmark in your life.'

'Be reasonable, Thelma,' said Bob. 'All I'm going to be doing is standing on Platform 4 at Doncaster waiting for the next train.'

'A landmark, Bob,' said Thelma. 'Think about it.' She hung up.

Terry was in sole possession of the waiting room and deep into his Alistair MacLean paperback. Bob shouldered open the swing door and paused as he caught sight of Terry Terry didn't look up. Bob cleared his throat.

'Are these anybody's seats?'

'It's a free country.' Terry still didn't look up.

Bob selected the seat furthest away from Terry, disposed his luggage about him and sat with his hands clasped on his knees. He studied Terry for a long moment, then said, 'I expect you feel the cold after the Med, eh?'

Terry turned over a page of his book.

'Why? Just tell me. Why did you get off here?'

'I thought it might be the one place Bob Ferris hadn't been to.' Terry's eyes didn't lift from his book.

'No, seriously,' said Bob. 'Tell me.'

Terry lowered his book, thought for a moment, then looked across at Bob. 'It's like what you said, Bob. You can't turn the clock back.'

'Oh no, hang on. It was you who said that. You said it first, mate.'

'Well whoever. It's true, that's the point. Apart from me folks, there's nothing for me back home. Five years is a long time . . . ' Terry shook his head sadly. 'Let's face it, there'll be more changes than Cloughy behind a shop counter. Bound to be. I'm not the same person I used to be. Nor are you. I mean it was simple then – birds, booze, the dance hall. Now it's . . . "the wife" scampi, supper dances and holidays in Malta. All my mates will have settled down now. With children and mortgages. Saving up their Green Shields for a new set of hock glasses.'

Terry paused dejectedly. More than anything Bob wanted to tell him that he was wrong. That it would all be the same. But it wasn't. Never would be. Never could be.

'Where's my place in all that?' continued Terry. 'I'd be like a square peg in a what-you-call-me. I used to think when I was first in the Army . . . I used to think "When I get back" . . . then I started to think, "When I get back, *what*?" I can't expect everything to have been in a deep freeze since I left. I envy you in a way. You've got your girl, and you've got your second car. Good lad . . . '

Bob's lip trembled. For a moment it looked as if he might need Terry's handkerchief again. 'I'm sorry, Terry.'

'Me too, Bob.'

'Funny, y'know. Since we've met we seem to have done nothing but apologise to each other.'

'Yes, I know. Sorry about that.'

'What – ' Bob hesitated. 'Well, what are you going to do?'

Terry pocketed his paperback. 'Well, I always thought I should . . . try down south. London, you know. Place to be, isn't it?' He shrugged doubtfully.

'Permissive society's still going on down there,' said Bob helpfully. 'Much more than up our way.'

'Aye, well,' said Terry. 'Might just catch the tail end of it.' Another doubtful shrug.

A station trolley whined past the door of the waiting room dragging a line of mail bins, then it was silent again.

'Well,' said Bob. 'Just so long as you – make out, Terry.'

'I'll manage. How about you?'

'Oh, I'll manage. Everything's fine with me, thanks.'

'What will Thelma say when you tell her you met me?'

'I've already told her. Rang her up. She was going to meet me at the station.'

'She must have been pleased. What did she say?'

'Said this was my moment of truth.'

Terry's top lip curled back. 'People don't have moments of truth in station waiting rooms. Especially at Doncaster.'

'She said that for a long time, the threat of your return has cast a giant shadow over her entire future happiness.'

'Very poetic, isn't she?' said Terry. 'I think I've read that somewhere.'

'She's assistant Librarian.'

'It was a film too, wasn't it. "Cast a Giant Shadow".'

'Kirk Douglas.'

Terry nodded. 'Mind you, I can appreciate her panic. That phone call must have put a cold draught up her knickers. I'll bet she'll be up there waiting at the platform barrier knowing it's only heads or tails you'll be on the train.' He grinned. 'Terry Collier strikes again.'

'Balls.'

Terry took in the bleak waiting room with a sweep of his hand 'Mind you, she won't believe this. She'll see us in some lush penthouse in Doncaster's Latin Quarter being seen to by a pair of West Indian models to the strain of "Begin the Beguine".'

'Get off,' said Bob. 'She knows me better than that. Trust. That's what we've got. It's a word you probably haven't come across, but it describes what exists between two people who are going to get married. It means not having to worry about what the other person's up to. Not having to be afraid . . . not having doubts . . . ' Bob faltered. 'Besides, Doncaster hasn't got a Latin Quarter, has it?'

Terry glanced at his watch. 'You've left it too late to find out. Your train's due in right now.'

Bob climbed aboard the 23.10 for Darlington, Durham and Newcastle and leaned back out of the door window.

'Change your mind. Come on home. After all it's *your* home as much as it is mine.'

Terry took a step back from the train. 'No. My mind's made up. I'll manage in London. It'll be more bearable now they're selling Newcastle ale. Anyway, I'm best out of it. For your sake.' Terry gave a wry grin. 'I don't want to cast my wiry little shadow over your happiness.'

Bob didn't know how to reply to that. He had an idea what Thelma would have said, though. Trains always took so long to pull out. Someone ought to write a book of witty things to say on station platforms. After all, how many ways are there to say 'goodbye'?

'Make sure no one runs off with your luggage.'

'It'll be okay in the waiting room,' said Terry.

'So,' said Bob. 'This is it then.'

'Aye. See you in another five years, maybe.'

'Cloughy will have a chain of shops by then.'

'And you'll have bought Mrs Morris five more birthday cards.'

'Yes, well . . . I'll say so long, then.'

'Be seeing you.'

Bob stuck out his hand. Terry gripped it briefly.

'God bless,' said Bob, lips crumpling.

'Cheers.' Terry walked away without looking back. Bob walked down the corridor to look for a corner seat. The doors slammed shut. The guard's whistle blew.

Thelma was waiting on the platform at Newcastle Central. Ordinarily she would have economised by waiting at the barrier, but she felt unable to stand the suspense of waiting for Bob to appear. She wanted to get her eyes on him as quickly as possible.

She scanned the windows of the carriages as they passed her but there was no sign of Bob. The train slid to a stop and the carriage doors began to open. Thelma started to walk slowly down the platform, standing on tiptoe now and then to try and spot Bob.

'Thelma?' The voice came from behind her.

Thelma composed her face into a severe expression of disapproval and turned around. Terry Collier was standing behind her, half-hidden behind a large gift-wrapped parcel.

Thelma's mouth dropped open. 'Wha-what are *you* doing here?!'

'I brought you a present,' said Terry. He thrust the

parcel into Thelma's arms.

'Where's Bob!'

'You're not going to believe this,' said Terry.

'Terry Collier, I'm warning you. If you're up to your old tricks again – '

Terry held up both his hands in a sign of peaceful surrender. 'Thelma, love. Bob's explained to me the way things are between you two. I'm not going to try and break that up.'

'What have you done with him, Terry? He was supposed to be on the eleven ten from Doncaster.'

'He was on the eleven ten from Doncaster. I saw him on to the train myself.'

'Then where *is* he?!' squealed Thelma.

'Well,' said Terry. 'Hey careful with that parcel. I don't think you're supposed to drop it.'

'Oh, blow the parcel. Here take it. I don't want a present from you anyway!'

'It's not from me. It's from Bob,' said Terry, handing the parcel back to Thelma. 'I'm just trying to explain.'

'And I wish you would!'

'You see,' said Terry, 'I'd left my luggage in the waiting room, and when I got back there, I saw Bob had left your present behind. I must have found it about the same time he realised he'd forgotten it. I jumped on the train to give it to him, just as he got off the train to fetch it.'

'So?'

'The train was already moving. He just came out of the waiting room in time for me to wave goodbye.'

'You mean you just left him there in Doncaster?'

'Didn't have any choice, love. Still, he's not alone. He's got all my luggage. Here – you'd better look after his briefcase.'

Thelma took the case from Terry. She was too stunned to object. 'But that was the last train,' she said. 'Bob will be stuck in Doncaster all night.'

'Oh, it won't be too bad,' said Terry. 'There's always the Latin Quarter.'

2

Home is the Hero

By the time Bob got back to Newcastle the next morning, Thelma had already gone to work. He drove round to Terry's to drop off his luggage and to find out what had happened at the station.

Terry told him how well Thelma had taken it. There was nothing else to do but go round to the library and try and patch things up. Work was out of the question.

Thelma was putting an armful of books back in their places on the shelves. As she turned the corner of the stack, Bob popped out from Crafts and Leisure. She turned her back on him, her mouth set in a thin red line.

'Thelma, please!'

'Ssshhh – !'

'I want to talk to you!' said Bob in a loud, urgent whisper.

'Well, you can't,' hissed Thelma. 'Not here.'

One or two people at the reading tables looked up curiously. Bob followed Thelma down the line of shelves.

'Why are you being so unreasonable?'

'I'm not being unreasonable.'

'Excuse me,' said a man. 'Is *The Godfather* back yet?'

'No, I'm sorry, sir.' Thelma turned on a sweet smile, then turned it off again as she looked at Bob. The man moved away.

'Why are you in such a state?'

'I am not in a state.'

'Yes, you are. You've just put *Human Sexual Response* under Hobbies.'

Thelma checked the title and took it back off the shelf. She pushed past Bob and threw a sharp glance over her shoulder.

'Don't you recognise the symptoms? It's shock. Delayed shock. The shock of knowing Terry Collier is back in this town, this conurbation. North of the Trent.'

A little old lady began to hover at Thelma's elbow.

'So, what of it?' asked Bob. 'Who's Terry Collier?'

'Your mate, your mucker, your oppo, your chum, your bosom companion.'

'Oh, *that* Terry Collier,' said Bob.

'You can save the sarcasm,' said Thelma. 'Yes, *that* Terry Collier. From the good old days. The lads. The Roxy Rams. Nudge nudge. Wink wink. Two buckets of brown ale and have you heard the one about the nympho and the traffic warden.'

The little old lady was tugging gently at Thelma's sleeve. Bob pointed at her.

'There's a bit of nudge nudge going on behind you right now.'

'What?' said Thelma. 'Oh . . . ' She turned around and put on her *Play School* voice. 'Can I help you?'

'Is *The Godfather* in yet?'

'No, not yet, Madam. I'm sorry.'

The old lady tottered away. Thelma smoothed out the bulge the old lady had made in her sleeve.

'Is it *my* fault he decides to come back? To his own home. In his own home town. In his own . . . conurbation?

Thelma buried herself with her books.

'That can't be right, surely. *Insight into Acupuncture* under Car Maintenance?'

Thelma pulled the book savagely from the shelf. 'It just seems funny to me that he comes out of the army now. Just six weeks before we're due to get married.'

'Ah,' said Bob. 'I was to blame for that. I wrote to the War Office saying 'Please could Corporal Collier have a compassionate discharge so he can come back home to drag me from the altar'.

'Very funny. But that's what he'd like to do.' Thelma moved round to the next book stack. Bob tagged along behind.

'He's changed, Thelma. He's not the same person. He's another person. He told me himself. Five years is a long time.'

A man in a raincoat and glasses tapped Bob timidly on the shoulder. 'Excuse me – '

'Sorry, it's not in yet,' said Bob.

'Oh,' said the man. He edged past them with a puzzled look.

Thelma put a pile of books into Bob's arms and looked at him accusingly. 'Why did the two of you break your journey last night? Why did you suddenly get off the train when you were half-way home?'

'I've told you why. I told you last night on the telephone.'

'Because *he* was putting the doubts in. That's why,' said Thelma. 'There will now be a short intermission for second thoughts.'

'Don't be silly.'

'Why else would you get off at Doncaster in the middle of the night?'

'I've already given you a perfectly reasonable explanation.'

Thelma gave him a withering look of disbelief, then took the top book from the pile Bob was holding and looked for its place on the packed shelves.

'All right then,' said Bob. 'I'll give you the real explanation. We were seduced by the distant sounds of merriment, laughter and depravity. "Ho, porter," we said. "What goes on?" "What goes on, sir? Why it's our midnight carnival. Mardi Gras." And within minutes we were caught up in the swirl of merry revelry. Young virgins knotted flowers in our hair. People swayed to the sound of primitive jungle rhythms, and couples copulated the entire length of the Doncaster by-pass– '

'Bob!' said Thelma.

Bob turned to see the little old lady behind him. From her wide eyes it was obvious she'd heard every word. Bob leant towards her confidentially. 'It's all in the book,' he said. 'Ask this lady for it.'

Bob walked out past the main counter. Thelma's pal was behind the counter. Not a bad-looking girl. On her good days.

'If you've never been to Doncaster at Mardi Gras, you've never lived.' Bob didn't bother to keep his voice down.

'Oh, Mr Ferris?' It was Thelma's pal.

Bob came back to the counter. 'What can I do for you, love – apart from take you to Doncaster?'

'Would you mind bringing back *The Godfather*? It's seven weeks overdue.'

Terry pottered barefoot into the kitchen with his army greatcoat over his pyjamas. He was cold, unhappy and irritable. He put a kettle of water on the gas then went and emptied the teapot down the outside loo. On his return he found the tea caddy was empty.

A frantic search of the cupboards failed to reveal a fresh packet of tea. Terry cursed. The kettle was now boiling. He draped the teapot over the spout to warm it, and then found the new packet of tea under the tea cosy. He'd put the cosy on top when he'd gone to empty the teapot.

Terry whacked in three spoonfuls of PG Tips and poured on the boiling water. Unfortunately the carelessly aimed stream hit the rim of the pot and sprayed hot droplets over his bare feet. Terry let out a howl of pain and hopped over to the armchair.

Bob popped his head round the back door and saw Terry clutching both feet in a passable imitation of a crossed lotus position.

'You oughtn't to do those Yoga exercises if they hurt that much,' he said.

'You dumb bugger,' howled Terry. 'I've just poured bloody boiling water all over me foot!'

'Oh, I thought you'd had an accident. Gave me quite a shock yelling like that.'

'I *have* had an accident,' snarled Terry.

'What you need is a cup of tea,' said Bob soothingly. He poured the rest of the hot water into the teapot, stirred it, then pulled the tea cosy down on top of it.

'What do you want anyway? And why aren't you at work?'

'I told them I'd be in this afternoon. Getting back so late, like. Had to go round to the Library to make it up with Thelma.'

'Couldn't wait till lunchtime, that, I suppose.'

'No,' said Bob, refusing to rise to the bait. 'Milk and sugar?' He put two saucers underneath the cups, one spoon in the sugar and one to stir with.

'Two big ones,' said Terry. He took the offered cup ungratefully. 'What I mean is, what are you doing back here?'

'Well, I've come to see you, haven't I?' said Bob stretching his elegant flared trousers underneath the kitchen table. 'Come to extend the hand of friendship and welcome on this, your first day of freedom.' Bob lifted his tea cup and toasted Terry.

'Huh.'

'Come on, cheer up,' said Bob. 'You're home aren't you? This should be a day of joy and celebration. For your family and friends – and the shareholders of the Scottish & Newcastle Breweries.'

'Joy and celebration, you what? Me Mum and Dad aren't even home. Five years I've been gone – well, not counting leaves. Five years of hardship, toil, solitude and self-sacrifice and what happens? I get home, the key's under the mat, the heat's turned off and the only thing in the fridge is a packet of frozen cod balls.'

'What, not even a note?' asked Bob.

Terry was lost in bitter reflection. 'They know I'm allergic to fish.'

'Not fish and chips, you're not.'

'That's different. Different sort of fish that.'

'Not like your folks to be away. Another cup of tea?'

Terry stopped nursing his toes, and hobbled over to

the table with his cup. He pulled out a chair and sat down.

'Bed wasn't aired. Milk was almost sour. No newspaper and the wireless needs a battery.' Terry sighed heavily. 'Good mind to sign on again.'

'Did you ring your Audrey? She should know where they are.'

'Didn't sleep a wink. Not a wink. Sat by the window and watched the dawn come up.' Terry took a sip of tea. A far-away look came into his eye. Bob knew he was in for a touch of poetry.

'You know Bob, watching the dawn come up over this town. Watching the sun rise over the roofs of the little terraced houses. All huddled together in lines up the hill. Watching it bounce off the brewery then up over the glue works and the distant shot tower of the lead factory – well . . . it must be one of the *ugliest* sights in the whole world.'

'You're lucky. Most days you can't see as far as that,' said Bob.

'Made me wonder why I'd ever come back. Actually started feeling homesick – for the Army. Started me thinking, you know – about the places. About the lads. Was with them a long time, some of them. Went through a lot together. Hughie Mclaren, now. He was with me since basic training. Next bed to me for five years.'

'I'm surprised people didn't talk.'

Terry gave Bob a withering look. 'You wouldn't understand the friendships that are forged in combat.'

'Combat?! Where?'

'Take Taffy Lewis for example. With me in Germany. I was there the night he brained a second lieutenant with a hock bottle.'

'Ah,' said Bob. 'That kind of combat.'

'Two years he got for that. In the glass house. Still . . . Clarkie was already in there, and Chippy was sent up soon after.'

'You got in with quite a nice set then?'

'What's that supposed to mean?'

'Well,' said Bob. 'The way you're talking, you'd

think you'd just been released from prison, not the forces.'

'They were a lot of good lads,' said Terry. 'But just unlucky. They got caught, I didn't.'

Bob smiled. 'What were you known as – "The Dirty Dozen"?'

'Great film that.' Terry took a sip of tea. 'All right, go ahead, but Taffy Lewis, now. I would have trusted him with my life.' He paused to remember Taffy. 'Not me wallet like, but certainly me life.'

'Well, all that's behind you now. Time to look ahead isn't it? Time to plan. To forge ahead. Get something behind you. Build a future.'

'Aye, well, it's easy for you to say that,' said Terry with undisguised bitterness. 'Some of us have been able to, haven't they? Some of us have been *able* to forge ahead, to *build* a future. While others of us were serving Queen and Country. Keeping these shores safe. So that *some* of us could *safely* get on with forging ahead and building a future while some of us *not* so fortunate couldn't.'

'I don't quite understand,' said Bob. 'Are you getting at me?'

'Well, you've obviously done all right. Mortgage and a car. And a few premium bonds, have you?' Terry rubbed his hands together like a money-lender. 'And I bet Thelma's got something tucked away in the Post Office for a rainy day.'

Bob pushed his cup and saucer away. 'You've never liked Thelma, have you?'

'It's the other way round.' Terry shrugged.

'No,' said Bob. 'You've always resented her. Oh, God . . . ' He raised his eyes to the embossed polystyrene-tiled ceiling. 'An hour ago, I was arguing with her on *your* behalf, and now I'm having a go at you about *her*! I can just see my life stretching ahead of me. My marriage'll be like a game of tennis – with you and Thelma serving for advantage points.' Bob tapped his chest. 'And *I'm* going to be the ball that's bashed from one to the other. Trying to love all. I'll just be a go-between. An emissary of hate.'

'Emissary' was a word Bob had borrowed from Thelma. He was quietly pleased to have found an opportunity to use it. He got up with a dignified gesture of resignation.

'I might as well make plans for the divorce now. No point in waiting till the last moment.' Bob made a mock appraisal of Terry. 'Mental cruelty is what I suppose you'd come under.'

'Well, it's certainly not going to be adultery!'

Bob was so far ahead with his plans for disaster that he missed the joke '. . . she can have the house, of course. Only fair.'

'Right.'

'Only fair . . . ' Bob looked at his watch. 'My God, look at the time. I'm supposed to be up there doing some decorating.'

'Is it worth it?'

'How do you mean?'

'Well, if Thelma's getting the house, why don't you let her hang her own wallpaper?'

From Bob's expression, it was apparent that Thelma was no longer a subject for funny jokes, ribald remarks or general merriment.

'You know what you are, don't you?' he said. You're what's referred to as just cause and impediment.'

'I'm a wounded ex-serviceman simply trying to make his way back into society,' said Terry stoutly. 'That's what I am.'

Bob gave him a reproving look and walked out into the hall. Terry grabbed the kettle that had been simmering on the gas.

'A society that obviously doesn't want me!' He shouted at the half-open door.

It was unfortunate that he chose to refill the tea-pot at the same time as he was savouring the bitterness of this final, savage shaft. The hot water missed the tea-pot.

'Jesus Christ, Oh, Jesus Christ, oh, Jesus Christ!'

Bob ran back down the hall and poked his head round the door. 'Now what's the matter?'

Terry was hopping about hugging his left foot. Bob

tried to keep a straight face. 'You want to be careful, you know. You can have nasty accidents with boiling water.'

'It's all your bloody fault in the first place! Go on, piss off!'

'Hey,' said Bob, grinning.

'What?'

'Why don't you go up to your Audrey's. She'll be surprised to see you, and when she says – "My God, where have you sprung from?" – you can say – "I've just come hot-foot from my house".'

Bob just managed to shut the door before the kettle hit it.

Actually, there was little else for Terry to do but go and see his sister up on the estate. She'd been there about four years. At first, there had just been three roads of semis. Now, the founding families were marooned in a maze of pale grey concrete roads with their own bus service.

At least, thought Terry, I'll be able to cadge a meal or two. He sniffed. No doubt about it, he was definitely getting a cold. He turned into Audrey's road. As he passed a TV repair van, a man in a white coat came out of the house opposite. 'Hello, Terry.'

Terry stopped. He felt cheered at being recognised. 'Hello, Stan.'

Stan clapped Terry on the shoulder and dumped a tool box in the back of the van. 'Mind, I haven't seen you for a long time. On leave, are you?'

'No,' said Terry. 'All through. Finished. Got back last night.'

'Gerraway.'

'Yep. A civvy now.'

'You're looking fit, mind,' said Stan.

'Full of bloody cold.'

'Aye, well, it's parky up here you know. You'll probably have forgotten. Wind can go right through you.'

'You're telling me.'

'You were in the tropics, weren't you?'

'More or less,' said Terry. There had, after all, been a

few sunny days in München-Gladbach.

'Where are you off to then?'

'Just away up to see our Audrey for a cup of tea.'

'Be havin' a few bevvies this week, eh?' said Stan, raising an invisible pint glass in a trembling hand. 'A few jars with the lads.'

'More'n likely,' said Terry.

'Aye, I reckon you'll be in for a grand time,' said Stan. 'Red carpet, the welcome mat. Home is the hero. The big hello, eh? Drinks all round.'

'Do you still go down there?' asked Terry.

Stan shook his head. 'No, the doctor took me off it,' he said. 'But have one for me.' He clapped Terry round the shoulder again and got into the van.

'See you.'

'Aye,' said Terry. 'See you.' Mean bugger . . . Still, he thought, when you run out of friends, there's always your family. He rang the bell of Audrey's house.

'Good God,' said Audrey. 'What are you doing here?'

'Marvellous. Is that all you can say to your little brother? After five years?'

Audrey stepped back to let him through the front door, 'Wipe your feet, I've just Hoovered the hall.'

Audrey went back to the kitchen. Upstairs, Terry could hear the noise of little children. He hung up his raincoat and went to the door of the kitchen. Audrey was busy ironing. Apart from a bloody great pile of washing on the table, the kitchen was neat and tidy.

'I've taken me coat off,' said Terry. 'I hope I'm not intruding.'

'That's all right,' said Audrey. 'If you want to make yourself useful, you can sit down and pair off all those clean socks.'

Home is the hero. Terry sat down. 'Where's Mum and Dad?'

'They're at your Uncle Norman's funeral.'

'Which Uncle Norman?'

'Your Uncle Norman in Carlisle.'

'Carlisle?'

'Yes, you remember. He had the, er – '

'Oh, aye. Yes. How is he?'

'How d'you expect him to be at his own funeral?'

'Sorry,' said Terry. 'Didn't hear you. Still, he had a good innings. He was eighty – something, wasn't he?'

'Ninety-four.' Audrey started on the collar of another shirt.

Terry was having difficulty in telling black socks from navy blue ones. He rolled them together. What the hell. If he couldn't tell the difference no one else would.

'When are they coming back, then?'

'Don't know. They were going to stay on with your Auntie for a day or two. She's ninety, y'know.'

'Ninety?'

'Yes.'

'It's hardly worth them coming home. If they hang on a bit, they could save themselves a double journey.'

'What a terrible thing to say.'

It must have been. Audrey actually stopped ironing for a full ten seconds.

'I'm sorry,' said Terry. 'I'm a little bit short of the milk of human kindness this morning. Got back in the middle of the night. The house was like ice. Bed wasn't aired, and I couldn't find a hot water bottle.'

'Probably took them with them,' said Audrey. 'Carlisle's not exactly your Costa Brava.'

'And on top of that I'm getting a cold,' said Terry miserably.

'Well, don't go breathing your germs round here. Not with the baby.'

'What baby?'

'We had another one six months ago,' said Audrey. She pointed to a large pile of clean nappies. 'What do you think those are – woolly handkerchiefs?'

'What make is it?'

'A girl. Emma Fleur.'

'*Fleur*?'

'F-L-E-U-R,' said Audrey. 'Like in *The Forsyte Saga.* It means flower in French.'

'I know what the French for flower is,' said Terry. 'I just didn't know about *her*.'

'Well we wrote and told you.'

'Ah, well, mail didn't always get through to some of the places I've been.'

'Don't know why,' said Audrey. 'You've been in Devizes the last six months.'

'Officially,' said Terry.

Audrey gave him an old-fashioned look.

'I've finished the socks.'

'Good. Why don't you put the kettle on? I suppose you want a cup of tea?'

'I was hoping I might get a late lunch.'

'Sorry, I've got a date at the hairdressers.'

Terry put the kettle on the electric stove. He hesitated. 'Do you – er . . . '

'What?'

'Well, do you think there's any chance of me staying here? I mean just till Mum gets back?'

'Why don't you stay at Bob's?'

'*She* wouldn't let me.'

'Who, his mother?'

'No. Thelma. The fee-on-say. She's put her foot down. Come on Aud – it's just awful back home. There's no food, nothing. And you can't get a decent picture on that set.'

'I just can't have you here with that cold.' said Audrey. 'If one of us gets it, we'll all go down with it. And Wayne's very chesty. The kettle's boiling.'

'That was quick,' said Terry. 'Who's Wayne?'

'Oh, for God's sake, Terry! He's your godson.'

'Oh, *that* Wayne. I thought you'd married again.'

'Well, he's nearly four now, and you owe him for three Christmases, three birthdays and one christening. We'll accept Premium Bonds. You never know your luck.'

'This must be what they call an open-handed welcome,' said Terry.

'The tea bags are in the cupboard right behind you, two will be plenty, and there are some cream crackers in the blue tin,' said Audrey. 'And be careful with the teapot.'

Terry made the tea and put the crinolined-lady tea cosy on top of it. He took down two alphabet mugs and got a bottle of milk from the fridge. He turned it upside down to get rid of the cream.

'You know,' he said. 'I didn't expect the freedom of the city. I didn't expect a champagne buffet with the Mayor and a march-past. But really, when you've been away five years, serving your country, you expect to come back to more than two tea-bags and a cream cracker.'

'You should have written,' said Audrey.

'Oh, aye. And what would that have entitled me too?' asked Terry. 'A heart-warming triangle of Dairylea?'

'Wayne had the last bit with his lunch,' said Audrey. 'But you can have some lemon curd if you like.'

'By the cringe!' Terry sat down disconsolately.

'Mind out!' cried Audrey. 'I've just ironed that lot!'

There is no doubt about it, thought Terry. It is nice to know you are wanted.

Bob Ferris looked out his bare picture window and saw Terry duck down behind the front garden wall. Since it was only two foot six high, his attempt at concealment was less than perfect. Bob went to the front door.

'Terry?'

Terry remained bent over. Bob walked down to the bent metal gate. The style was called 'Valencia'. Thelma had preferred 'Seville' but he'd managed to persuade her that the extra-curly, curly bits would be difficult to repaint.

Terry looked up at him. 'Oh, hallo!'

'Thought you'd got your tie caught in the manhole cover,' said Bob.

'No, er – I was just tying my shoelace.' Terry straightened up with an embarrassed shuffle that failed to conceal the fact that he was wearing slip-on shoes.

'Ah . . .' said Bob understandingly. 'Came up to see the house, did you?'

'Is *this* your house?' asked Terry with a great show of surprise. 'I didn't know you lived here. I was just taking a short cut back from our Audrey's. Well, well, well, so this is your house. What a coincidence.'

'Especially seeing you've come miles out of your way,' said Bob. He opened the front gate for Terry and waved proudly at the house. 'Well, there she is.'

Terry took a pace back and scanned the façade. He looked impressed. 'Looks quite a canny house, though but . . . '

'We haven't given it a name yet.'

'You'll need one though, won't you? Or you may never find it again.'

'What d'you mean?'

Terry swept a hand up and down the road. 'Well look at them, they're all the same, aren't they? Rows and rows of them.

'Oh, no, no. These are quite different. Our living-room's sixteen by twelve. Those down that end are fifteen by thirteen.'

Terry looked hard, but couldn't see any distinguishing features. 'I must be blind,' he said.

Bob showed him around upstairs first. None of the rooms were furnished. Terry couldn't work out how Bob planned to open the bedroom door once he had got the bed inside. I'll give him a year, thought Terry, and then he'll have plastic moulded panels on all these flush doors.

'We're going to put a bee-day in there,' said Bob showing Terry the bathroom.

'They've got 'em in Germany,' said Terry. 'Great for washing your feet. You can do yourself an injury cocking your leg up into the washbasin.'

Bob led the way down the stairs. They looked unfinished, but what with the two-inch-wide door jambs and the one-inch skirtings, Terry concluded there must be a drastic shortage of wood.

The living-room, with dining nook, was carpeted. A new sofa in its polythene wrapper stood against one wall. Bob had been busy putting up new shelves around a service hatch that opened into the kitchen.

'Under-floor central heating, of course, and we've decided to be all electric. Lots of points everywhere, dimmer-switches on the lights – what are you looking at?'

Terry had laid the side of his face against one of the walls. 'Are you sure this is plumb?'

Bob walked over and laid his face alongside Terry's. 'Of course it is. What makes you think it isn't?'

'Well, if you can't see it, I'm not going to tell you. Nasty crack in the plaster.'

'That's just settling down. Always get a bit of that in new houses.'

Terry sucked his breath in sharply. 'Just hope it's not structural.'

'Listen,' said Bob. 'You're bound to get a few teething troubles. Like having a new car.'

'Ah. Had trouble with that as well?'

'Not really. Well, apart from the starter motor.' Bob watched Terry slow-march the length of the room. 'What are you doing?'

'Just measuring,' said Terry. 'I only make it fifteen. You've been done.'

'What?!' Bob started to pace out the room himself. He stopped halfway. 'Yes, well it depends what size shoe you take, doesn't it? You're two sizes bigger then me.'

'I'll bring me tape measure,' said Terry. He lifted the service hatch and peered into the kitchen. As he turned back to make another uncomplimentary remark to Bob the hatch slammed down on his fingers. Terry let out a howl of pain.

'Jesus wept!'

'I forgot to tell you about that,' said Bob. 'That *does* need fixing.' Then added soothingly, 'Put some cold water on it.'

'Cold water?! I've broken me bloody fingers!!'

'No, you haven't, no you haven't. If you can wiggle it about like that, you're all right.'

'All right?! Jesus – '

'Just keep them moving. Here – '

'Don't touch me!'

'Just think about something else. Look at these windows.'

'Bugger the windows.'

'Bags of light. It's a feature of these houses. Open-plan.'

'Means you can't hide from the gas man,' said Terry sourly.

'Nobody's going to do that on this estate.'

'They won't be doing much else either the way you can see right through from back to front. I'd rather have a bit of privacy.'

'Privacy? Listen, mate. This is Woburn Abbey compared to what we were brought up in. When you think where we lived as kids – why, if you sneezed, they said "Bless You" three doors away. The privvy's inside and upstairs, not out in the yard with a tin bath hanging on the wall.'

'All right. Admitted. But there was some character about those houses. There's something depressing about these estates. It's the thought of you all waking up at the same time, all eating the same low calorie breakfast cereal – with added raisins. The same rows of books from the same book club on your shelves, the same miniature bottles of booze on your bar next to your Sparklets soda siphon. All coming home at half-past six, switching on the same programme and having it off on the same two nights every week.'

'I beg your pardon?'

'Put it in your diary. By the time you've done the garden and put the rest of the shelves up, and she's run the bag-wash down to the launderette, you'll be lucky if you even manage that.'

'I don't see how you'd know,' said Bob. 'But anyway, look – we haven't had a chance to personalise it yet. Once everyone moves in and chooses their own decorative schemes and their own curtains. Thelma has a flair for things like that. We're having mauve and seaweed green.'

'At least that's unusual.'

'We were going to have yellow, but we found out they were having that next door.'

'Well, that's it, isn't it? That's the problem. You've said it all.' Terry walked to the front window and looked out along the road. 'It seems sad when you realise the only way people can tell the difference between you and everyone else is by the colour of your curtains.'

'So what's wrong with that?' said Bob with rising indignation. 'What's wrong with being the same as everybody else? What's wrong with trying to make some modest progress? I've worked bloody hard the last five years, and I've got this to show for it, and the car – '

'And a thirty-year mortgage round your neck.'

'I can pay that. It's still my house. Might not mean much to the Burtons, but it means a lot to me. It's okay for you to sneer, but what's so special about *your* life style? You're homeless, carless and single. What does that amount to? Terry Collier. Bachelor Pedestrian.'

Terry looked at Bob, then turned away. It was obvious that Bob had scored a direct hit. He'd meant to put Terry down, but not that much.

'I'm sorry,' said Bob. 'That wasn't a very nice thing to say.'

Terry puckered his lips but said nothing. He stared out of the window. Bob suddenly felt awkward.

'It's stupid anyhow. Why should you be interested in all of this? No need for a fellow like you to get lumbered with a wife and mortgage. Not your scene. Can't imagine you married with all those birds out there. All those good times to be had – not to mention the birds. *I* was always the one falling in love all over the place, not you. You were the cool one. Kept your head. Safety in numbers. The born bachelor.'

'Aye, you're right.' Terry's voice was heavy with resignation. He stiil kept his eyes averted.

'Naturally independent.'

'True. True.'

'You see? There you are then.'

'Just one little problem.'

'What's that?'

'I'm married,' said Terry.

'You're what?'

'I'm married,' said Terry. He turned to face Bob in case he needed to lip-read. 'I – am – a – married – man.'

Bob stared back at Terry. His mouth was wobbling about like it had on the train.

'But – '

'Well, go on. Say something then.'

'I – '

'Don't tell me you've lost your tongue. The Joker of Jesmond. The Wit of Walker. The Sage of Scotswood. Surely you can think of something to say.'

'I'll, er – '

'You'll what?'

'I think I'll pop down to the off-licence and get a few bottles of Brown,' said Bob.

Bob came back with a carrier bag full of Brown Ale and they squatted on the floor to drink out of plastic cups. Terry couldn't understand why they couldn't sit on the sofa – especially as it was covered. He concluded that perhaps it first had to be christened by Thelma's majestic bum.

'Right now,' said Bob. 'Start at the beginning. Don't skip anything. Tell it from the start. I want to hear it all.'

'Bob,' said Terry patiently, 'This is the story of my marriage, not the serial on *Woman's Hour*.'

'It's the story of the century, mate. It's fantastic. It's like me getting a peerage – or Darlington winning promotion.'

'I'm glad you're going to get so much fun out of it, Bob. Perhaps you'd like to ask your mates round. I could give a talk at the Institute. I can illustrate it with coloured slides – '

'I've got a projector.'

' – And you can all sit around peeing yourselves at my misfortune.'

'Misfortune?' The smile faded from Bob's face.

'The wounds are deep. Scars haven't healed yet.'

'I'm sorry. I didn't realise.'

'I've only just learned to live with the pain.'

'Well, then forget it. I mean, don't talk about it if it hurts too much. You don't have to tell me everything. Just give me the recorded highlights.'

Terry lowered his plastic cup. 'You can't wait can you?'

'Sorry.' Bob affected disinterest. 'Just give it to me in your own time.'

Terry got to his feet and stuck his hands behind his back like the Duke of Edinburgh, and his chin on his chest like Churchill.

'During my military career, two things happened to me which have left an imprint on me for the rest of my life.'

'Your leg?' said Bob.

'Apart from that. That I can live with.' Terry gave it a quick rub. Presumably to drive the pain away. 'No,' he continued. 'The first was the night I got pissed out of my mind in Hamburg and got tattooed on my left buttock.'

'What kind of tattoo?'

'And the second, was the rainy day, four years ago come this November, when Jutta Paumgarten, spinster of München-Gladbach and yours truly got wed.'

'Incredible.'

'Fact nonetheless.'

'Stranger than fiction.'

'The plain, unvarnished truth.'

'Was she, um – ?'

'Funnily enough, no, she wasn't *um*.'

'A rich dad.'

'Not especially,' said Terry. Had a few pfennigs put away, but nothing much. Just a chemist's shop on the Wendlichstrasse. Not exactly your Gunter Sachs. Your Baron von Thyssen.'

Bob could not have looked more incredulous if he had discovered Einstein's Theory of Relativity. 'You mean it was love?'

'That's your last alternative, is it?' Terry looked annoyed. 'She's not pregnant, she's not loaded, so this must be love. Thank you.'

Terry wandered over to the shelves and cast an unsympathetic eye over Bob's handiwork.

'Come off it, Terry, I'm only going on what I know of you. Your priorities were always firmly worked out. "Do you or don't you, darling?" And as long as they did, you weren't fussy. You'd have had a frog if it had stopped hopping long enough.'

'Get away.'

'Come on, now.'

'I'm not denying I put it about a bit,' said Terry defensively. 'I'm just saying that I'm capable of deeper emotions than "wham, bang, thank you mam". I'm not the person you used to know. I now know that there's more to life than the merely physical. I know there's more to people than just the way they look. I've changed.' Terry sat down beside Bob again.

'So sex didn't come into it,' said Bob, filling up Terry's plastic cup.

'Of course sex came into it. I haven't changed that much. All I'm saying is that when I walked down the aisle, I was looking beyond bed. Maybe it wasn't love. Maybe I was looking for something else.' Terry shrugged. 'At the time, married quarters seemed a whole lot better than a metal bunk in Hut 14.'

'We had *no* idea,' said Bob. 'Wasn't in the local paper. And your parents never mentioned it.'

'Well, they wouldn't, would they? They were dead against it. You know how me Dad feels about the Germans. He won't even accept a lift in our Audrey's Volkswagen.'

'So what went wrong?'

'What went right, you mean. I suppose the main trouble was communication. No point of contact. You can't spend all your time in bed.'

'Didn't you have anything else in common?'

'Difficult to tell. She didn't speak English, and I

certainly wasn't going to learn German.'

Bob watched Terry down his beer and reach for another bottle. 'Perhaps a child would have helped,' he said. 'Or an interpreter.'

Terry didn't reply.

'I'm very sorry. I really am.'

'Aye, well – we live and learn.' Terry gave a wry smile. 'It's just that – well, when you see somone in their new home, you're inclined to get a bit bitter. I'm sorry, I wasn't trying to be rude about your house.'

'Of course, I understand. It was my fault for being so – insensitive.'

'We're apologising to each other again.'

'Sorry,' said Bob.

Terry stood up. He rocked a little on his gammy leg. Bob got to his feet and steadied him.

'Playing you up, eh?'

'Just now and then.' Terry let out a long sigh. 'Yes, it would have helped if I'd had a house to come home to. I don't want to land myself on relatives.' He shivered. 'If this does turn out to be another bout of malaria, it's hardly fair to them.' Terry turned and limped out of the room.

'Where are you going?'

'Thought I'd go down to the cafe by the bus terminal. Buy a hot cup of Oxo. If I could stand near the tea urn I might get some warmth.'

'Terry – you know you could stay at my place if it wasn't for – '

Terry silenced him with a raised hand. 'Please I don't want to cause any more trouble between you two.' He picked up his coat and opened the front door.

'Wait a minute,' said Bob. 'I've got an idea.'

Thelma was still at the library when Bob got there. She'd opted for two evenings every week to bump up her salary – and so put more away in the Post Office. Bob explained the situation very carefully, and very sentimentally. So well, in fact, that it brought tears to his eyes. Thelma lent him her handkerchief.

'Poor Terry,' said Thelma. I never thought I'd hear me saying that.'

'I'd never thought *I'd* hear you say that.'

'I am human, Bob. I do have some compassion.'

'Even for Terry,' observed Bob.

'For any human being who's suffered. I suppose there's no chance of them – ?'

Bob shook his head.

'It's such a risk marrying foreigners. Especially Germans. They're so – physical.'

Bob nodded. 'You're right. Yes. He said their relationship was very – physical.'

'I see. You've been into all that, have you?' An old-fashioned look.

'We touched upon it. He poured his heart out.'

Thelma took back her handkerchief. 'And is he still terribly upset?'

'He's only just learned to live with the pain. And then there's his leg.'

'What's wrong with his leg?'

'He never talks about it.'

'Poor Terry.'

'And he got precious little comfort coming home. Folks away . . . '

'It's not fair.'

'So I thought the best thing would be for him to come and stay with me.'

'Then you can think again!'

'But he needs comfort,' pleaded Bob. A helping hand. A shoulder to lean on.'

'He's not leaning on *your* shoulder. Giggling away into the small hours. Discussing – physical things. The good old days when you were both free.'

'So where's this compassion of yours gone?'

'It hasn't gone. I'm just saying the answer isn't to have him staying with you. Filling you full of the perils and pitfalls of married life. I've got a much better idea.'

'Oh, yes?'

'He can stay at my place.'

'Like hell he can!'

'It's the perfect answer.' Thelma had the marvellous gift of being able to totally ignore objections to her bright ideas. 'In these situations a man needs a woman's sympathy.'

'But your parents are away.'

'So there's plenty of room.'

'But you never let me stay there when they're away. I'm always having to make pre-dawn departures. Losing sleep. Risking the breathalyser.'

'That's because of our situation. Because of the neighbours. It doesn't matter about Terry. He'd be a guest, not a lover.'

'He'd be more than a guest given half a chance.'

'Well, he's not getting half a chance with me!' Thelma bristled with indignation.

'I'm not saying he would. But your feelings don't enter into it. You must remember what Terry's like when he's had a skinful. He can't take "no" for an answer. He gets the red mist.'

'Don't worry. I can handle Terry.'

'That's what he'll be hoping! It won't make any difference to him that you and I are engaged. Won't stop him chancing his arm. Won't stop him laying siege at your bedroom door.'

'Bob, I'm making a real effort to understand Terry. To get to know him. That's what you wanted. I was unreasonable because I wasn't prepared to do that. Now I'm making the gesture. To be a friend of your friend.'

'I want you to be a friend of my friend. I just don't want my friend getting too friendly that's all.'

'I see,' said Thelma. 'What happened to our trust, then?'

'Trust?'

'Trust, Bob. Isn't that what we're supposed to have? It describes what is supposed to exist between two people who are going to get married. It means not having to worry about what the other person's up to. Not having to be afraid. Not having doubts.'

'I know. That's exactly what I told Terry.'

'So?'

'It's not worth the risk,' said Bob.

When Bob got back to the new house, Terry was stretched out on the sofa. Terry had decided not to wait for Thelma's inauguration ceremony. He'd also finished all the beer. Bob explained how Thelma had reacted.

'Well, I'm glad we're all friends together. Can't say I'm not touched, Bob. Can't say I'm not surprised, either.'

'Aw - you know what women are like. Soon as they hear about some personal tragedy, it brings out the mother instinct.'

'Well, I don't mind being mothered by Thelma for a few days. Could start a whole new chapter in our relationship.'

'That's what I thought,' said Bob. 'That's why I put my foot down.'

'You what?! Terry sat up with a start.

'I refused the offer - on your behalf.'

The message sank in. 'You don't *want* me to be friends with Thelma.'

'Of course I want you to be friends. I - just don't want you staying there, that's all.'

'You don't trust me. I'm your best mate and you don't trust me.' Terry stood up.

'Of course I trust you.'

Terry gave Bob a sly prod in the belly. 'You think I'd go there and try it on. You think in the middle of the night, I'd be . . . '

'Laying seige.'

'Laying siege?'

'At her bedroom door.'

'I wouldn't need to lay siege, mate. Those flush doors are only two thin bits of ply filled with paper!'

'That's why I said "no".'

'Thank you. Well, I'd better get going.' Terry began to button up his coat. 'Don't want to miss the last bus. I want to get to the cafe before they run out of Oxo.'

'I've got it!' said Bob. 'Of course! You can stay here!'

'Here?'

'Don't know why I didn't think of it before. Thelma wanted you to stay at her place – well, this is her place. And it's mine too. Central heating, radio, tea in the kitchen, and we've got a bed too!'

Bob began to unfold the sofa to form a double bed. There's blankets and sheets in the drawer underneath. I often stay here when I'm decorating.'

'Oh, aye.'

'And sometimes Thelma comes over and – well . . . '

'Gives you a hand. Right. Got it.'

Bob was visibly embarrassed. 'Well, you know how difficult it is at her place.'

'Of course. The neighbours.'

Terry helped Bob arrange the sheets and blankets, then he tried the bed for size.

'Well, it's very comfy, I will say that.'

'It will be our spare bed. You may as well get used to it.'

Terry looked doubtful.

'You can't go limping off into the night with galloping malaria can you?' said Bob.

'Right,' said Terry. 'You're on.'

'I'll come round early in the morning with some eggs and bacon and the paper.'

'Smashing.' Terry started to take off his shoes.

'Oh, one thing,' said Bob. 'Turn the light out before you get undressed. We haven't got any curtains, remember?'

'Got it.' Terry walked to the front door with Bob.

'Cheers.'

'Hey, Bob.'

'What?'

'Do you really not trust me with Thelma?'

'No,' said Bob. 'I bloody don't. Nite, nite.'

Terry closed the front door happily, reassured about his sexual menace.

Bob of course had been scheduled to spend the evening decorating at the house. He'd told Thelma that Terry had been helping him. Naturally Thelma took that to mean that a lot more had been done. And, just as naturally, Thelma was keen to see it. And also prepared to show her appreciation of the effort Bob was making.

She made her way over after she'd shut up the library and been to the launderette. There was no point in getting there *too* early. She let herself in quietly, took off her shoes and tip-toed into the living-room. There were no street lights outside yet, but there was just enough light from the house across the way to see the sleeping figure on the bed.

'Bob?' she whispered.

No reply.

Thelma tip-toed across to the shelves and felt their smooth surfaces with one hand, and unbuttoned her blouse with the other.

What a darling. He'd finished them. And all she'd done was to bitch about how long everything was taking, and be generally unreasonable.

Well, she thought fondly, there was always one way to make up for it. She undressed and slipped very carefully into the bed and snuggled up against her loved one's back.

'Don't wake up, pet,' she whispered, and got a snore for an answer.

Bob got up especially early, borrowed six eggs and two rashers of bacon from his Mam, bought a *Daily Mirror*, and drove round to the estate. He was careful not to slam the car door, and he let himself in without making a sound. He planned to surprise Terry with a slap-up breakfast. But as Burns himself said, even the best laid plans 'gang oft agley' and Bob's was no exception.

He laid the two egg-and-bacon breakfasts on the

kitchen side of the hatch and lifted it with a flourish.

What he saw was his bride-to-be playing 'this little piggy' up Terry's back in an effort to wake him. What Thelma saw was the startled face of her future husband stuck in the hatch, when his body was in the bed beside her. What Terry saw, when his sleep was shattered by Thelma's scream, was that he might not get his promised breakfast.

Thelma leapt out of bed in her briefs and bra, snatched up her clothes and shot off to have a nervous breakdown in the bathroom.

'What have you done!?' Bob's purple face was framed in the hatch.

'Nothing,' protested Terry, still dazed with sleep and deafened by Thelma's scream. 'I was out like a light all night.' He rubbed his eyes. 'What the hell is Thelma doing here?'

'You devious bastard,' snarled Bob.

'Bob – you surely don't think we – '

'What else can I think!!'

'Trust,' said Terry. 'You told me yourself. It means not having to worry what the other person's up to. It means not having to be afraid. Not having doubts.'

As Bob opened his mouth to reply, the hatch slammed down shut on both his hands.

There was no doubt about it, thought Terry. Bob would really have to get it fixed.

3

Cold Feet

Terry thought it was better to leave Bob and Thelma to sort out their pre-marital problems in the privacy of their own home. Two fingers of the hand he'd caught in the hatch the night before were still giving him jip, so he decided to go to the doctor's.

He was relieved to find his house still standing. Although it was a full ten minutes to opening time, there were fourteen people lined up outside the surgery. Terry scanned their faces for signs of fatal diseases, and wondered how many had just come to pick up prescriptions. Not that it really mattered. He didn't have anything else to do that morning.

They filed into the disinfected waiting room and sat down on the metal chairs. Terry recognised the aspidistra. It was still on the table in the window where it had been five years ago. He thought he recognised some of the tattered magazines too. He flipped through several of the women's mags but they were all full of the same rubbishy advice, fair-isle knitting patterns, pictures of Princess Anne and recipes for lemon meringue pie.

Terry carefully counted the people in the room and memorised the grey face of the middle-aged man who'd been ahead of him in the queue outside. If he lost count, it would be his turn after Pale Face had gone in. If he lasted that long.

Terry nursed his hand and tried to will a little more pain into it. He laid his head back against the wall and projected himself through a series of complex operations, followed by a slow convalescence in the care of a glamourous multi-racial nursing staff on a sun-drenched Greek island retreat.

A noise like a bee's fart dribbled into his subconscious and brought him winging back. It was the buzzer for the first patient. Two people got up. A good start anyway. Two down and twelve to go. Terry drifted off into another scene where this lady doctor in long black boots and glasses began testing the reflexes of his damaged hand. He was just about to tell her about his thigh – when he came to with a start.

Everyone had gone except the grey-faced middle-aged man and a woman with a plaster cast on her neck. There was another long dribbling fart from the trapped bee over the door. The woman got up and went through. Terry looked at the clock and saw it was ten fifteen. The door opened again and Bob walked in. His right hand was bandaged like Terry's.

'Snap,' said Terry, holding up his own right hand.

Bob looked right through him and leafed through the litter of magazines. He pulled out a copy of the *Daily Telegraph* Colour Supplement and sat down opposite Terry.

'Morning,' said Terry.

Bob appeared engrossed in the pictures.

'We seem to keep meeting in waiting rooms.'

No reply.

'Did, ah – Thelma explain – about last night?'

Pale Face looked up from his 1963 copy of *Yachting World* with a flicker of nervous interest.

'I mean, if she did,' continued Terry. 'You must know it was all an accident, so it's pointless you sitting there in a black huff.'

No reply.

'What *did* she say then?'

Without looking up, Bob said, 'I'm not prepared to discuss what she said. I am not interested in anything you might have to say. I do not wish to speak to you ever again – so please, stop trying to engage me in conversation.'

Strong stuff.

'Well, we can't just sit here like a couple of ninnies.

He's got a broken collar-bone in there at the moment – you know how long they take. Then there's this gentleman.'

'Oh, I won't be long,' said Pale Face. 'I'm only collecting the wife's prescription.'

'I wouldn't be too sure,' said Terry. 'You don't look too good to me. If I were you, I'd get it seen to.'

Pale Face took shelter behind his copy of *Yachting World*. Bob reached for another magazine.

'Look, Bob. Be reasonable. Talking to me is better than reading a 1957 edition of *Autocar*. Did she, or did she not explain?'

Bob sat back and mastered an overwhelming desire to brain Terry with one of the surgery chairs. Finally he said, 'Thelma is not speaking to me. Thelma is having a nervous breakdown.'

'You should have brought her along with you,' said Terry cheerfully. 'She could have had my turn.'

Bob raised his bandaged hand. 'If it wasn't for this, I'd smash your stupid face in.'

Terry raised his own hand. 'What? You mean you'd hit an injured man?'

Bob's verbal log-jam broke. He leaned forward. 'I offered you my hospitality. I offered you my house. Because you had nowhere to go. Because I was sorry for you. I even got up early this morning to come and make you breakfast – '

'I suppose Thelma ate mine.'

'I brought you the morning paper, bacon, eggs. Large, brown, organic eggs. From free range chickens. And what do I find when I get there? *You're* in bed with my fiancée!'

The copy of *Yachting World* trembled.

'Look, Bob – '

'Are you denying it?!'

'I don't deny being in *bed* with her, but I *do* deny *knowing* I was in bed with her. Bob, look, nothing happened – well, as far as *I* know, nothing did. It's obvious she didn't know she was in bed with me. I mean, granted we're mates, and we went to the same school – but that's where the resemblance *ends*.'

'Thank you very much.'

'Use your loaf. It's obvious. She came up to stay with *you* last night. Saw me asleep, and thought I was you. Didn't want to wake *you* up, so she got into bed beside me and went to sleep.'

'Without noticing I'd lost a good two stone? Where had I been all day – in a Turkish bath?'

'It was dark. I was asleep. Out like a light. I was so tired, and so ill, I wouldn't have cared if it had been Raquel Welch beside me. Mind you – I might have kicked meself in the morning, like.'

There was another bee-fart from the buzzer. Pale Face sat fast in his chair and pretended not to hear. Terry and Bob both looked at him.

'I think it's your turn,' said Terry.

The middle-aged man got up reluctantly and went to the door. 'You won't be coming back this evening will you?'

'No,' said Terry. 'Buy the book.'

The man left.

Terry spread out his hands in an appealing gesture. 'Bob, I'm the last person Thelma would think of cuddling up to. That's why she's having this – breakdown. Not because *you* found her in bed with me, but *she* found herself in bed with me.'

Bob's anger seemed to weaken as he considered the logic of Terry's argument.

'Come on, now,' pressed Terry. 'I'm right, aren't I?'

'I don't know.'

'Bob, nothing happened. Nothing.'

'Swear it, cross your heart and hope to die?'

'Not so much as a nudge.'

'Cross your heart?'

'Cross my heart. Scout's Honour. Cub's salute. I didn't even know she was there until she screamed in my ear. I wondered what the bloody hell was happening. It was like the last trump!'

'Well . . . '

'Mind, I can see how it must have been a shock for *you*.'

'At the time,' said Bob. 'At the time. The idea takes a bit of getting used to.'

Terry smiled. 'How's the hand?'

'I think I've broken it.'

'You can't have. Not if you can wiggle it about like that.'

'It's very sore.'

'So's mine. Mind you, the main reason I'm here is to get some malaria pills.'

'Come on. You haven't got malaria!'

'From the services,' said Terry stoutly. 'I spent two years in the Mediterranean, you know.'

'I'd have thought you'd have had webbed feet, not malaria,' said Bob. He was smiling now.

Terry relaxed. He crossed the room and sat beside Bob. 'She's not *really* having a nervous breakdown is she?'

'Well, she's very upset. Luckily, it's her half-day. I'll have to go round later and patch things up. Funny things, women, aren't they? If it's not one thing, it's another.'

'Usually the other,' said Terry reflectively.

'I seem to have been through so many hang-ups since you got back,' said Bob. 'And you've only been back two days!'

'Yes, I know,' said Terry. 'I'll have to leave. It's the only way. I'll emigrate.'

'Don't be silly. You're not to blame – not entirely, anyway.'

'Thanks. At least that's something.'

The buzzer sounded. Terry got up. 'You do believe me then?'

'Yes. Of course I do.'

Terry smiled. 'Perhaps you and I could have a swift half later on. Unless you want to hold Thelma's hand over lunch.'

'Okay, you're on.'

Shake?'

'Shake.' Bob stuck out his hand.

The reconciliation was unexpectedly painful. They had both forgotten that their right hands were bandaged.

When Bob arrived at the pub, Terry had already called up the first two halves. Bob joined him in a left-handed toast. Both of them now sported a clean, clinical bandage on their right hand.

'Have you, er – been in touch?' enquired Terry.

Bob nodded. 'Force eight gale warning.'

'With sunny periods expected later?'

'Maybe. Eee, it's a game, though, isn't it?'

'Don't tell *me*,' said Terry. 'I've been through it all once.'

'Everything's such a *drama*.'

'Same with my marriage. Except, of course, in our arguments, we could never understand one another. Mind, I knew what the rude words meant, like . . . '

'Couldn't, er – '

'Jutta,' said Terry. 'Yoo-tah.'

'Couldn't Jutta speak any English at all? I mean apart from the rude words you must have taught *her*.'

'She had a few useful phrases,' said Terry. 'Like – "Where are you going?" – "What time will you be in?" – "Give me more money" – you know. Warm, friendly sort of things.'

The two lads sat down at one of the tables in the public bar.

'Thelma's like that. She gets so – ,' Bob shrugged. 'Hysterical. It's your female insecurity, of course. She was like this when I broke off the engagement six months ago.'

Terry looked surprised. 'You mean again? *Apart* from the first time, like?'

'Yes,' said Bob. 'And there was another one in between those two. Another break.'

Terry looked at Bob and made a rapid reassessment of the situation in the light of this unexpected revelation.

'Well, Jesus,' he said. 'You can hardly blame the poor cow – I mean, poor lass for feeling insecure. That ring must have been on and off her hand like a yo-yo. Now you see it, now you don't. She must feel like Pavlov's dog.'

'Who's dog?'

'Pavlov's dog. You know. They used to ring this bell and take away his dinner.'

Bob frowned. 'I always thought Pavlov was a ballerina.'

'Well, she probably was. I only know she had this dog who didn't know whether he was coming or going.'

'Oh, be fair now. It's not as bad as that. Every couple has their ups and downs. Nothing's cut and dried. People have to be certain in their own minds. It's a big step to take.'

'Why did you break it off?' asked Terry. 'I mean, last time.'

'Irreconcilable differences,' said Bob.

Terry waited, but Bob didn't elaborate further.

'So how come it's all on again?'

'Our name came up on the housing list.'

Bob's matter-of-fact tone shook Terry.

'Bob, look. I've got no axe to grind. I'm not trying to stir things up, but that's hardly a basis for marriage now, is it? Loving someone – needing someone – putting someone up the stick, fine. But you don't just get married because someone on the Council writes to say your number's come up.'

'It wasn't just that. And it's not like that at all. Anyway that's all in the past. There are no more doubts. No more uncertainties.'

'I see,' said Terry. 'So at this moment in time, that little ring, after its many journeys up and down her digit, is now firmly in place.'

'Definitely,' said Bob. 'The banns are being read this Sunday, and the invitations have already gone out.'

'Well, that's it, then,' said Terry. 'It's settled.' He signalled to the barman for two more halves. 'No point in discussing it. I mean, what with the printer's charges and the cost of an announcement in the *Northern Echo* – let's face it – that represents too large an investment. Can't let that go to waste.'

'Terry, I've gone into this question of marriage very seriously. I'm well aware of the dangers of marrying for the wrong reasons. Thelma and I have been very mature about this. We've not panicked ourselves into rushing things.'

'I agree,' said Terry. 'After sixteen years of friendship and three engagements, no one can call *you* impetuous.'

'Sixteen years? It's not been as long as that, has it?'

Terry nodded. 'I can remember the day. Park Road Juniors. It was me that brought you together – well, indirectly. Old man Hayward wanted to split the two of us up, so he had a reshuffle and moved her desk next to yours.' He sighed. 'Lost me place by the radiator.'

'Oh, yes,' said Bob. 'I remember. Ironical, isn't it? I mean, the three of us have been reshuffling around ever since.'

They started on the fresh glasses of beer.

'You've always been falling in and out with her,' said Terry. 'You used to row even then. The first time was over some plasticine she had in an old Four Square tobacco tin. It disappeared and she said you'd stolen it. You said you hadn't, of course.'

'Of course.'

'But she didn't believe you.'

'Naturally.'

'And she asked to be put back on the other side of the room.'

'How can you remember all that?'

'Well, I stole the plasticine.'

'And you've been coming between us ever since.'

'Only for your own good.'

'It was you who spread the rumours about her going to the allotment with Frank Cheever.'

'Oh, yes?'

'Yes. And it was you who told me that her brother had been sent to Borstal – and that her mother was in a looney bin. You've been stealing Thelma's plasticine for sixteen years – metaphorically speaking.'

'Meta – what speaking?'

'Never mind.'

'You can tell you're marrying a grammar school girl,' said Terry.

'And I count myself lucky, too. That's when I almost lost contact.'

'You mean when she went to Heaton Grove Grammar?'

'Yes. While you and I went up into the Blackboard Jungle. That was when I became her social inferior.'

'Listen,' said Terry. 'At that school we were everybody's social inferior.'

Bob went misty-eyed. 'She was so – unobtainable. I used to watch her through the railings. Skipping with her skirt tucked into her navy blue knickers . . . As Paul Anka so aptly put it at the time – 'So near, yet so far away" . . . '

'Get off,' growled Terry. 'It was Billy Fury.'

'Of course it wasn't.'

'Billy *Fury*!'

'Paul *Anka*. A quid on it.'

'Done.' Terry slapped a pound note on the table. 'The title was "Halfway to Paradise". Sung by Billy Fury. "I want to be your lover but your friend is all I stay. I'm only half – " '

'What does *that* mean? "Your friend is all I stay"?'

Terry raised his voice in annoyance. 'I want to be your *lover* but you'll only let me be your *friend*!'

'Hey – !'

Terry turned as someone tapped him on the shoulder. It was the owner of the pub. As big as Mick McManus but twice as ugly. He pointed to the door.

'You two fairies – *OUT*!'

The best idea seemed to be to leave there and then and worry about their reputations later.

The two lads went round to Terry's sister Audrey. Terry

was still fuming when they got there.

'Hallo, Bob. Nice to see you.'

'Hallo, Audrey.' Bob kissed her on the cheek.

'Don't I get a kiss, then?' asked Terry.

'Just make sure you wipe your feet.' Audrey turned back to Bob. 'We got your invitation. I'll R.S.V.P. you as soon as I get a moment.'

'Thanks. Don't forget to send it to Thelma's place.'

'Soon as I get this bandage off, I'm going to go round there and land that bloke one,' growled Terry. 'They don't treat you like that in the Black Horse.'

No one was listening. He followed the others into the living-room.

'I see the reception's at the County,' said Audrey. 'That'll be nice.'

'Yes. It's a nice hotel.'

'Doesn't matter how big he is. I picked up a few tricks in the Army. The bigger they are – wallop . . . '

'How d'you feel about the big day, Bob? Are you nervous?'

'Not really.'

'He's terrified,' said Terry. 'He's got cold feet. Correction. In his case, it's cold *flat* feet.'

'Hah, hah, hah. As a matter of fact, I'm rather looking forward to it.'

'Of course you are. Don't be so cruel, Terry.'

'What do you mean?' Terry tried to look hurt.

'Has he been stirring it as usual?'

'He hasn't helped,' said Bob.

'Well, take no notice of *his* marriage guidance counsel.' Audrey gave Terry a sharp look.

'I know what it's all about,' said Terry. He tapped his chest. 'I've been through it.'

'And I know what it's all about, too,' said Audrey firmly. 'I've been married four years, and I've got two kids and a bad back to show for it. I know marriage isn't like a breakfast food commercial. You have to work at it – day after day.'

Terry slumped down into an armchair. 'I tried. God

knows, I tried.'

'Everything but learn the language,' said Bob.

'You didn't lift a finger to save your marriage.' Audrey turned to Bob. 'It was madness him being married in the first place – ' She frowned. 'What happened to your hand?'

'The same thing that happened to mine.' Terry waved his bandaged hand in a vain effort to win Audrey's attention. 'He's got a kitchen hatch that eats people.'

'Teething troubles,' said Bob. 'New houses are like that. I'm getting it fixed.'

'Well, don't let Terry do it,' said Audrey. 'He may be able to change a fuse, but he doesn't know one end of a nail from the other.'

'Perhaps,' said Terry. 'But I'm rapidly becoming an expert on service hatches.'

Audrey turned her back on him. 'You'll have a lovely marriage, Bob. You'll make a good husband, *and* a good father.'

'Ah, yes . . . if only *we'd* been able to have children.' Terry sighed heavily.

'Don't let him give you any of that "how he's suffered" bit. The heartbreak and the anguish of it all. Get him to tell you why his marriage broke up,' said Audrey. She looked at Terry. 'That'll give you an idea just how *anguished* he was.'

Terry stood up. 'Now *that* hurts, Aud. That hurts more than you'll ever know. Excuse me . . . ' He pushed between them and went upstairs for a leak.

Bob turned to Audrey. 'I only heard he *had* a wife yesterday. Did you ever meet her?'

'Once.'

'What was she like?'

'Well . . . ' Audrey wrinkled her nose. 'Very physical.'

'Ah, yes. That's what he said.'

'You mustn't let it worry you, though.'

'I don't, I don't – still,' Bob grimaced. 'It shakes you when you hear something like that. I mean, happening to someone you *know*.'

'You and Thelma will be all right.'

'We have rows, you know. All the time.'

'And you'll have lots more when you're married,' said Audrey. 'With a few breaks in between to get your breath back. But you'll last the distance.'

Bob sat down on the settee. Audrey sat on the arm.

'You're happy though, aren't you Audrey?'

Audrey shrugged and picked at her apron. 'I suppose so. We don't fight so much since I took up Yoga. Every time Ernie starts a row, I just sit there in the Lotus position with a serene smile on my face. Drives him absolutely potty.' She stood up. 'I'm going to have to leave you to look after yourselves. Got to pop down to the shops.'

'It's all right,' said Terry. 'I found the cream cracker.' He came back into the room eating it.

Audrey flashed him the look that only elder sisters can give younger brothers. Terry slumped down in the armchair opposite Bob, and made a V-sign at the door as it closed behind Audrey.

'Terry . . . '

'What?'

'How exactly did your marriage end?'

'Same way as your engagement. Irreconcilable differences.'

'But what exactly? Was it the rows? Another woman? Another fella – or what? I mean, what was the last straw, so to speak?'

Terry bent his head in bitter recollection. It was a while before he spoke, and when he did, it was in a low voice. 'I suppose it all built up to a climax in June 1970. June the 14th, it was. Nine thirty local time. I had a seventy-two-hour pass, and I was spending the weekend with her at her family's place. They were all there. Her father and mother, sister, her two brothers, uncles, God knows how many other relatives. All sitting round the telly after dinner. All full of veal and sauerkraut. Poppin' their cans of Dortmunder beer. And then it happened . . . ' Terry shrugged helplessly and raised his hands.

'The thing that snapped the final thread that held our chance of happiness together.'

Bob frowned. 'What was it? I don't get it. What happened?'

'What happened?' Terry looked incredulous. 'On June the 14th, *1970*?! I would have thought that date was printed indelibly in the mind of every Englishman worthy of the name. England, TWO, West Germany, THREE. That's what happened.'

Bob sat stunned. 'Oh, my God . . . of course!'

'Can you imagine it?' asked Terry. Do you have *any* idea what it was like to be in Germany that night? *West* Germany? Especially after England was leading *two* goals to nil. I mean I was out of my *mind*! Standing on the sideboard singing "Rule Britannia" – "Land of Hope and Glory" – their *faces*! And then . . . the *shame*. The *humiliation*. To have them all leaping up and down – eyes glazed with National Socialist fervour. It was the old "Deutschland über Alles" all over again. The old jackboot. I thought they were going to rush out and invade Poland.'

'Don't . . . don't,' said Bob. 'I've only just learned to live with it myself.'

They both slumped back dejectedly.

'You can realise how I felt at that moment,' said Terry. 'I just got up and left. Quite unnoticed. Just got me bag and walked out of her life for ever.'

Bob looked at him with a new understanding. 'No one can blame you for that, Terry. I think I might have done the same. It was bad enough here. I had to go to bed for two weeks.'

'So – that was that . . . total disaster.'

'Something like that takes a lot of getting over,' said Bob.

Terry nodded. 'It does. It does . . . '

'I mean, you just can't shrug it off and forget. Pretend it never happened.'

'You have to go back to square one. Start again.'

'Pick up the pieces,' said Bob.

'Begin afresh . . . '

A brief silence fell between them as they were each lost in their own thoughts, then Bob said, 'Mind you, I think Chivers has made a difference.'

'You're right,' said Terry. 'If only he'd been there then. He might have saved my marriage.'

Audrey returned to find the lads still glumly contemplating England's disastrous World Cup defeat in Mexico. She made them a cup of tea, then stood herself upside down against the wall for an hour of Yoga. She always did it before Playschool started.

Bob decided to phone Thelma. As the phone was in the living-room, Terry had the pleasure of watching him squirm.

'Well, do you *want* me to come over? . . . Well, that's up to you . . . No, I don't mean *that* . . . Do *you* want me to come over . . . I see, you *don't* want me to come over . . . I do, I *do* . . . That's why I offered to . . . '

'God preserve us,' said Terry disgustedly.

'I only *asked* in case you didn't want me to,' continued Bob. 'I *want* to . . . That's why I *offered* . . . Well, I didn't just want to *come round* . . . Well, in case you didn't want to *see* me . . . Well, you might have been lying down – or having one of your migraines . . . '

It was obviously the wrong thing to say. Terry watched Bob's face cloud with constipation as Thelma gave him an earful.

'I didn't mean one of *your* migraines,' said Bob lamely. 'I meant – one of your *migraines* . . . '

It was all too much for Terry. He burst into song – badly off-key. '*Luuvvv is a many-splendoured thing* . . . !'

Bob covered the phone. 'Shut up, will you?'

' – "*It's the April rose, that only gerr-ows* . . . " '

Bob raised his voice. 'No, pet. I'm not with Terry. It's the radio. I'm at Audrey's. I'm just having tea with Audrey – '

'*In the ear-lee spring* . . . '

'No, she can't speak to you at the moment. She's

standing on her head. . . That's right. Hang on a minute. I'll just turn the radio down.'

Bob reached for the tea cosy and rammed it down over Terry's head. 'Stop stirring it you – ' He bit off the word 'bastard'. He didn't want to shock Audrey out of her trance.

'There, that's better,' said Bob into the phone. 'Hello? Thelma? Hello?' He slammed down the receiver.

'Hung up on you has she?'

'Yes. Thanks to you . . . ' Bob dumped himself back onto the sofa and folded his arms crossly.

'Just as well,' said Terry. 'There's no way of ending conversations like that.'

'Take that bloody tea cosy off. You look ridiculous.'

'Temper.' Terry left the tea cosy where it was. 'Well, are you or aren't you?'

'Am I what?'

'Going *over*. Dear, oh, dear – after all that. *Are* you going over, or aren't you?'

Bob sat there with a sullen expression as Terry mimicked the wheedling tone he'd been obliged to use on the telephone.

'You're *not* going over. You're not going *over*, because once you *get* over, you *might* wish you hadn't *gone* over.'

'Why don't you shut your face, Terry Collier?'

Terry looked round in surprise at his inverted sister. 'And why don't you come down from there? You look terrible. Can't do you any good to have all that strawberry yoghurt rushing to your head.'

Audrey folded her legs down and stood the right way up. She looked at Bob sympathetically. 'Still upset, is she?'

'It's too difficult to explain,' said Bob.

'No need to, love. She rang me up this morning and told me all about it.'

'Oh, great,' said Terry. '*That's* why I've been getting the cold shoulder. *I'm* the outraged party. The one who's hard done by.'

'Take that tea cosy off your head,' said Audrey. 'You

look ridiculous.'

'Good.'

'And it's unhygeinic.' Audrey whipped the tea cosy away and put it back over the teapot.

'She doesn't want me to go over,' said Bob.

'Well, at least that call wasn't a total waste of time. You saved yourself a journey.'

Audrey and Bob ignored him. He might as well have been in another room.

'And she's stopped work on that cardigan she was knitting me.'

'Downed needles, has she?' jeered Terry.

'Terry!' snapped Audrey.

'It was a fawn one. For weekends.'

'I hate people who wear cardigans . . . '

Bob looked at Terry. 'So you hate your Dad do you? And your Grandad – and all your uncles too? Because *they* all wear cardigans.'

'Not *your* sort of cardigan. Not the sort Thelma'll be knitting *you*. All chunky, double-knit beige and fawn and Rugby clubs and Sunday-morning open-air drinks and barbecues and cocker spaniels and gin and tonics and Crosse & Blackwells type of cardigan.'

'Don't take any notice of him, Bob. He's the original angry young man. Only now, he's ten years out of date. Like his hair and his shoes.'

'And what's that supposed to mean?' Terry got up aggressively.

Audrey squared up to him. 'You're a born knocker. Terry Collier, the alternative voice.' She didn't budge an inch.

Bob moved to her side. 'Yes. Except people like him don't offer any alternatives. They're just against things. Against everything – not just other people's cardigans.'

Terry was outnumbered, but he wasn't about to be talked down. He tapped his chest. 'I'm against things that threaten my personal liberty. I don't want to be submerged – to be suffocated by society. By – '

'Marriage,' said Bob. 'Go on, say it. That's what all

this is leading up to, isn't it?'

'I don't know what you're talking about.'

'Marriage,' repeated Bob. 'You know – this blessed union – Holy Wedlock. All this is just another of your not very subtle attempts to kick me in the matrimonial groin.'

'Not true,' said Terry. 'All I'm trying to do is warn a friend. A very *close* friend. About not rushing headlong into things which I have learned from bitter experience to think about twice. *I* know all about Holy Necklock, mate.' Terry put a strangle-hold on an imaginary opponent. 'Three falls or two submissions.'

'Your marriage may have been like that,' said Bob. 'But my marriage is going to be a thing of great beauty – '

'And a joy for-a-fortnight,' added Terry sarcastically.

Bob shook his head. 'No wonder *yours* never got off the ground. You've got too much meanness inside you.'

'Too much aggression and hostility,' said Audrey.

'Yes.' Bob smiled. 'It's little wonder your marriage collapsed on the strength of a late Gerd Muller goal.'

Terry looked at them both in an effort to find a grain of sympathy in their faces. All he could see was a wall of misunderstanding. He turned on his heels and left the room abruptly. As he went through the door, he looked back briefly.

'I tried,' he said. 'God knows, I tried. I hope you remember that.' He banged the door behind him.

'Terry!' called Bob. He looked at Audrey. 'I shouldn't have said that, should I? I'd better stop him before he goes.'

'Don't fret,' said Audrey. 'He won't leave till he's had all there is to eat in the kitchen.'

Audrey poured Bob another cup of tea.

'I do worry, you know, Audrey. Just look at the number of people that we know that have split up. We all left school around the same time, shared twenty-firsts and engagement parties – and now everyone's separating. Here *I* am, just getting it together, while all my contemporaries are taking it *apart*.'

'Well, don't count Terry's fiasco.'

'Oh, it's not just him,' said Bob. 'I mean, all sorts of people.'

Terry returned with the tin of chocolate biscuits from the kitchen. He sat down and pointedly ignored their presence.

'Even the Sandersons have parted.'

Audrey looked surprised.

'It's true. And last week, Frank Clarke ran off with an usherette from the Regal.'

'I nearly left Ernie about eighteen months ago,' said Audrey. 'But I just couldn't find the time.'

'Then there was Tony and Joan. Do you remember? They went on a cruise with Doug and Glynnis. Now it's Doug and Joan, and Tony and *Glynnis*!'

'And your banns are being read this Sunday?' asked Terry. 'With all these warning signals flashing round you?'

Bob didn't look at him. 'I'd better be going,' he said to Audrey. 'I've got to check a few details with the Reverend Gordon.'

'What happened to the Reverend Newman?' asked Terry.

'He left the parish,' said Bob curtly.

'And his wife,' added Audrey. 'It was in all the local papers.'

'Who for?'

'An eighteen-year-old petrol pump attendant. In hot pants,' said Audrey severely. 'Left a wife, three kids, and twenty-one books of Green Shield stamps.'

'Thanks for the tea, Audrey.' Bob kissed her on the cheek.

'I hope it all goes well, Bob.'

'Aye,' said Terry. 'See you in church.'

Bob looked alarmed. 'What do you want to come for?'

'It's a free country isn't it?'

'Listen,' said Bob. 'If you're going to – '

Terry held up a hand. 'All I want to do, is pop in, commune with my Maker, and hear the glad tidings along with everyone else. After all,' said Terry devoutly, 'it is *my* parish church as well, you know.'

Bob decided not to tell Thelma.

There was no doubt about it. If you closed your eyes, you could have been in Westminster Abbey. It was the Reverend Norman Gordon's voice. Since becoming the incumbent of St Mark's, its plummy, magnetic, High Church quality had brought about a 100 per cent increase in the congregation. Counting Bob and Thelma, that made twenty-eight worshippers of varying degrees of fervour.

All of them now knelt with lowered heads while the Reverend Gordon intoned the words of the General Thanksgiving. All except Bob. He was looking nervously over his shoulder. Thelma stuck a sharp elbow in his ribs.

'Bob!' she hissed.

'What?'

'What are you *doing*?'

'Nothing.'

'Well, pray.'

That was the only thing left for Bob to do. Pray. Pray for Terry Collier to be struck down on his way to church by the Divine Wrath of God. Failing that, a double-decker bus would do.

Bob was still on his knees trying to establish a direct line to the Almighty long after everyone else had sat down. Thelma tugged him up by the collar.

'Sorry,' whispered Bob.

'He's *looking* at us.' Thelma's lips were fixed in a smile. Arthur Worsley couldn't have done better.

Bob sat up attentively as the Vicar opened his hymn-book.

'We will now sing Hymn number one hundred and sixty – "Holy, Holy, Holy, Lord God Almighty".'

The ragged singing could be heard outside the church as Terry approached. The verger was pinning an announcement to the church noticeboard inside the porch. He squinted at Terry through his small, steel-frame glasses.

'You're Cyril Collier's lad, aren't you?'

'Aye, that's right.'

'Young Terry.'

'Not so young now. Are you still top of the Bowls Club?'

'Oh, your Dad's got the edge on me now. How's life in the Army?'

'Okay. I've done my stint.'

'Best time I ever had,' said the verger.

'Takes some beating,' said Terry. He cocked his head towards the door. 'Sounds as if I'm late for the kick-off.'

The verger looked surprised. 'Don't tell me you're going in?'

'Well, I haven't come all this way just to read the notices,' said Terry. 'I've been baptised, you know. I know what it's all about. You're looking at a bloke who nearly got a full book of Sunday School stamps.' Terry took hold of the heavy wrought-iron door handle.

The verger shook his head. 'Who'd have believed it. "God works in mysterious ways – " '

' " – his wonders to perform", ' said Terry. He tapped his head. 'You see? It's still all up there.' He paused to listen to the hymn-singing. 'I remember that too. Used to be a hit in *my* day. Must get in – don't want to miss the sermon.' He lifted the latch.

'You'll find plenty of seats at the back.'

'Seats in all parts!' cried Terry. He pulled open the door and left the verger cringing in the porch.

The hymn ended. The congregation sat down. Terry selected a pew at the rear of the church and sat in the aisle seat opposite an elderly lady.

'On Tuesday,' intoned the Reverend Gordon, 'Sister Elizabeth Hayes will be giving a talk on her work in Teheran with the Voluntary Service Overseas.'

Bob and Thelma squeezed hands secretly. Bob was now quite relaxed. Terry, obviously, had not managed to get out of bed.

'Next Saturday is, of course, the day of our Jumble Sale, and the Church Hall will be open from Thursday onwards to all those who wish to deposit articles for sale. On Friday evening, in the Scout's Hall, Mrs Punshon will be giving a welcome repeat of her illustrated lecture on "Birds of the Farne Islands", and I am told there will be several new slides, some of them in *colour*.'

Terry leaned towards the elderly parishioner across the aisle. 'Sounds as if it's going to be quite a week.' He winked at her.

The lady edged along the pew in an attempt to get out of earshot. As she did so, Bob became aware of Terry's presence by extra sensory perception. He turned round and caught a glimpse of Terry lounging in his aisle seat at the rear. It was not a pretty sight. Terry's hair looked like a bombed haystack. One wing of his collar had got tucked under his tie, the other wing was airborne, and his suit looked as if it had been slept in. Terry grinned and wiggled the fingers of his good left hand.

All Terry got back was a silently snarled 'Get out' underlined with a vicious jerk of Bob's head.

'What's up?' hissed Thelma.

'Nothing,' said Bob, hissing back. 'Got a crick in my neck.'

'Well, sit straight, for goodness sake!'

Bob composed himself as best he could.

'Today,' continued the Reverend Gordon, 'we publish the banns of marriage between Judith Mary Caldicott, spinster of this parish, and David Randall Pierce, bachelor, of the parish of Christ Church, Tynemouth. This is for the first time of asking.'

Thelma turned to smile at the young couple who were in the pew behind them, then she leant towards Bob. 'It's us next.' She squirmed excitedly.

'Now this,' boomed the Reverend G, 'is for the second time of asking, and is between Thelma Ingrid Chambers, spinster, and Robert Andrew Scarborough Ferris, bachelor, both of this parish. If any of you know cause or just impediment why these two souls should not be joined together in Holy Matrimony, you are to declare it or forever hold your peace.'

There was a snort of suppressed laughter.

'Who's that laughing?' hissed Thelma.

Bob looked round. Thelma looked round. Everybody looked round. Terry had slipped even further sideways in the pew as he shook helplessly with laughter. He waved his bandaged hand limply in Bob's direction.

'Robert Andrew *Scarborough*?! Ohh – that's too much!'

It was.

On the following Monday, Bob went to evening surgery. There weren't so many patients this time. Attendance tended to drop off towards nightfall. For one thing, it meant you couldn't take the morning off work to find out if you could get a note to be off work. Bob imagined the invalid thousands nursing their fallen arches and clutching their hernias in front of 'Crossroads'.

Bob was the last one in to bat. He'd stayed on late at work to make up for the time he'd lost on the previous Friday. Making it up with Thelma.

The buzzer sounded. It was now three tones flatter and weaker than before. The poor little bugger of a bee that was trapped inside was obviously farting himself to death. One of the two women ahead of Bob got up. That left a lady of about 45, with a shopping basket, her own copy of *Woman's Realm*, a blue rinse and the sniffles.

The door to the waiting room opened and Terry walked in. He paused in the doorway as he saw Bob and stuck out his bandaged hand defensively. Bob glowered at him and looked out of the window. Terry took the other bay window seat on the far side of the aspidistra.

'Evening,' said Terry cheerfully.

Bob didn't reply. The woman patient gave a shy acknowledgement. She wore those swept-up sort of glasses with diamante clusters in the corners. The kind you *don't* get on the National Health.

'Come to get the bandage off, have you?' Terry was obviously totally unrepentant.

'Yes,' said Bob sullenly. He didn't want to make a

scene.

'Me too.' Terry peered at him under the intervening greenery. 'Well, the deed's done. The banns have been bandied abroad. Count-down's commenced. M minus 19. M for Marriage – get it?'

'Very witty,' muttered Bob. He wondered how hard he could hit Terry with his left hand.

'So how's Thelma?'

'I wouldn't know. Thelma isn't talking to me.' Bob tried to keep his voice low.

'Saints preserve us! Now what?'

Bob leaned back against the net curtains to get a clearer view of Terry. 'Now *what*? I don't know how you've got the nerve to show your face! You made a laughing stock of me in church yesterday. You reduced the whole service to a shambles.'

'Not completely.'

'I've never felt so ashamed or embarrassed in my whole life!'

'Don't blame *me*,' whispered Terry. He leaned back into the line of sight. 'Blame your parents.' He grinned. 'Robert Andrew *Scarborough*. Why *Scarborough*?'

'Because –' Bob's eyes flickered towards the lady with the blue rinse. He lowered his voice even more. 'Because that was where I was . . . ' He got into difficulties and went back to try again. 'Well, they once told me that *that* was where I was – you know . . . '

Terry and Bob both glanced at the woman. She didn't appear to be listening.

' . . . Conceived.'

Bob's voice was barely audible, but the sound waves caused a flutter in the pages of *Woman's Realm*.

'Gettaway.' Terry's face was full of amused disbelief.

'It's true.'

'You mean they could work it out that precisely?'

'Apparently.'

'Did they only have it away on their summer holidays, then?'

The lady patient blew her nose loudly, presumably to

remind them of her maidenly presence. Terry glanced at her casually, then looked at Bob. 'Well?'

'SSShhhh,' said Bob. 'No, of course they didn't. They were *living* there. My Dad was stationed there at the end of the war. They called me that out of – well, sentiment.'

'I see,' said Terry, speaking far too loudly. 'Good job he wasn't posted to Barrow-in-Furness.'

The buzzer dribbled flatulently. The woman gathered up her belongings and gratefully took to her heels.

'Of course, I've never used it,' said Bob. No one ever knew about it till now.'

'Just as well,' laughed Terry.

'Anyway let's forget it.'

'I doubt if the congregation will.'

'Well, *they're* not the sort of people who are going to shout it from the rooftops.'

'But I am, I suppose.'

'I don't care *what* you do,' said Bob peevishly.

'My lips are sealed, Robert Andrew. I promise.'

'Good.'

'But what about Thelma? Are her lips sealed – perhaps for ever? Is there any chance of *her* breaking the Angry Silence?'

'Listen, we've had a little row. My fault for telling you about the service. It's nothing serious. Nothing I can't handle.'

'You may as well get used to it. There'll be plenty more.'

'I'm going through with this marriage, mate. Nothing's going to stop me.'

'I know, Bob, I know.' Terry sighed. 'I've known that ever since Park Road Juniors. Your fate with her was sealed long before the eleven-plus.'

Bob pushed the aspidistra back out of the way. 'This may sound funny after what's happened in the last couple of days, but I'm *grateful* to you. I really am. You've forced me to re-examine. To reassess. To re-appraise everything. Well, I've done that, and now I'm reassured. All my doubts are ironed out. I'm confident.

My mind's made up.'

'Good,' said Terry. 'Because if you *were* going to have any doubts, *now's* the time to have them. Not in two weeks' time when you walk up the aisle. I mean, when the Reverend Gordon asks – "Do you take this woman to be your lawful wedded wife?", you can't say – "Not necessarily!" '

'Terry,' said Bob patiently. 'I've had cold feet – more than once. But that was in the *past*. In my heart of hearts I *know* Thelma's the girl for me. Always has been. Always will be. I've never been more certain of anything in my whole life – '

The bee inside the buzzer made a last dying effort.

' – *I think* . . . ' Bob concluded lamely. He looked back over his shoulder at Terry as he left the room.

Terry sat back and lit a cigarette. He knew a mate in trouble when he saw one. Luckily he'd come home in time. He was going to have to work hard in the next two weeks.

4

Moving On

Bob was waiting outside in his car when Terry came out of the doctor's. He pushed open the car door as an invitation to Terry to get in.

Terry held up his unbandaged right hand and flexed the fingers experimentally.

'Snap,' said Bob, holding up his own, now fully restored.

'I'll have to watch out then.' Terry grinned.

'Are you heading back home?'

'No. Audrey's offered to put me up for a few days. Mind, I have to cut the lawn and do the baby-sitting, though. Earn me keep, like.'

Bob switched on the ignition. 'Fancy a drive? Just to have a look round?'

'Aye, that's not a bad idea,' said Terry. 'I'd like to see how the place looks these days.' He stuck out a finger. 'Tell you where we could start. That coffee-bar we used to hang around at.'

'The Marimba?'

'That's the one. Had that waitress with those gigantic knockers and green fingernails.'

'It's a launderette,' said Bob.

'Never.' Terry looked shattered. 'I remember we used to get those big vanilla ice-creams with little green specks on top.'

'Green specks? You mean pistaccio?'

'No,' said Terry. 'Nail varnish.'

'Sit well back,' said Bob. 'You're in for a few surprises.' He put the car into gear and drove off towards town.

Terry had already noticed from his few bus-trips how dramatically the high-rise blocks had changed the whole horizon of the town. Everything seemed to have got out of proportion. Probably because the architects had been working on big, double-elephant drawing boards. With long pencils.

Bob pulled up opposite a glass-walled office block. 'Know where we are?'

Terry looked around for a familiar landmark. 'Vaguely,' he said. 'Just can't place meself.'

'Well, buried under that pile of glass and concrete is the ghost of the Go-Go Rock Club, Members Only, Closed Sunday, Licensed till 3.0 p.m.'

'Oh, not the Go-Go? The North's Premier Music Mecca? Hell's flames, is nothing sacred?'

Bob shook his head. 'They do say, that if you come here on the night of a full moon, you may catch a glimpse of a headless electric guitarist – drifting through the deserted typing pool to the strains of "Roll over Beethoven".'

Terry's eyes misted over with damp nostalgia. 'Take me to the canal,' he said.

Bob parked in a litter-strewn back street behind some scarred, sooty warehouses. They walked over the waste-ground to the edge of the canal.

The black, oily water was barely moving.

'Remember when we used to fish here?'

'Yes,' said Bob. 'Sunday afternoons. If we didn't have a fixture.'

'Let's come back here next Sunday. Let's get some rods and come for the afternoon.'

'No point,' said Bob. 'No more fish. Pollution.'

'But we've always had pollution,' said Terry. 'We *invented* pollution. Long before it became fashionable.

'Yes, but they pulled down the flour mill and put up a chemical factory. There's not a fish alive between here and Tynemouth.'

'What – not even a stickleback?'

Bob shook his head.

'Bloody disgrace,' said Terry. 'Big business. They pollute our rivers, blacken our air, dump their refuse just anywhere – with a total disregard for people like you and me.' He put his last cigarette in his mouth and threw away the crumpled packet. 'How about Hockley Woods?'

'I think that's still there,' said Bob.

'Yes, well, all the same, we'd better hurry.'

The woods *were* still there. There was even the same huge, splendid old oak tree. They did however have to climb over a fence to get to it. They sat down between the great roots at its base.

'I used to spend whole summers here,' said Terry. 'Sun was always shining. Climbing trees, hiding in the gorse bushes, blackberrying . . .'

'Trying to get some girl's gymslip off . . .'

'Speaking of gymslips,' said Terry. 'Do you know, I really think that's the tree where Isobel Ritchie and I used to have a tree house.' He pointed straight ahead from where they sat.

'Get away,' said Bob. 'They'll all have grown miles by now. It could be any one of them.'

'No,' Terry insisted. 'I'm positive. I can tell by the shape of the branches.' He got to his feet. 'Her initials and mine should still be on the trunk.'

Bob followed Terry over to the tree. Terry walked round it, then looked up.

'I was right. Look, there they are. I.R. – T.C.'

They both gazed up at the ragged, but lovingly carved initials on either side of a heart pierced by a primitive arrow. The letters were now a good seven feet off the ground.

'Incredible,' said Bob. 'And somehow very sad.'

'Aye,' mused Terry. 'She'll have varicose veins by now.'

'Hey – *you*!!'

The lads looked round to see a man approaching. He was paunchy, but still impressively large, in a Vyella check shirt and cavalry twill trousers. Beyond him, Terry caught a glimpse of houses through the trees.

'Would you mind telling me how you got in here?' huffed the man. He had curly ginger hair and small teeth.

'Over the fence,' said Terry helpfully.

'Did you by God – what the hell do you think you're doing?!' The man's face went bright pink.

'Er, nothing,' said Bob, sensing trouble.

Terry looked bewildered. 'Hang on, hang on. Why're you getting so shirty? Isn't this Hockley Woods?'

'It was,' said the man. 'It is now the Hockley Woods Estate – ' He pointed through the trees. '*That* is my house, *this* is my garden, *you* are trespassing, and *I* am going to call the police!'

There was nothing for it but to drown the past in several pints of ale. They drove to the Black Horse, their favourite local, and got stuck in. When Terry had become suitably immune to the slings and arrows of outrageous fortune, he gazed glumly round the pub's warm dark interior.

'Wonder this is still standing,' he said. 'I'm surprised they haven't slapped a demolition order on it. They could pull it down and put up a new Civic Centre.'

'Don't need to,' said Bob. 'The new Civic Centre's been built on the site of the old Roxy.'

The news shook Terry so much he actually spilt some beer. 'Oh, no, Bob. Not the Roxy Ballroom.'

' 'Fraid so.'

'Aw, hell's teeth! That really is going it a bit!' Terry took a long half-pint swallow to shore himself up.

'I should have broken it to you gently,' said Bob. 'Still – you had to find out sometime.'

'But, I mean – that's terrible,' said Terry. 'The National Trust should have put a Preservation Order on the place. Part of my life – part of *your* life, *belonged* to the Roxy.'

'I know.' Bob sighed. 'I suppose the National Trust needs a better reason than that.'

Terry sagged against the bar and shook his head sadly. 'No more Roxy . . . what's the point of going on?'

'I expect, in time,' said Bob, 'on new moons, you and I will haunt the Civic Centre. Twisting our way through the corridors.'

'Accompanied by Art Sibley and his singing sax.'

Bob didn't have the heart to tell Terry that Art Sibley had died – and was already out front in that great Palais in the Sky. And still probably playing half a tone flat.

'It was the first dance hall I ever got into.'

'Yes, I remember,' said Bob. 'I let you in the back way.'

'Such memories . . . ' Terry sighed. 'That's where I first learned to dance. Where I first acquired some social poise. Some witty repartee . . . '

'Do you remember the girls we used to invite to come with us ?' asked Bob.

'Yeah – and when they said "Yes", we used to say – "Great. Meet you inside".'

'Well, if you didn't pay for them, you didn't have to stick with them.'

'Right,' said Terry.

Bob smiled. 'Nowadays that's called "maximising your opportunities while minimising your investment". Did you know I once won the Roxy's "Holiday for Two Bossa Nova Contest" ?'

'Really ?'

'Yes. I thought the holiday was going to be in Brazil –'

'Home of the Bossa Nova.'

'Correct – but their budget wouldn't stretch that far. We ended up with a week in Redcar.'

'Redcar's still there, I suppose ?'

'It was at the last election,' said Bob.

'Well very little else is. There's hardly any of our memories intact – except the Juvenile Court.'

'It's funny, you know,' said Bob. 'You're the one that's made me realise just how much this place has changed. When you're here all the time you don't seem to notice it so much. I suppose it's a good thing in a way. Progress. Expansion. There's lot's more opportunities up here now.'

'Precious few opportunities on display at the local

Labour Exchange,' said Terry. 'That is unless you want to work for British Rail as a Parcels Clerk, or hose down a coal yard.'

'Oh,' said Bob. 'You've been down to the Labour, have you?'

The question caught Terry with his guard down. 'What? Oh – well, I mean, you've got to call in, haven't you? For the Insurance Card, like.'

Bob was embarrassed for him. 'Ah, yes – of course,' he said helpfully. 'I thought for a minute you might have been looking for a job.'

'No, no, no. It was just for the Insurance Card. You need that, you see.' Terry recovered his aplomb. 'Even if you're self-employed.'

'Right,' said Bob. 'Still, I imagine you'll have to think about some kind of job sooner or later.'

Terry held up a hand. 'No hurry, no hurry. Not short of a bob or two. Not on the breadline. Still got my savings – *and* my terminal leave pay. Don't have to rush into just *any* old job. Want to sort things out first. Not even sure I want to stay *here*. Not now they've pulled down the Roxy.'

Bob frowned. 'Not stay here? Where would you go?'

'*Go*? Why I could *go* anywhere. This town may have a new Civic Centre, but that doesn't hide the fact that it's a dead-end. Especially for someone who's seen a bit of the world. Knocked around a bit. Travelled. Broadened his horizons.'

'You mean as far as München-Gladbach.'

'Further than that. Lots further than that.'

'But you *belong* here,' said Bob. 'You always said this was the only place you felt comfortable.'

'Oh, but that was years ago. When I didn't know any better. Before I had a chance to – well, see a bit of life.'

Bob looked concerned. 'But what could you do?'

Terry shrugged. 'I'll have to turn me hand to whatever comes up.' He saw the doubt on Bob's face. 'Look – there was a bloke with me in the Army. Lad called Hughie McLaren. Really good mates we were. Now he had no kind of an education or anything. He'd just been learning to be a baker up in Berwick. I said to him once – "What are you going to do when you get out, Hughie?" – and do you know what he said?'

'No. What did he say?'

'I'll never forget it. We were in the Guard House together at the time. On *guard*. He said – "Anything I like".'

' "Anything I like"?'

' "*Anything I like*". Not – "Well there's not much I *can* do except bake bread in Berwick" – no. *He* wasn't going to lie down and let Life walk all over him. No. "Anything *I* like". That's what he said. Marvellous!'

'A lesson for us all,' said Bob. 'I can just see the headlines now. Ex-Berwick baker named as next Foreign Secretary.'

Terry eyed Bob sourly. 'Who's doing the knocking now eh? That's *typical* of your small town mentality. If you don't believe in yourself, you'll never amount to *anything*.'

'I believe in myself.'

'Bollocks. Do you know where Hughie was demobbed?'

'No, tell me.'

'Aden. Long way right? *Hughie* didn't take the plane home. He hitch-hiked home. All the way from Aden.' Terry looked impressed, even if Bob didn't. 'Bloke like that could do anything. And so could *I*.'

Terry tapped his chest. 'Trap furs in Canada. Drive to Katmandu. Row across the Atlantic . . . '

'But Terry – your roots are *here*.'

'Roots? I was *uprooted* from here five years ago. Uprooted and dumped down into some draughty barracks. Thanks to you.'

'Ah, but without which,' said Bob indulgently, 'you would never have seen Life. Without which you would never have had the urge to row across the Atlantic – or drive to Katmandu in a baker's van.'

Terry looked so riled Bob thought he was about to lay

one on him, but his anger slowly subsided.

'Okay. Go ahead. Laugh,' he said. 'One day . . . I'm not saying I will – but I just might.'

Bob decided that a little more tact was called for. Especially as Terry was obviously sincere in his idiotic beliefs. 'Of course you might *one* day – and good luck to you. But in the meantime, you should give yourself time to adjust. Time to sort things out. And to do that, you need some security. Something coming in. Can't just rely on your savings. And you won't get far just babysitting for Audrey and cutting her lawn.'

'Listen, if I need a job – for a stopgap, like, I can always go back to Ellison's. Old Darby told me – "Terry lad, when you come out, your job'll be waiting for you. No problem".'

'Well – there is just a little one.'

'What's that?' asked Terry.

'Ellison's was pulled down two years ago. 'Bout the same time as the Roxy.'

Terry's mouth fell open. 'You're having me on.'

'No, honestly. They went bankrupt.'

'*Ellison's*? I don't believe it,' said Terry.

But he obviously did. It seemed to be the biggest blow he'd received all evening. Bob hadn't thought that Terry might have been secretly counting on getting his old job back. And now it was difficult to ask him. As Terry lapsed into a sombre silence, it was hard to know what he was thinking about. Bob decided he was probably working out how many gallons of petrol he'd need to get to Katmandu.

Bob drove Terry back to Audrey's in silence. Her husband Ernie had been in for supper and had gone out again. Audrey made some coffee for the two lads and carried on with her mending. Terry took his cup from the tray and sat down glumly.

Audrey looked at him over the top of her sewing glasses. 'You look as if you'd lost a pound and found sixpence.'

'We've been on a sentimental journey,' said Bob. To all

the old, familiar places.'

'Fatal,' said Audrey. She carried on sewing.

'There's nothing left. Nothing . . . ' Terry could hardly muster the will to stir his coffee. 'Bob's just told me about Ellison's going bankrupt. Who'd have thought it?'

'Well, Bob saw it coming, didn't you, Bob?'

'Ye-es.' Bob seemed curiously reluctant to take credit for his foresight.

'Yes, you got out before the crunch came. Very sensible. Very shrewd. Best move you ever made.'

'Yes.'

'I mean,' continued Audrey. 'Look how well you've done since.'

Even Terry had noticed Bob's manner. He was not normally one to hide his light under a bushel.

'Yeah,' said Terry. 'Come to think of it. Whereabouts *are* you working now?'

'Oh – with another company.' Bob shifted uncomfortably. 'Another line of country altogether.'

'Oh, yeah – what's the name of it?'

'Well –,' said Bob.

'Thelma's Dad runs it,' said Audrey. 'Building and Civil Engineering. That's what you're in now, isn't it, Bob?'

Bob eyed Audrey with a noticeable lack of gratitude. Terry's face brightened at the opportunity of getting a bit of his own back.

'Ahh . . . I *see* . . . '

'No, you don't,' said Bob. 'You don't *see* anything.'

'How *sensible*,' said Terry. 'How *shrewd* of you to get out before the crunch came. No wonder your engagement to Thelma went smartly back on again. Might lose a job as *well* as your bride-to-be.'

'It's not like that, if you must know. I get no favours from Mr Chambers. I pay my way. I have to prove myself as much as the next man.'

'Bollocks. The next man's not going to marry his daughter, is he?'

'You can think what you like,' said Bob. 'It's not a subject I'm prepared to discuss any further.'

'You cunning bugger.' It was an oblique compliment, but Bob didn't take it as one.

Audrey felt it was time to effect a rapprochment. 'Perhaps Bob might be able to fix *you* up with something, Terry.'

'I don't need any strings pulled for me,' huffed Terry. '*I* don't need the old pal's act!'

'It's not what you *do* in life, love. It's *who* you know. Believe me. Ernie and I found *that* out the hard way.'

'I'll manage, thank you,' said Terry. 'Just you wait and see. One day . . . '

Audrey looked up. 'One day, what? When?'

Bob couldn't resist the chance to score. He smiled over the top of his coffee-cup. 'He means one day, he and Hughie McLaren will be washed ashore on the sands at Whitley Bay. The first men to have crossed the North Sea on a tea tray. They'll be in the Guinness Book of Records.'

Audrey didn't get it. 'Who's Hughie McLaren?'

Terry gave a tired sigh.

'Audrey,' said Bob with mock concern. 'You haven't heard of Hughie McLaren? A legend in his own lifetime? He travelled from Aden to Aldershot on a camel. You *must* have heard of him, surely.'

'That's right,' said Terry. 'Laugh. Go on – laugh.' He gave Bob a pitying look. 'What else can you do? Hughie taught *me* a lot. He taught me that there was a lot more to life than a salary and the superannuation fund – and an endowment policy when you're sixty-five.'

Audrey looked baffled. 'Why did he go from Aden to Aldershot on a camel?'

'He didn't,' said Terry, dismissing Bob with a wave. 'Take no notice of him. What does *he* know about anything?'

'Nothing,' conceded Bob happily. 'I'm just an innocent abroad.'

Audrey put down her sewing and began to gather up

the cups. 'Well, whatever else, at least you're a qualified electrician, Terry. You shouldn't have much trouble in getting a job.'

'Yes, seriously,' said Bob, and meaning it. 'I *can* ask around if you want.'

'I don't want you to do anything,' said Terry. 'I don't want any help from anyone. '*I've* got a few ambitions, mate. A few ideas. A few plans. And getting a job round here doesn't fit into any of them.'

Bob looked at Audrey. 'I think he really does mean to drive to Katmandu.'

'Where?'

'Never you mind where,' said Terry. 'Have you got a map of the new bus routes?'

The next morning Terry put on his best suit, made sure his tie was straight, and took a bus to the address he'd got from the Labour Exchange.

It was a large building site, and well fenced-in. Terry studied the impressive picture of the project at the main gates. Offices, shops and a multi-storey car park. He made his way to the pre-fab site offices.

In the outer office, a blonde school-leaver sat at a table behind a typewriter and several telephones. The walls were covered with plans of the site.

'Can I help you?' The voice was not unpleasant.

Dim, thought Terry. But definitely possible. 'Er – is Mr Busby around?'

'You want to see him, do you?'

'Well – he wants to see me. I'm an electrician.'

'Oh, one of ours?'

'Not yet. I've got an appointment.'

'Oh – well, he's not here.'

'And he didn't say anything – about me coming, like?'

'No.'

'Are you expecting him back?'

'Don't know. He didn't say.'

Thick as a post. Terry turned towards the door. 'Okay. Thanks. Don't blame me if this place isn't finished on time.'

'Hang on a minute,' said the girl. She got up, knocked twice on the door to another office and went in. Terry could hear someone talking on the telephone. He inspected a tasteful nude calendar then dropped the pages hurriedly as the girl returned.

'His assistant will see you in a moment.'

Terry took a better look at her. As she sat down he got a pleasing flash of mini-skirted thigh. Not bad. Dim as a Toc H lamp but she might just know what end went where. He sat on the corner of the table. The girl gave him a sidelong glance and began to type a letter.

'Been some changes round here, though, but,' said Terry.

'Yes.'

'Aye. You notice it, you know – when you've been away for a few years like.'

'Yes.'

'Aye. You notice the difference coming back.' Terry was hoping she'd ask 'Where from?'

'Yes.'

He played his trump card. 'Especially from overseas.' He rubbed his right thigh slowly.

The girl took a good look at Terry's clothes. 'I thought you were going to say "prison".' She carried on typing.

Terry decided to try a different tack. 'D'you go dancing?'

'Now and then.'

'Where d'you go then?'

'What do you want to know for?'

'Well, I see they've pulled down the Roxy.'

The girl looked puzzled.

'The Roxy Ballroom.'

The girl shook her head.

'Don't tell me you've never heard of the Roxy *Ballroom*,' said Terry.

The girl gave him another disenchanted appraisal. 'I might have,' she said. 'But I don't go in much for Olde Tyme Dancing.'

Terry sat there completely shattered. One of the telephones rang. The girl answered it.

'You can go in now,' she said.

So be it. Terry eased himself off the desk. She would never know the chance she'd missed.

As he walked in through the door to the inner office, Terry wished the ground would open up and swallow him. Instantly. Sitting in front of him, behind a desk, was Bob Ferris.

'Terry?!'

'Ah – '

'What in the world are you doing here?'

Terry fumbled desperately for some plausible explanation. 'Well, I was, er – '

'Sit down, sit down,' said Bob. 'Make yourself comfortable. Nice of you to drop in.'

'Ah, well – yes, I was just passing like – so I thought – '

'You might as well look in and say "Hello".'

'Well, sort of.'

'Great,' said Bob. 'Like a cup of tea?'

'Gasping.' Terry began to feel better. 'That's why I dropped in, really.'

'Hang on.' Bob raised his voice. 'Wendy?'

The girl came into the room.

'Could you bring us two cups of tea? Oh, and a biscuit for Mr Collier.'

'Yeah, okay, Bob – er, I mean Mr Ferris.'

As Wendy went out, Bob winked at Terry. 'Reckon you'd do all right there. Want me to put a word in?'

'Not really,' said Terry. 'She looks under age.'

'Can't chat for too long,' said Bob. 'I've got to see a bloke out there who's come about a job.'

'Ah . . . '

'Yes, some spark. Still, he can wait a bit. They're two a penny at the moment.'

'Oh, really.' Terry tried to sound disinterested.

'Yes, can afford to pick and choose now.'

'Didn't realise that this firm belonged to your father-in-law.'

'Subsidiary,' said Bob. 'There are four firms in the group.'

'Do you normally interview people for all of them, then?'

'Not normally, no. That's Frank Busby's job. He's out on the site somewhere, so I'm sitting in for him. Two telephones, a four foot six wide desk, and drunk with power.'

Bob laughed. Terry found it hard to raise a smile.

'Look, Terry – I know you're looking for something different, but well – if you change your mind, I mean I could – I mean Frank Busby could always – '

'Thanks, Bob, but the fact is I've made my decision. I'm not staying. I thought you should be the first to know. I'm moving on.'

Bob looked genuinely surprised. 'Moving on? Where to?'

'Well things aren't quite finalised yet. The first thing is to look up Hughie.'

'Oh, Hughie McLaren.'

'That's right. And from there, we'll just play it by ear.'

'Are you sure you're doing the right thing?'

'Well, it's not just a snap decision, you know.'

'I see,' said Bob. 'When are you leaving?'

'Oh, this week sometime.'

'I see. Nothing's fixed.'

'Nothing definite. But there's no point in hanging around, is there?'

'No, I suppose not.' Bob sat back in his chair and considered Terry's surprise announcement. Terry didn't look too happy about it. And Bob didn't feel too happy about it either.

'You'll miss my wedding,' he said.

'Yes, I know. I thought about that. Still – your in-laws won't be sorry. Nor will Thelma.'

'I will be.'

'I'll send you a funny telegram.'

Bob smiled. 'Could be quite pricey from Katmandu.'

'I doubt we'll have got that far by then.'

You're not really going there, are you?'

Terry shrugged. 'Depends.'

'I don't understand it,' said Bob. 'You've only just got back, and now you're off again. Didn't know you had so much gipsy in your soul.'

'Must be something in the blood. The last five years have given me a taste for excitement. For the thrill of adventure. For the mystery and the danger of the unknown. A taste for exotic places.'

'Oh, aye . . . '

'That's why I have to join Hughie.'

'Where's he?'

'Berwick-on-Tweed.'

Bob laughed. 'There's not much mystery and danger in Berwick-on-Tweed. You can go on a day bus trip. The way you were talking, I thought at the very least he'd be a mercenary in Mozambique.'

'Berwick is where he lives, you pillock. That's just where we're going to meet up to plan the next move. Buy stores, and maps and suchlike.'

'Of course.' Bob grinned broadly.

Terry stood up. 'You keep sneering at me. It's that sort of attitude that's driving me away.'

'Sit down,' said Bob. 'I'm sorry. I'm not trying to drive you away. I don't want you to go away at all.'

Terry stayed on his feet. 'That's nice of you, but my mind's made up. It's definite.'

Bob's mouth puckered with regret. 'Well, if it is, all I can say is – good luck and God bless.' Bob came round the desk and shook Terry's hand warmly.

Wendy knocked on the door and came in with their tea and biscuits on a tray. 'Oh, congratulations,' she said to Terry. 'You got the job.'

Bob frowned. It took a second or two for the penny to drop. 'Don't tell me *you* were the bloke outside waiting to see me about a job?'

'If I was,' snarled Terry. 'Which I wasn't, you know what you can bloody well do with it!' He threw a lethal glance at Wendy and slammed the door on the way out.

'Well!' said Wendy. 'He's got a cheek.'

'What?' Bob was still stunned.

'He took all the blinking biscuits!' said Wendy.

As soon as he finished work, Bob drove round to the Black Horse to see if Terry was there. He tried Terry's parents' house and then drove over to Audrey's. Terry wasn't there either, but he'd left the spare front door key on the kitchen table.

Bob sat down to talk it over with Audrey and her husband Ernie.

'Sheer loss of face, isn't it?' said Ernie. 'It's his pride that's been hurt.'

'I'm sure he didn't *really* want to go.'

'Of course he didn't, Bob.'

'Loss of face,' said Ernie. He'd seen *Bridge on the River Kwai* five times.

'So much has changed for him, you see,' said Audrey. '*You*'re doing well, and so are a lot of his old friends. All he's got to show for five years in the Army is two stripes and a broken marriage.'

'And a tattoo on his left buttock,' said Bob.

'So that's why he always locks the bathroom door,' said Audrey. 'He never used to.'

Ernie looked interested. 'What's it look like?'

'I haven't seen it,' said Bob.

Audrey's nose wrinkled in disapproval. 'It'll be something crude, I don't doubt.'

'Still,' said Bob. 'At least we've got a distinguishing mark for them to mention on Police Five.'

The postcard came two days later. A view of Berwick Castle. Audrey phoned Bob.

'What's it say?'

'Nothing much,' said Audrey. 'Just a reminder that we owe him a pound for the hire of a motor-mower.'

'Did he put his address?'

'Yes.'

'But no mention of any plans – or that Hughie What's-his-name?'

'No,' said Audrey. 'If you ask me he only wrote to let us know where he is so we'd all write begging him to come back.'

'I could drive up on Saturday, if you like. Have a chat with him. See if I can persuade him to come back.'

'No chance of you doing it before then, is there?'

'Why?' asked Bob.

'Well, we need a baby sitter for Friday night.'

On the Saturday, Bob got a special dispensation that enabled him to lay down his lambs-wool paint roller and drive up to Berwick.

A fisherman directed him to a cramped terrace of stone dwellings. Bob checked the address on the postcard and pushed open the gate of Number Fourteen. A 'Bed & Breakfast' sign hung in the ground-floor window. Bob rang the bell.

A hunched-up woman with her hair in curlers poked her head round the front door.

'Yes?'

'Is there a Mr Collier staying here? Mr Terry Collier?'

'Aye, there is, but he's oot the noo.'

'Do you know when he'll be back?'

'High tea's at six. He'll no miss that.'

'Thank you,' said Bob.

'You're welcome.' The woman shut the door in Bob's face.

Hardly your Merry Widow type of landlady, thought Bob. More your Mrs Quasimodo. He and Terry had once shared an adolescent fantasy in which they left home to become lodgers in a house run by Lana Turner.

Bob looked at his watch and went back to his car. He had four hours to kill before Terry came galloping back to put on his nose-bag. Bob decided to drive down to the sea-front. The wind was coming in from the north east and bitterly cold. Bob had forgotten to bring a coat with him. He drove back into the comparative shelter of the town and looked in the windows of several ironmongers and a toolshop. It made him feel he wasn't totally wasting his time – especially as he saw several things he'd need to buy later on.

The doors to the local cinema were locked, and the programmes didn't start till 5.30 p.m. There was nothing for it but to go into a café. Bob managed to make one iced bun and six coffees last an hour and a half then found that the café didn't have a lavatory.

He drove around for a bladder-bursting twenty minutes trying to find a public lavatory but too embarrassed to ask, and finally ended up on the seafront again. Having relieved himself in the Gents, he bought a Mickey Spillane paperback and a copy of *House Beautiful* to take back to Thelma.

It was while he was parked on the sea-front that the tide came in and sent a shower of salt seaspray all over the car. Bob cursed irritably. The last thing he wanted was premature corrosion setting in. Battling the rust that was built-in during manufacture was bad enough. He remembered a carwash sign he'd passed on his frantic search for the Gents toilet. No problem.

There were about six cars waiting to go through the wash. As he joined the tail-end of the queue, Bob glimpsed a white-coated attendant drying off the cars as they emerged from the sprays. He settled back with his Mickey Spillane, edging forward slowly in first gear as the cars in front passed through the wash.

When Bob's turn came, he checked all the windows and went back to his book. Water flooded all over the car and the huge blue nylon brushes drummed up the bonnet and over his head onto the boot then went into reverse gear. As they lifted clear, Bob drove out of the wash and stopped. The blurred figure of the attendant leaned over and began to wipe away the water that was draining off the windscreen. Bob looked up from his book and found Terry Collier staring in at him, his chammy-leather frozen in mid-wipe.

Bob parked outside the workman's café on the other side

of the road and waited inside till Terry had finished work. When Terry finally came across, he still had his damp, white garage overalls on. He sat down opposite Bob and looked at him sullenly over the plastic salt and pepper and the Daddies Sauce bottle. Bob pushed them to one side and leant his folded arms on the table.

'It's a smashing idea you've got. It's really great.'

'Go to hell,' said Terry.

'No, really – I envy you.'

'Envy me what? Filthy overalls and chapped hands? Terry thrust them under Bob's nose. 'They don't wash those cars in Fairy liquid, you know.'

'I don't mean that.' Bob tried to sound encouraging. 'I mean the whole idea of what you're doing. Travelling around. Doing different jobs. Meeting different people.'

'Don't bloody patronise me, Ferris.'

'I'm not. Honestly I'm not.'

'You bloody well are.' Terry sat sideways on his chair, half-turned away from Bob. 'You came here to have a good laugh. To humiliate me again. Not content with interviewing me for a job, you have to drive all the way up here in your Brabham Viva, to catch me on the end of a squeegee.'

'I swear to you, Terry, that's absolutely not true.'

'Well, it's a bloody long way to come just to wash your car!'

'I came to see *you*. I didn't know where you worked. Your landlady didn't tell me. I was killing time till you went back for tea.'

'In a car-wash?'

'Well, there's not much else to do in this place.'

Terry eyed Bob bitterly. 'At least it will give you something to talk about. Something to amuse your new friends at the Squash Club.'

'I don't play squash.'

'Well – whatever . . . '

'Terry, listen. Believe me, I really *do* envy you. You're getting it together. Nothing wrong in that. It's the whole Easy Rider bit. Getting straight. Taking off. Moving on.'

'Yeah,' said Terry. 'Except all I'm doing is wringing out.'

'Listen – Elvis Presley worked in a car-wash. Well, in song, anyway. It's part of this whole new idea of personal freedom. The Youth kick. They don't want possessions, a job, a home. They just want to be on the open road to New Mexico – or freaking out with a guru in – '

'Yeah, I know. In Katmandu.'

'Or wherever,' said Bob. 'You know the sort of thing – "By the time I get to Phoenix" – "Twenty-four hours from Tulsa". All you need is a sleeping-bag and a harmonica.'

'I don't play the harmonica.'

'Details,' said Bob. 'We're talking in broad concepts. Maybe you could live in a commune.'

Terry moved to face him squarely. 'Bob, I'm sorry to shatter your romantic notions, but I'm not about to give up my worldly goods to go traipsing about with a sleeping-bag and a harmonica. For a start, I've got no worldly goods to give up, and I'm not working in a car-wash as a tribute to Elvis Presley. I'm working to pay for my room and board in that grotty old house.'

The café-owner slapped down two Pyrex cups of watered-down Camp coffee. A third of it was already in the saucers.

'The point is,' said Bob. 'You've made the gesture. Okay – so it's a rotten job. But it's worth it. You've made *me* think twice about getting . . . well, suffocated. Bogged down. You've made me realise life *has* got more to offer.'

'Has it?' Terry poured the coffee from the saucer into his cup and added sugar.

Bob leaned forward intently. 'Why don't we get together and go off and grab some of it?'

Terry didn't seem to understand. 'You and *me*?'

'Yes. The two of us.'

'Forget it.'

Bob borrowed Terry's spoon and stirred sugar into his own cup. 'Do you think *my* life is so exciting? Decorating, choosing table linen, saving every penny, planting hedges, staying up all hours with a dreary correspondence course.'

'What in?'

'Quantity surveying.'

'Jesus Christ . . . '

'Exactly. Do you think that's living? Of *course* I nurse romantic notions. To visit the places I've only seen in the colour supplements. To meet the girls I've watched on Hawaii Five-O.'

'But I thought you had everything settled,' said Terry.

'None of us are what we seem. I don't want to be one of the people who only experience life second-hand. You've made the break – now it's time *I* did. Before it's too late.'

Terry took a long look at Bob and shook his head sadly. 'No, Bob. No, no. *You* are the one that's right. I'm the one that's got it all wrong. We *need* a home, roots – security. That's the only thing that makes sense. *I* was wrong because I couldn't accept what I am. Couldn't accept that the world on the telly wouldn't ever be mine – unless I could grow Georgie Best's feet or Tom Jones' tonsils.'

'Don't say that, Terry. What did your mate, Hughie, say about what he was going to do? "Anything I like". *We* can do anything we like. I can cash in my Post Office Book, sell the car – '

'And what about Thelma?'

'She'll have to understand,' said Bob. 'This is something we both have to get out of our system.'

'I know what *I* have to do,' said Terry. 'And that's to take you back home. Where we *both* belong.' He waved to the café-owner.

'Another cuppa, Terry?'

'No thanks, Hughie. How much do I owe you?'

Hughie walked over to the table. 'That's two now, two your mate had, plus a couple of rock cakes. Call it thirty altogether. Terry paid him. Hughie wiped down the table with his greasy apron and took the empty cups away.

Bob followed him with his eyes, then whispered, 'That's not – you know – ?'

'Yes.'

'But not *the* Hughie.'

'Yes.'

'You mean Hughie *McLaren*?'

'Yes.'

'But – ,' It was all beyond Bob. 'What happened?'

Terry shrugged. 'He put his childhood sweetheart up the stick, married her and they live on a caravan site with twins. He's got a ninety-five per cent mortgage on this place, and if he works sixteen hours a day for the next thirty years, he'll just about have paid off the tea-urn.'

Both lads lapsed into silence as Hughie brought Terry's change.

'Do you fancy coming over later?' he asked Terry. 'After Maureen's got the kids off, we could maybe have a game or two of Monopoly. Or play poker for match-sticks. Long as we keep it quiet, like.'

Terry and Bob got to their feet, and Terry gripped Hughie's arm. 'I'd love to, Hughie, but I'm off away home.' He walked to the door.

Bob followed.

'Take care of yourself,' said Hughie. He looked as if he'd just been marooned on a desert island.

'I'll maybe pop up and see you,' said Terry.

Hughie nodded. 'You know where to find me.'

They drove away from Berwick in silence. Terry didn't look back once.

'Nice to see you back,' said Ernie.

'And to *be* back,' said Terry. He settled into Ernie's favourite armchair.

'Fire's not too hot, is it?' asked Ernie.

Terry shook his head. There was no point in freezing to death just to trim Ernie's electricity bill.

Ernie wore a black bow tie and a hired evening suit that was too tight under the armpits. 'We were all worried about you going off like that. We didn't know what to do – did we, Aud?'

'No.' Audrey had just walked into the room in a long dress and wobbly earrings.

'Still, I'm back now,' said Terry.

'Yes.'

'And no harm's done.'

'No, we were lucky,' said Audrey. 'We managed to get the party shifted from Friday to Saturday.'

The front doorbell rang.

'I'll go,' said Ernie.

'How do I look?' Audrey spun round for inspection.

'You'll do,' said Terry.

'I've just checked upstairs. They're both fast asleep. If Wayne wakes up, you've got to be firm with him. I don't want you bribing him with a box of After Eights like you did last time.'

'I'll manage.' Terry remembered the grotty little kid on the Dover train with her chocolate-starved rabbit. 'I'm getting rather good with kids.'

Ernie brought Bob into the room. Bob was kitted out with a black bow tie as well. He had a small parcel in his hand.'

'Audrey, you look smashing.'

'Thank you. Makes me feel better than "you'll do".' She threw a sharp glance at Terry.

'Catch.' Bob tossed the parcel to him.

'Thanks.'

'Half a bottle of Wodka. From Varrington.'

'You're all being suspiciously nice to me.'

'That's because we're all glad to see you, aren't we?' Bob looked at Audrey.

'It's just time,' said Audrey. 'Are we going in your car?'

'Are you not staying here with me, then?' Terry looked a little put out.

'Not when I'm dressed like this,' said Bob. Audrey invited Thelma and me to go along with them.

'Oh, aye . . . '

'Sort of little celebration.'

'To which I am not invited.'

'Well, *you* haven't got a bow tie and evening dress.'

'Bloody good job too,' said Terry. 'I'd hate to look as ridiculous as you do in yours.'

'I'll go and get my wrap,' said Audrey, and swept out of the room.

Terry took a swig of vodka from the bottle.

'Listen,' said Bob. 'About that job. I had a word on the phone with Frank Busby, and it's still open. Union rates as basic plus bags of overtime, and there's a – '

'You never give up, do you?'

'What do you mean?'

'I mean poking your nose into my affairs. Worrying about my welfare. Making assumptions.'

'What have I said now?'

'All right, so I'm back home,' said Terry. 'That doesn't alter my thinking on certain fundamental principles. I haven't come back here just to end up working as a sparks for some tinpot jerry-builder. With you prancing round the site every five minutes flaunting your new-found status and your pocket slide-rule.'

Bob took a step backwards. 'You ungrateful sod. I put my reputation on the line recommending you for that job. *Knowing* how you might make things difficult for me. Well, never again, mate. Never again!'

'Oh, for God's sake, stop it you two.' Audrey had returned with her simulated fur wrap.

'Why I bothered to rescue you from the total obscurity of a Scottish car-wash, I'll – '

'You rescue *me*?!' screeched Terry. 'It was me who had to drag *you* back – practically by the scruff of the neck? *You* were the one who wanted to go "a roamin' through the gloamin' " with a sleeping bag and a harmonica.'

'I – !!'

'Harmonica!' jeered Terry. 'I can't play one, and you haven't got one. What a fiasco *that* would have been.'

'I could have bought one,' said Bob. 'And you could have learnt to play. Anyone can do anything, remember? But *who* was it who got cold feet? Not *me*, mate. *I* was prepared to drop everything and take off there and then.'

Bob turned to see what Terry was looking at over his shoulder. Thelma was standing alongside Audrey and Ernie in the doorway to the living-room.

'We're ready to take off, too,' said Thelma, in a voice that forecast high winds later.

Bob couldn't have looked more chuffed if he had been mounting the scaffold. He threw a hate-filled glance at Terry and followed them out.

Terry clutched the vodka bottle to his chest and sank further into the armchair. He felt totally abandoned, but he smiled happily to himself. At least it was nice to know he'd ruined Thelma's evening too.

5

Birthday Boy

Terry's Mam and Dad came back from Carlisle on the Sunday. Audrey wasn't sorry to see him pack up and go. Especially after the way he'd ruined their evening out. Thelma hadn't stopped bickering all night.

So Terry went back to tea in bed, and rock cakes in the oven, and spotted dick and two helpings of everything and it was all marvellous.

'Come on,' said Mrs Collier. 'Stir yourself, lad.' She had brought Terry his morning cup of tea along with the morning paper and a letter.

Terry yawned an enormous yawn that made his face look all mouth. He sat up on one elbow, scratched his head, wiped his hand over his face, scratched his armpit and yawned again.

'What time is it?'

'Half past eight.'

'Half past *what*?!' Terry looked outraged. 'I thought you said I could sleep late?'

'This is late enough. I don't know how I'm going to get through today. And I've *got* to do this room out. It hasn't been touched since you got back.'

'Aye, well, I meant to . . . '

Mrs Collier surveyed the wreckage and wrinkled up her nose in disapproval. 'Smells like a – can't quite think of that Army expression of yours.'

'Like a Maltese brothel?' suggested Terry helpfully.

'Terry! My goodness – my, it's made you very coarse, the Army has. Made you very crude. No – I was going to say like a gorilla's armpit.'

'*Mother*! That's hardly the height of gentility!' Terry picked up his cup of tea and made a point of raising his little finger.

'All I'm saying is – don't bring your vulgar barrack room ways and your Maltese brothels, into *this* house.' She paused. 'It's no good, we'll have to have some fresh air in here.'

Mrs Collier slid the window wide open top and bottom. A draught of cold air that had come all the way from the Russian steppes hit Terry's bare chest. He shrank back.

'By the cringe! Hey up, I'll catch me death!'

'This room smells of last night's beer and last week's socks.'

Terry pulled the bedclothes up around his neck. 'Should smell sexy,' he said. 'Should smell of my after-shave – which according to the bottle makes me dangerous to be with.'

Mrs Collier sniffed the air cautiously. 'What's it called – "Pickled onions for men"?'

'No, they're under the bed.' Terry reached down and handed the jar to his mother. 'Sorry, I've lost the lid. I'm referring to a thing called "Quiver", and I was hoping, that on today of all days, someone might have bought me a refill.'

'What is today of all days?'

'It's a day,' explained Terry, 'when I didn't expect to be woken up at half past eight in the morning. It's a day when I might have expected a modest amount of affection and attention to be lavished on me. A day on which I should have been woken gently. At noon – with bacon and eggs, fried bread and Marmite, and a copy of *Sporting Life*.'

'This house isn't a resettlement centre for disabled ex-servicemen, my lad. It's about time you got your thinking cap on.' Mrs Collier found the lid of the pickled onion jar.

'Mother – don't you know what day it is?'

'Thursday.' Mrs Collier started to straighten up some of the debris.

Terry caught hold of his mother's wrist. 'I mean what day – historically? Just pay me some attention, will you?

Down dusters for a minute. What happened in 1944 – not counting the Second World War and all that? Something that we've celebrated ever since.'

Mrs Collier thought hard for a moment. 'Is it nice or nasty?'

'A happy event,' said Terry peevishly. 'Something which – amongst the grief and confusion of war, brought you a ray of sunshine and hope.'

'I remember I saw *Gone with the Wind* for the third time.'

'Try again,' said Terry. 'Is there no other vivid experience which springs to mind?'

'Well – I remember I had a terrible time carrying *you*.'

'We're getting warmer. And then – ?'

She got it at last. 'Eee, I didn't forget, pet. I didn't forget that.'

'Of course you forgot.' Terry slid miserably under the bedclothes.

'No, I bought you a card. I've got it downstairs somewhere.' Mrs Collier frowned. 'Now what did I do with it . . . ?'

The front doorbell rang twice.

Mrs Collier looked out of the window. 'Oh, that's Bob's car – and look at you. Still not dressed!'

Terry surfaced with renewed hope. 'Ah, friends. *Real* friends don't forget.'

'I'll go and let him in. Many happy returns, pet.' Mrs Collier gave Terry a pat on the cheek and went downstairs.

Terry spotted the letter lying on top of the newspaper and ripped it open in the hope of finding a birthday card from a well-wisher. It was an advertising brochure.

Terry read the blurb out aloud. '*Gender* . . . the most up-to-date comprehensive manual on adult sexual instruction. No obligation . . . send fifteen pounds.' He tossed it onto the floor. 'Happy birthday . . . '

Bob came into the room and stopped dead. He sniffed the air with some distaste. 'My God, your room smells like a Turkish wrestler's jock-strap.'

'Oh, give it a rest,' said Terry. 'I've just had me Mam in. And don't open the window any wider. It's like the Russian front in here.'

Bob surveyed Terry sprawled out in the crumpled bed. 'Bye, some people have it easy, don't they? Breakfast in bed, the papers . . . what's this?' He stooped to retrieve the glossy brochure.

'It's a manual of sex instruction.'

'Oh, Thelma and I did that.'

'What – wrote it, or posed for it?'

'No, you twit – we gave them your *address*. You see, if we get a friend to buy a copy, we get ours at half price.'

'How thoughtful of you.' Terry snatched the brochure back and thumbed through it. 'How can it be "No obligation" when you've got to send fifteen quid?'

Bob looked uncertain. 'Well, I suppose you, er, send the fifteen pounds for the manual, but . . . '

'Yes?'

'But you're under no obligation to follow the instructions.'

'Brilliant,' said Terry.

'Look, I haven't got time to bother about that now,' said Bob. 'I'm on my way to work but there was something important I wanted to say to you.'

Terry sat up and beamed expectantly. 'What is it?'

'Well, listen – you know we were going to meet in the Black Horse tonight.'

'Yes . . . '

'Well, I've just remembered that today's a special occasion.'

'Oh, not so special as *all* that.'

Bob sat on the bed, pulled out a small package and handed it to Terry. 'Here – d'you like those?'

'Aww, Bob – you shouldn't have . . . ' Terry opened the box, touched.

'Bloody expensive,' said Bob. 'You wouldn't believe the price if I told you.'

'It's the thought that counts,' said Terry. He unfolded the tissue paper and found a pair of earrings. He looked up at Bob with a frown. 'They're earrings!'

'Of course they're earrings! Do you *like* them?'

'Well, I'm not a bloody gipsy,' said Terry. 'What are you getting me for Christmas – a caravan?'

'They're not for you, you twit! They're for *Thelma*.'

'Thelma?!' Terry felt his temper rise.

'Of course. It's her anniversary present. Do you think she'll like them?'

'Anniversary of *what*?'

'Of our engagement.'

'You've had three,' said Terry acidly. 'Which one is this?'

Bob wrapped up the earrings and ignored the question. 'They're nice, aren't they?'

'Very nice.' Terry sank back into the bed. 'So that's the special occasion, is it?'

'Yes,' said Bob. 'Means I won't be able to meet you for a drink tonight. I'm taking Thelma to the pictures. They're showing *Gone with the Wind* at the Regal.'

'And it soon will be, too,' muttered Terry.

'Do you know I've never seen that film?'

'Isn't that incredible?' Terry's sarcastic delivery was lost on Bob.

'Not really,' said Bob. 'It was made years before I was born.'

'No, I meant incredible coincidence,' said Terry. 'I meant that my own *mother* also put Clark Gable and Vivien Leigh before me.'

Bob looked puzzled. 'I don't get it . . . '

'Don't bother . . . *so* . . . this is your special occasion?'

'Yes.'

'Marvellous. I'd have thought you of all people . . . aye, well, we live and learn.' Terry gave a weary shrug and sank deeper into the pillow.

'What's the matter?'

'Nothing,' said Terry lightly. He gazed at the ceiling.

'Well, something's the matter.'

'I've just told you. Nothing.'

Bob checked the ceiling. Everything seemed normal.

'Look,' he said. 'I know you well enough by now. I can tell by the way you say "nothing", that *something's* wrong.'

'Oh, really?'

'Listen,' said Bob. 'I haven't got all day. Are you going to tell me what's the matter, or aren't you?'

'If you don't know *already*, there's no point.'

'Well, give me a clue.'

Terry relented a little. 'What day is it?'

'Thursday.' Bob got up off the bed.

'I mean the date. Historically. Not counting Madam's triple anniversary.'

Bob shook his head. 'Sorry. Don't get it. Must get to work. Hope you don't mind about tonight. I'll give you a call tomorrow.'

'So you don't remember, then?' said Terry with growing desperation.

'Terry, I'm supposed to be at *work*. I can't think what you're on about – unless you mean it's your *birthday*.'

Before Terry could react, Bob shut the door firmly behind him, then opened it again almost immediately.

'Sorry, kidda . . . '

'I should think so.'

Bob walked back to the bed and picked up Thelma's present. 'Forgot the earrings. See you.'

As Bob went out, Mrs Collier came in with a birthday card in one hand and a pine aerosol in the other. She handed the card to Terry. 'Here you are, love. I told you I'd got one. Left it behind the clock.' She gave the room a vigorous burst of disinfectant.

Terry looked at the back of the card first. His mother hadn't erased the price. 'Four and a half pence? You've been lashing out haven't you?' Terry opened the card to read the verse. 'Ohh, Mam . . . you could have *signed* it.'

'I'll do that later,' said Mrs Collier. 'When I'm not so busy.' She sprayed a pile of discarded clothing and gathered it into a bundle which she held at arm's length. 'Do you want these washed or destroyed?'

Terry didn't answer. He read out the copperplate verse inside the card. '*On this day of love and joy – I send a toast to my dear Boy –*' Terry shut the card and ad-libbed the rest. 'I wish him luck, I wish him well – I wish his bedroom didn't smell.'

At tea-time, Terry found himself alone in the house. His mother had left buttered bread between two dinner plates and had put the jam and cake tin on the table along with the tea-tray. Terry made himself a pot, turned on the radio and spread the raspberry jam on thick. It was clear that sugar was going to be his only solace.

The radio was tuned to Anne Nightingale. 'And here,' said her voice, 'Is the last batch of birthday requests for today. For Tony, Larry, Sheila, Tommy, Ricky, Charmaine, Dick, Ian, Jenny, Sasha, Andrew and – Barney. Hope you all got *lots* of cards and presents, and maybe a birthday cake and a party. Many Happy Returns to all of you, and I hope you enjoy this new single from – '

Terry gave the 'Off' knob a vicious twist and flicked his solitary card into the empty grate. There was a knock at the back door.

'It's open,' he yelled.

Bob entered the kitchen cautiously. 'It's only me.'

'Oh. I thought it was Harrods with a vanload of presents.'

'I brought you the evening paper.' Bob dropped it onto the table.

Terry fished some coins out of his pocket. 'How much is it – three pence?'

'I don't want the money.'

'Oh, no,' said Terry. 'Always believe in paying my way.' He slammed the coins down on the table.

'I'll swap it for a cup of tea,' said Bob.

'Help yourself. You might need some more water, though.'

Bob checked the contents of the teapot then poured himself out a cup. He sat down at the table. Terry started to eat his bread and jam.

'Just on my way back from work,' said Bob.

Terry carried on eating. Bob took a rock cake out of the tin, stuck a match in the top and lit it with another match. He pushed the rock cake towards Terry. 'You see? I remembered. Happy Birthday, kid.'

Terry gave Bob what he hoped was a withering look and unfolded the evening paper.

'Well, aren't you going to blow it out?'

'I'll bloody well blow *you* out in a minute,' growled Terry from behind the paper.

Bob blew out the match. 'You might at least take a joke. Enter into the spirit of things.'

Terry put down the paper. 'Why not?' His voice was heavy with sarcasm. 'We can have jelly, and ice-cream, put on funny hats and play Musical Chairs.'

'Or Statues,' said Bob. 'I prefer Statues – still, it's *your* party.'

Terry picked up his knife, considered stabbing Bob, then decided to spread jam on another piece of bread.

'What was that other game we used to play?' asked Bob. 'Hunt the Thimble – now that was fun.'

'I can think of something more difficult than that,' said Terry. 'Hunt the Birthday Card.'

'Did you not get a lot of cards, then?'

'*None* from you, an unsigned one from me Mam, and one from Audrey's kids.'

'Well, that's two.'

'Theirs doesn't count. It said "Get well soon".'

Bob got up and retrieved Terry's card from the grate. 'Must have fallen off the mantelpiece.' He put it back.

'Perhaps they know something *I* don't know,' said Terry. 'Perhaps I'm suffering from some incurable disease and they're keeping it from me.'

'I doubt it,' said Bob. 'Besides, they can cure almost anything these days.'

'Except loneliness.' Terry loosed a monstrous sigh.

Bob came back to the table. 'Do you remember your twelfth birthday? Round this table – in this room?'

'Yes,' said Terry. 'I got cards, and presents. I got a speedboat. And we had a party.'

'And a good one, too. You were just at the transitional stage. You were going off "Hunt the Thimble" and onto "Hunt Deirdre Birchwood".'

'Deirdre Birchwood . . . ' Terry cast his mind back. 'My God . . . '

'That party marked the borderline. Between the age of innocence and the age of puberty.'

'Our behaviour was on the borderline too,' said Terry.

'Yes. We played "Dustman's Knock" – the same as "Postman's Knock" only dirtier. And then there was "Photography".'

Terry looked puzzled.

'You turn the lights out and see what develops.'

'Oh, I see. Joke . . . joke . . . '

'I remember it as if it was yesterday,' said Bob. His eyes glazed over.

'Well, I don't recall it being *that* exciting. I know some bugger overwound my speedboat.'

'It got better when your Mam and Dad went round to Uncle Wilf's.' Bob grinned impishly. 'I poured a bowl of pink blancmange over Deirdre Birchwood's bra.'

'Oh, I remember *that*,' said Terry. 'I had my hand inside at the time.'

They paused to contemplate their memories of Miss Birchwood's pubescent superstructure.

'She was a big girl, for twelve years old,' said Bob. 'To have a bra you could get blancmange in.'

'And your hand,' added Terry.

'Fantastic . . . ' Bob smiled. 'Mind, by the time she was sixteen, she was wearing scaffolding.'

'Yes,' sighed Terry. 'I'd have given anything to have been underneath when *that* collapsed – but by then she wasn't talking to me anymore.'

There was another moment of silent reflection on the opportunities now lost forever, then Terry looked at the clock.

'Don't you have to take Thelma and her new earrings

to the Regal?'

Bob checked his watch. 'Not yet. I've got the tickets. Reserved seats.'

'Ahh . . . how thoughtful.'

Bob reached for the evening paper. 'Let's see what your stars have to say. As today's your birthday, you should have a special horoscope.' Bob hunted for the right page. 'What's your sign again?'

'Pisces . . .'

'Hold on . . . ah, here we are. Pisces . . . "A good time for chucking things out – like old grudges and inhibitions, and making a fresh start.'

'You're making it up.'

'I'm not,' said Bob. 'That's what it says here. You can read it yourself if you like.'

'Okay, go on.'

' – "Take a closer look at your career and social possibilities and you will discover new openings".'

'Great,' said Terry. 'I haven't got a career, I haven't got a job, and as I haven't got any friends, I haven't got any social possibilities. So *that* stargazer's right up the shute to start with.'

'That's why it's a good time for making a fresh start,' said Bob. 'There's a bit more.'

'I can't wait.'

' – "Tonight, in a harmonius atmosphere, pleasant memories return".'

'Well, if you call the Snug at the Black Horse a harmonious atmosphere, I suppose he's right. Especially as I'll only have memories to keep me company.'

Bob looked over the top of the newspaper. 'The trouble with you Pisces people is that you lack stability and precision. You're like fish. You drift aimlessly through life, and are prone to melancholy.'

'I'd rather be a fish than a goat. That's what you Capricorns are – bloody billygoats.'

'I've got other signs rising,' protested Bob. 'I'm certainly not Capricorn by temperament. And I wouldn't have *been* Capricorn if I hadn't been premature. I'd have been Aquarius if my mother hadn't got crushed in the January sales.'

'Who cares, anyway,' sneered Terry. 'It's a load of old gunge, that star business. Codswallop. Every paper you read tells you something different. It can be time for a new romance in the *Daily Mirror*, or the moment to launch a new business venture in the *Daily Express*.'

Bob's faith in astrology remained unshaken. 'They give the names of celebrities who've got birthdays this week.'

'Oh?'

'Mmmmm . . . '

'What d'you mean – mmmm?'

'Well, no one really famous was born *today*. The best they can do is James Ogilvie.'

'Who the hell's he?'

'Exactly,' said Bob. 'He happens to be the son of Princess Alexandra and the Honourable Angus Ogilvie.'

'Bet *he* isn't short of presents today.' Terry gave Bob a bleak look.

Bob puffed out his chest. 'I share birthdays with Bruce Forsyth and Prince Edward of Gloucester.'

'Well, well, well. Do you really? Who'd have thought it?'

An uneasy silence fell between them. Terry plucked the burnt match out of the rock cake and took a birthday bite.

Bob tried a new opening gambit. 'Is that all you plan to do tonight? Go down to the Black Horse, I mean?'

'Nothing much else *for* me to do.'

'I see. Well, I mean – if you're *definitely* going to be there, I'll meet you.'

Terry stopped munching. 'What about your command performance at the Regal?'

'I'll pop across during the intermission. There'll be time for a swift half.'

Terry considered the idea. 'Okay,' he shrugged. 'See you in the Snug.'

'Right.' Bob got up. 'Must go – cheers.' He patted

Terry on the shoulder. 'Hey – come on. Perk up!'

'I am perked up.' Terry sat there looking as miserable as sin.'

'Pisces,' said Bob. 'Prone to melancholy.' He looked back as he was half-way through the door. 'Penny for your thoughts?'

Terry shook his head. Bob closed the door quietly. Terry put two big rock cakes side by side on his plate like a pair of breasts and sat looking at them.

What ever happened to Deidre Birchwood? he asked himself. But then – what ever happened to blancmange?

Thelma's mother's lounge had been specially cleared for the party. A barrel of beer stood on the sideboard ready tapped, and there were plenty of glasses and a whole tableful of mini-sandwiches and mini-sausage rolls, all mortally wounded by wooden cocktail sticks.

Thelma had a thing about mini-sandwiches. The smallness of the portions somehow elevated the social status of the occasion. The stuffed olives, and the pickled onions shrunk to the size and colour of mothballs, were especially prized. They added 'tone' to any proceedings. Slightly creased, paper decorations hung limply across the ceiling. Bob had made a bit of a mess folding them up after last Christmas. There were also several balloons to complete the atmosphere of carnival.

Thelma and Bob had invited Mary and Raymond, Hugh and Janey, and Podge Rowley. They all knew Terry from way back, and were all more or less the same age. Thelma had also invited a couple of younger girls – Debbie and Clare to partner Podge and the surprise guest.

They all stood around in a pleasant state of anticipation, trying to make their regulation glass of Cyprus sherry last.

'Hey, Bob,' said Podge. 'How will we recognise him? Will he be wearing a red carnation?'

'Oh, he hasn't changed that much.'

'It's a good five years since I've seen him,' said

Raymond. 'Must be.'

'At least,' said Mary. She was engaged to Raymond. 'I don't think I'd know him if I bumped into him in the street.'

'Oh, come off it.' Raymond nudged her. 'You used to go out with him.'

'*Ages* ago.'

'So did Janey,' said Harold.

'But not for long,' said Janey. She was engaged to Hugh.'

Raymond turned to Bob. 'I think we ought to leave all his ex-girl friends here, while *we* go down to the pub.'

'Thanks very much.' Thelma's mouth compressed into that thin red line which Bob knew so well.

'It's not a bad idea,' said Podge. 'We could have a game of darts. Two a side, three hundred and one up, start on a treble, finish on a double.'

'You're on for a quid,' said Raymond.

Bob stepped in hastily. 'Now come on, lads. You can give up the Stick and Bottle for one night. This is supposed to be a surprise party.'

'But I *always* play darts on a Thursday,' said Podge.

'It's the welcome mat,' insisted Bob. 'The red *carpet*.'

'Every Thursday,' said Podge. 'Never miss.'

Bob widened his appeal to include them all. 'Look – he's been away for five years. He's lost contact with all his friends. He thinks he hasn't *got* any friends. And today is his *birthday*. So let's make him feel at home. Let's make him feel we're glad to see him again. Give him a drink, a pat on the back, a smile, a chat.'

'Really gee him up, like,' said Raymond.

'Show him we *mean* it,' said Bob. 'Okay?'

There was a general chorus of assent from the girls.

'All right,' said Hugh. 'We'll do our best.'

'And *then* we'll go down to the Stick and Bottle,' said Podge.

'You *men*!' Mary gave them a look of reproof. 'Thelma's made all this lovely food. And there's all the beer you need to drink right here.'

Raymond squeezed her round the waist. 'We thought you might like to see your ex-lover alone.'

Mary pushed him away. 'He wasn't my lover. There was never anything between me and Terry Collier.'

'Frequently,' said Podge with a sly grin.

'Hey – watch it!' Raymond was sensitive to outside comment about Mary's previous lovelife. Fact *or* fiction.

Thelma decided to take charge. 'I think Debbie and Clare should go and fetch him. Bob, you run them down to the Black Horse. They can come back by taxi. Make sure you give them the money.'

'Neither of us have ever met him, you know,' said Debbie.

'Well, that's the whole *point*,' said Thelma. 'Two attractive young girls he's never seen before – suddenly falling for him.'

'He'll go out of his mind,' said Bob. He could just imagine Terry's reaction.

'About your height, but thinner, right?' Clare was a bit unhappy with the description she'd been given.

'Thin, fair-haired and forlorn,' said Bob. 'But not bad looking. He's quite a likely lad. He'll be in the Snug. That's the little room between the Saloon and the Public Bar.'

'Okay.' Clare picked up her handbag. 'Are you ready, sexy?'

'I'm wild, if you're willing,' said Debbie.

The two girls did a bump and grind routine all the way to the hall to ragged cheers and whistles from the boys. Bob followed, pausing to bow in the doorway and throw a theatrical kiss.

'This is one time,' said Thelma, 'I'd give anything to be a fly on the wall.'

If Thelma's wish *had* come true, with her luck, she might well have been the fly Terry batted savagely with his bag of crisps. The poor little sod bounced off the partition, fell to the floor with its feet in the air and took no further interest in the proceedings.

Terry sat up at the bar with a pint of ale at his elbow. He opened the bag and dipped into the Bovril-flavoured crisps. There *was* a time, he thought, when they tasted like potatoes. He sat there munching in solitary state till another young man came into the Snug. He was about the same age as Terry, and he also had fair hair and a mournful expression. Tom the barman appeared.

'Hallo, Colin.'

'Evening, Tom. Pint of lager, please.' Colin gave Terry a nod. 'Evening.'

Terry grunted in reply.

'All right?' asked Colin.

'Can't complain.'

'Aye, well . . . '

'Could be worse.'

'Yeh – always could.'

'Always someone . . . '

'Worse off than yourself.'

'True . . . true . . . '

'That's how to look at it.'

'Aye. Count your blessings.'

'Look for the silver lining.'

Tom brought Colin his pint of lager. Colin paid for it then lifted his glass.

'Cheers . . . '

'Cheers,' replied Terry.

They both took a swallow and contemplated each other and their surroundings. Neither of the other two bars were very busy.

'Not a lot happening tonight,' observed Colin.

'Not much, no.'

'You waiting for someone?'

'Only Candice Bergen and Julie Christie.'

'Oh, aye . . . '

'Always bloody late, those two.'

Colin nodded understandingly. 'Brigitte Bardot's the same. Been waiting three hours already.'

'Long way from St Tropez.'

'Especially when you're on a donkey, like.' Colin

took another sip of lager and wiped his lips. 'I reckon you must be going to the same party as me. On Elizabeth Taylor's yacht.'

'Yeah, well, I have to. She was a bit upset when I didn't turn up on her birthday.'

'I could give you a lift,' said Colin. 'Sammy Davis Junior's picking me up in his helicopter.'

'Nice of you to offer. Problem is I've got Jackie Kennedy calling round with the Onassis' hovercraft.'

Colin consulted the pub clock. 'Mind, we'll have missed the cocktails.'

'Aye, but we'll still be in time for the grand gala fancy dress ball.'

Colin nodded. 'I like *your* outfit,' he confided.

Terry gave a modest shrug. 'Yes, well, I thought I'd go as an ordinary working-class bloke from the North-East. With no job and no prospects.'

'Very lifelike,' said Colin. 'It suits you.'

Terry couldn't quite work that one out. He decided not to try. 'What're you going as?'

'Ghenghis Khan.'

'Ahh . . . of course,' said Terry. 'I should have guessed.'

'I left me horde outside. Had a hell of a job trying to find a place to park, mind.'

'That's the trouble with big hordes,' said Terry.

They drank on in silent contemplation of the glittering event. Terry held out his bag of crisps.

'Want one?'

'Oh, ta, thanks. What flavour?'

'Bovril.'

Colin took a palmful. 'Prefer Smokey Bacon meself.'

'This is all they had,' said Terry. He drained his glass.

Colin tapped it. 'Want another?'

'Why not? Cheers, great, a special, please.' Terry slid off the bar stool. 'Just going to see a man about a dog.'

'Oh . . . right.'

'Have another crisp,' said Terry. He went through the door to the Public Bar.

As the door closed behind him, Debbie and Clare walked through the street door to the Snug. They looked at Colin, then at each other.

'Hardly your Robert Redford,' muttered Clare. 'Still, it could be worse.'

The two girls came and leant on the bar on either side of Colin. His mouth was full of crisps, and his glass was half-way to his lips.

'Hello, stranger,' purred Debbie.

Colin nearly choked. 'You what?'

Clare ran a finger down his spine. 'My friend said "Hello". Aren't you pleased to see us?'

'You what?' Colin took another nervous sip of lager as the girls crowded him.

'Can I have one of your crisps?' asked Debbie. She didn't wait for Colin's reply. 'Mmmm . . . ' Debbie savoured the crisp provocatively. 'Bovril . . . '

'I prefer Smokey Bacon, meself,' said Colin.

'So do *I*,' murmured Clare. She ran her hand over Colin's arm.

Colin hurriedly finished his lager before any got spilt.

'Are you, er – all on your own, then?' asked Clare.

Colin shrugged. 'Sort of . . . '

'All alone and nobody to love you?' Debbie looked at Clare. 'It's not right, is it?'

Clare shook her head. 'No. Still, never mind. How would you like to come to a party with us?'

'A party?'

'Yes. With *us*.' Debbie linked arms with Colin.

Colin looked wary as Clare took his other arm. 'Where is it, this party?'

'Ah . . . that's a surprise.'

'There's lots of food,' said Debbie.

'And lots to drink.'

'And we may even turn the lights out.'

'You what?' said Colin.

The two girls took a step towards the door but Colin found himself unable to walk.

'Don't you trust us?' asked Clare.

'It's not going to be *that* kind of a party, is it?' asked Colin – hoping very much that that was *exactly* the kind of party it was going to be.

Debbie tightened her grip on his arm. 'Why don't you come and find out?' She gave him a look full of Eastern Promise.

'Tom,' called Colin. 'Cancel that Special.' He went weakly forward like a lamb to the slaughter.

Terry walked back into the Snug just in time to see his new drinking partner leaving with a girl on each arm. Colin looked back at him apologetically.

'Make some excuse to Liz for me, will you? And to Brigette, if she turns up.'

The street door closed to the sound of laughter. Terry slumped back onto the bar stool and sat there completely shattered by what he had just seen. He picked up his bag of crisps. They had all been eaten.

Tom came and picked up the empty glasses. 'Cheer up, lad. There's a lot worse off than you.'

'Name bloody one,' said Terry. 'Name bloody *one*!!'

Colin insisted on paying for the taxi that brought them to Thelma's house. Apart from a light in the front hall, the house was in darkness.

Debbie opened the front door with a key.

'It seems very quiet for a party,' said Colin.

'Won't be later on,' said Clare. She took a scarf from the hall-stand. 'Here – put this over your eyes.'

'You what?' said Colin.

'It's a *surprise*,' said Clare, knotting the scarf behind his head. 'Not too tight, is it?'

Colin shook his head.

'Right, give me your hand. Open the door, Deb.'

They led the blindfolded Colin into the darkened front room to be welcomed by a rousing chorus of 'For he's a Jolly Good Fellow'. On the last '*us*', Bob switched on the lights, everyone clapped and cheered, and Debbie pulled the scarf from Colin's face.

Bob stared at him in amazement. 'Who the hell are

you?!'

'You what?' said Colin.

Mary shook her head. 'I was right. I'd never have recognised him in a million years.'

'You're right,' said Podge.

'Just what d'you think you're up to?' demanded Bob angrily.

'Nothing,' said Colin. 'These two girls invited me to a party!'

'Well, you've come to the wrong one.' Bob turned to Debbie and Clare. 'This isn't Terry – this is an imposter!'

'You what-er?' said Colin.

'Oh, dear,' said Deborah. 'You did say thin, fair and forlorn.'

'And he was the only one in the bar,' said Clare. '*Now* what are we going to do?'

'Next time *I'll* organise things,' said Thelma.

Clare turned to Colin. 'We thought you were Terry Collier.'

'Ah – no . . . I'm Colin Ferguson. You must want the other bloke that came in as we went out.'

'Yes . . . sorry,' said Bob.

'Oh, that's all right,' said Colin. 'But now that I've come out of me way, like – d'you mind if I stay?'

Fuelled by the goodbye look Thelma gave him, Bob drove down to the Black Horse like a bat out of hell. Terry was still in the Snug – sunk almost irretrievably into a deep Piscean slough of despond. Bob slapped him heartily on the shoulder, and paused to get his breath back.

''Lo, kidda . . . I thought I might have missed you.'

Terry gave Bob a wintry look then glanced at the clock. 'That was a long first half wasn't it?'

'First half?'

'Of the film.'

'Film?'

'*Gone with the Wind.*'

'Oh, *that* film. Yes. *Yes*. It, er – started late.'

Tom the barman came to take their order.

'Drink?'

'Oh – yes. My round though,' said Bob.

'In that case, I'll have a large whisky.'

'Two large ones, Tom.'

'What d'you think of the film?'

'Ah – yes,' said Bob. 'Long. Tends to be a bit drawn out.'

'Yes,' said Terry. 'Have they burnt Atlanta yet?'

'Atlanta?'

'You *know* . . . '

'Oh, ah, yes – *Atlanta*. No, I don't think so. I think that's in the second half.'

Terry frowned. 'Funny. Thought that was in the first half.' He shrugged.

'Ah, well, they revised this version, didn't they?' said Bob. 'Changed the colour and everything.'

Tom brought them two large whiskies. Bob picked up his glass with a sense of relief. 'Cheers, kidda. Happy Birthday – and Many Happy Returns!'

'Is it your birthday?' asked Tom. 'Have this one on the house.'

'Marvellous,' said Terry. 'Always happens when I'm not paying for it.'

Tom grinned and walked away. The two lads sipped their whiskies.

'Hasn't been a very good birthday for you, has it?'

'No different from most of the others,' said Terry gloomily. 'But then I've been starved of love and affection ever since I was born.'

'Bollocks,' said Bob. 'You were spoilt rotten – you still are.'

Terry ignored him. 'No,' he mused. 'My parents didn't want me. That's what makes me such a loner. People sense it. I've got no friends. No *real* friends at all now . . . ' He looked reproachfully at Bob. 'If I ever *had* . . . '

'Rubbish.'

'There was a bloke in here earlier on,' said Terry. 'We got chatting, like – getting on quite well, you know.

Talking about this and that. Sharing my crisps. Having a jar together. The two of us were on our tod, you see.'

'Uhuh . . .'

'I go out for a Jimmy Riddle, and get back just in time to see this bloke being swept out the door by two teenage *ravers*! No *mention* of how about making up a foursome. All I got was the elbow. He'd woofed all me bleedin' crisps, and he didn't even leave the pint he'd offered to buy. Rotten sod . . .'

Bob decided not to tell Terry about Colin. 'Listen, it's not as bad as all that.'

'Oh, no?'

'You have friends. Stacks of them. People who *care* about you. Who want to see you again.'

Terry laid a hand on Bob's arm. There was a look of genuine concern in his eyes. 'Bob. You and I used to be close friends. I mean, we've known each other for a long time. You'd tell me wouldn't you?'

'Tell you what?'

'Well, if I had bad breath, or B.O. – or intolerably sweaty feet – or even all three.'

'Terry, there's nothing wrong with your personal hygiene – nothing radical, anyway.'

'Because if it meant getting under the tap with a big bar of Lifebuoy, I wouldn't let pride interfere.'

'Oh, for God's *sake*, Terry! Just because a few people forgot it was your birthday.'

'A *few*?!'

'Well, *I* didn't. Drink up. I've got a surprise for you.'

'What kind of surprise?'

'A surprise kind of surprise. Come *on* – there are people waiting!'

Terry looked confused. 'But what about Thelma? What about the second half of *Gone with the Wind*?'

'Bugger *Gone with the Wind*.' Bob downed the last of his whisky and pulled out his car keys.

'You'll miss the burning of Atlanta,' said Terry.

'Bugger that too.' Bob walked to the door.

Terry followed, buttoning up his raincoat. 'Still, when

you don't turn up in the Dress Circle, I imagine Thelma may start to smoulder a bit.' He looked back at the barman. 'G'night, Tom. Listen, if Candice Bergen and Julie Christie turn up, tell them I left with a friend.'

Thelma peered through a crack in the curtains. 'Light's out!' she hissed. 'Here comes Bob's car.'

Podge obligingly plunged the room into darkness.

'Has he got Terry with him?' asked Mary.

'Yes!'

'About bloody time,' muttered Podge. He was fast giving up hope of getting down to the Stick and Bottle for his game of darts.

Bob had persuaded Terry to put on a blindfold at the outset of their journey, so Terry had no idea where he was. Bob helped him out of the car.

'Can't imagine what this is all in aid of,' growled Terry.

'Don't cheat, now,' said Bob. 'It's all part of the surprise.' He opened the front gate and steered Terry up the garden path to the front door. 'Mind the step – that's it . . . '

Bob steered Terry into the pitch-black room where everyone stood waiting, doing their best not to laugh.

'Can hear a lot of snickering going on,' said Terry.

'Take no notice,' said Bob. 'Here – can you see anything if I put the lights on?' He did so.

'Black as a darkie's – '

'Quite,' said Bob hurriedly. He beckoned Debbie and Clare to come and stand beside Terry. 'Put your hands out in front of you – slowly now.'

Terry did so, and made contact with Debbie. He ran his hands over her face and hair, then down over her arms and breasts then down to her waist. Debbie did her best not to feel ticklish as Terry felt his way back up to her breasts again. He gave them an experimental squeeze. Debbie took it very well.

'It's a girl,' said Terry after a few moments deliberation.

'Very perceptive of you,' said Bob.

There was a snort of suppressed laughter from Debbie as Terry touched a sensitive area. He pulled her towards him. 'It's not Deirdre Birchwood, though. I wouldn't have been able to get this close.'

Thelma crossed her fingers and hoped Terry wasn't about to do or say anything outrageous.

'Now try behind you,' said Bob.

Terry turned and brushed against Clare. His mouth opened in delight as he ran his hands over her more generous bumps and hollows. 'Hey, I'm beginning to like my birthday,' he said. 'It's rather like reading a dirty book in Braille. And a lot more fun than sharing a choc-ice with Thelma at the Regal. Which one is yours?'

Thelma's mouth snapped shut with displeasure. The others tried not to laugh. Bob decided to hurry things along to avoid further indiscretions.

'They're yours. Both of them. They're a present – for your birthday.'

Terry sniffed the air. 'Scheherazade . . .'

'What?'

'That perfume. Scheherazade. Someone's wearing it.'

Clare shook her head. Debbie nodded to Bob and pointed to her neck. Terry followed his nose and took hold of Debbie again. He smelt her neck.

'That's it. Smashing . . .'

'You recognise the perfume, do you?'

'Anywhere. Janey Freeman used to wear it.'

Bob and Thelma looked at Janey. Janey looked at her husband, Hugh.

'You remember her. Don't you?'

'Who?' asked Bob with growing dread.

'Janey Freeman.' Terry cuddled Debbie and Clare. 'We had a very – physical relationship. Yes . . . She went and married that Hugh Blenkinsop. What a great long streak of wet weak lager *he* was.'

Hugh bristled.

'I don't remember him,' said Bob weakly.

'You should,' said Terry. 'You couldn't stand the sight of him.'

Hugh gave Bob and Thelma a deep-frozen glare and walked Janey to the door. Bob hastily barred the way.

'Er, I think that's enough of this game,' he stammered.

'Yeah,' said Terry. 'The two of them used to knock around with Mary Hodge and that Raymond What's-his-name. Mary, Mary . . . *she* wasn't so bloody contrary. I know that much.'

There was a gasp of annoyance from Mary.

Bob waved his arms desperately. 'All together now – 'For he's a jolly good fell-ow, for he's a jolly good fellow . . . ' Bob tailed off when he found that he and Colin were the only two singing.

Terry pulled off his blindfold and found himself face to face with Hugh and Raymond. 'Hello, lads. Have you come to wish me a Happy Birthday?'

'Stuff your birthday, Collier,' said Hugh.

'And stuff *you*,' said Raymond.

They grabbed hold of Janey and Mary and pushed past Bob.

'Podge!' Terry shook him warmly by the hand. 'And *Thelma*!'

Debbie and Clare began to move away.

'Hang on you two,' said Terry. He turned to Thelma with a bewildered look. 'I can't quite work out what you're doing here.'

'What *I'm* doing here? *I'm* playing hostess at a party in *your* honour. That's why the room's done out, and why all these drinks have been bought. That's why I spent the afternoon slicing cucumber and buttering bread and stuffing vol-au-vents!'

'Oh,' said Terry. 'I thought you were at the pictures.'

Thelma gave a gasp of exasperation and hurried after the others. 'Janey – Mary – wait!'

Terry called out after her. 'I like your earrings – '

'Aye, well,' said Podge. 'Time's a bit tight. I'll just try the Stick and Bottle.'

'Could you drop us off near the ice-rink?' asked Clare.

'Pleasure,' said Podge. He clapped Terry on the shoulder. 'Good to see you.'

'You're not all going, are you?' Terry looked pleadingly at Debbie and Clare. 'We were just getting to know each other.'

'You found out too much already,' said Debbie. 'G'night, Bob.' They left with Podge.

Bob looked long and hard at Terry and shook his head slowly. 'How *do* you do it. It must be a gift.'

'Do what? What have I done?'

'You know what you were saying earlier – about not having any friends?'

'So?'

'Well, you've got even less now.' Bob walked out of the room to help Thelma calm things down in the hall.

Terry turned to see Colin behind the food table in the window. He'd already made a start.

'Evening,' said Colin. 'Try the vol-au-vents. They're very good.'

'I suppose I'd better,' said Terry. 'Seeing they've been stuffed on my behalf.'

The front door slammed ominously. There was the sound of several cars driving away followed by two voices arguing in the hall.

'Funny lot, your friends,' said Colin.

'Ex-friends . . .'

'Ahhh . . .'

Bob and Thelma walked back into the room. Their faces were flushed and they both looked very fed up. Terry wished he could put things right, but it was clear from Thelma's expression that only throwing himself off the Tyne Bridge would do.

'I wish you'd told me that you were going to give me a surprise party, like I mean – going to all this trouble . . .'

Bob closed his eyes in despair. Thelma flopped down into an armchair and bristled.

'If I'd *told* you,' said Bob, 'it wouldn't have been a surprise, would it? It would have been a nice, pleasant, *successful* party, but it wouldn't have been a *surprise*.'

'I think I'd, er – better be off,' said Colin.

'Oh, no,' said Thelma. 'All this has got to be eaten.

Apart from the stuffed olives and the pickled onions. They can go back in the jar.'

Colin obediently drew up a chair and began shovelling it in with both hands.

'Bye, but you've made some cracking grub, Thelma, love.' Terry waved a plateful at her. 'I'm sorry I spoilt it all for you. I really am.'

'Oh, I don't blame you, Terry. Not entirely. After all, it was *Bob's* idea.'

'Thank you very much,' said Bob.

'Oh, why don't we just forgive and forget,' said Thelma tiredly. 'Give him his present.'

'Present?' Terry looked touched. 'Aww, don't say you've bought me a present as well.'

Bob took a parcel out of the sideboard and handed it to Terry.

'Now you make me feel *really* bad. I mean, first a party, and now a *present*.'

'Just unwrap it,' said Bob.

'I'm moved,' said Terry. 'I can't pretend I'm not.' He pulled off the wrapping paper and lifted the lid of the box. 'Well, well, well. "Quiver for Men". Soap, talc, deodorant, after-shave. Awww – I really don't deserve it.'

'I know,' said Thelma.

'Wait a minute,' said Terry uneasily. 'Soap, talc, deodorant, after-shave. This isn't some kind of a message, is it?'

'Yes,' grinned Bob. 'Happy *Bath-day*.'

6

Guess Who's Coming to Dinner

'I don't know how much more tea you intend to drink,' said Mrs Collier. She carried a fresh cup in from the kitchen and set it down by Terry's elbow.

Terry lay deep in one of the parlour armchairs with his feet up on the arm of another. He was surrounded by a litter of magazines and newspapers, and appeared to be engrossed in the day's list of racing fixtures. He hadn't shaved for three days, he hadn't combed his hair, and he hadn't got his slippers on. He wore one blue sock, one black sock with a hole in it, creased, baggy trousers and a greasy vest.

Mrs Collier put her hands on her hips and surveyed the unappetising spectacle presented by her only son.

'I see Midsummer Star's in the 4.30 at Wetherby. Lester's not riding him though . . . '

'That's the fourth pot I've made.'

'Mind you, he did well at Haydock Park last week.'

'Oh, don't put your cigarette ends in the saucer!' Mrs Collier took it away from under the cup.

'Me ashtray's full,' said Terry. 'Oops – !'

'It was. Now it's all over the floor,' Mrs Collier went to fetch a dustpan and brush.

'Aw, come on, Mam,' protested Terry. 'I'm not having tea at the Dorchester.'

'They wouldn't let you in the front door, my lad. They wouldn't let *you* have tea in their *coal* cellar!'

A look of pained surprise crossed Terry's face. 'What's the matter with me?'

'Well, you haven't shaved – '

'Run out of razor blades.'

'And your hair hasn't seen a comb since I don't know

when. You'd better not go near the back door. If the dustmen call, we might never see you again.'

'Aww, Mam. I'm not *going* out. And I've washed me face and hands.'

'Aye, yesterday.' Mrs Collier finished sweeping the carpet. 'I'm disgusted with you.'

'All right. I'll have a bath before I go out.'

'Don't know where you get it from. Certainly not from your father and me. Supposing someone called? Like that nice lady from Avon Cosmetics – or that young man with contact lenses who predicts the end of the world and sells that Watchtower thing.'

'I wish he could predict what's going to win the 4.30 at Wetherby.'

'I'm surprised you've got nothing better to do than just lie around all day.'

'Mother,' said Terry patiently. 'I've been in the Army five years. Serving my country – '

'Oh, don't start all that again. I'd have thought the Army would have at least taught you to have some pride in your own appearance.' Mrs Collier took the dustpan and brush back into the kitchen.

Terry scratched both armpits and called out over the back of the chair. 'What you see here is a reaction if you like. To the years of hardship and discipline – and danger.'

'You don't know what the words mean.'

'I'm entitled to take it easy,' called Terry. 'I need to catch up on essential reading and to reflect on the meaning of life.'

Mrs Collier appeared in the doorway. She was wiping the ashtray. 'The only reading you've caught up on is the *Football Monthly* and all those other magazines with nude whatsits on the cover.'

'You shouldn't have looked.'

'You're just letting yourself go. In your dress *and* your manners.' Mrs Collier returned the ashtray to Terry, and put a clean saucer under his cup of tea. 'You spend half the day in bed and the other half in front of television. The only time you get any fresh air is when you go down to the betting shop. And when you speak it's only to ask for more tea or the bottle opener. Go on like this and you'll end up like Andy Capp.'

'I've had a very *active* day, if you must know,' said Terry. 'Both physically *and* mentally. I fought the flab with Terry Wogan, and I walked all the way to the Black Horse at lunchtime. And there's been a very intellectual morning and *après-midi* on the box. I've watched gliding in the Dolomites, building a dam in Syria, *and* Intermediate Spanish – *muchas gracias*. It's amazing what you can learn from these school programmes.' Terry wagged a finger at his mother. 'If you hadn't gone down to the launderette, you could have seen the metamorphosis of the frog. Biology.'

'Yes, well, I was doing your clothes – biologically.'

'Then why don't you sit down and have a cup of tea?' suggested Terry. 'I could do with another one.'

Bob called in on his way home from work. He looked extremely smart in a new three-piece suit with flared trousers, block shoes, Brutus shirt and broad tie.

'Just thought I'd drop in, he said. 'How's our working-class hero?'

'You can see for yourself,' said Mrs Collier. 'Look at him. Did you ever see such a sight?'

Terry shrank down behind a copy of *Sporting Life*.

'Just look at Bob, now. Look at the nice suit he's got. And how nice his hair is. Bob's well groomed. That's what Bob is.' Mrs Collier prodded her son. 'Terry – I'm talking to you.'

Terry lowered his paper and studied Bob with a mixture of loathing and contempt. He fixed his gaze on Bob's trousers. 'They're a bit tight, aren't they? Like a cheap hotel.'

Bob frowned. 'Cheap hotel?'

'Aye. No ballroom.'

'Terry! That's coarse and quite unnecessary,' said his mother. 'I've told you before about bringing your barrack-room behaviour into this house.'

Terry went out of sight again behind the *Sporting Life*.

'Would you like a cup of tea, Bob?'

'If it's no trouble, Mam.'

Bob and Terry both addressed each other's mother in the same way.

'I've already made Sunshine five pots today, pet. One more won't make any difference.' Mrs Collier threw a sharp glance at her son as she went into the kitchen. 'If it goes on like this, we'll have to buy a plantation.'

Bob looked down at Terry. 'Have you been in that chair all day?'

'Now don't *you* start. I'm just having a break. Catching up on some essential reading – and some quiet reflection.'

'You look like a younger version of Andy Capp.'

'Thank you,' said Terry. 'You're the second person who's said that today. I happen to *like* Andy Capp. I'm *proud* of *my* background. My social class. *I'm* not full of bloody middle-class pretensions – just because you've got an office job and a fiancée who lives in a mock Tudor semi with a monkey puzzle tree in the front garden!'

'I haven't got any pretensions,' said Bob. I'm just open to new ideas. New concepts. There's nothing wrong in trying to improve yourself. To get out of the rut. That's what *you* ought to do. You ought to meet new people, new faces. I'd like to introduce you to *my* new friends – but how can I? How can I take you into their homes looking like you do now? What *would* they say? "Sherry, Bob? And what will your friend have – methylated spirits?" '

'I don't want to go into their little Wimpey-Wates sandwich boxes. Their snooty two-car garage semis. I don't *want* to meet your new friends.'

Bob sat down opposite Terry. 'You know, I don't think you appreciate how much the whole pattern of social life has changed since you've been away. It's different now – and I want you to be part of it. I want you to smarten yourself up – so I can take you out with me – anywhere. But – ' Bob shrugged. 'If you *prefer* to sulk at home, barricaded behind your class prejudices – fine. That's okay with me.'

'I don't mind going out with you, Robert,' said Terry mildly. 'In fact, if you asked me nicely, I might even *shave*. Where are you planning on going?'

Terry's reply caught Bob by surprise. 'Er – ah, well, we can't go anywhere tonight. Thelma and I are playing badminton with Hugh and Janey.'

'You used to call that "shuttlecock" when you played it in the yard. Okay, tomorrow, then.'

'Tommorow's out too, I'm afraid. 'We're having supper with Frank and Kristina – at Philip and Camille's.'

'Where are you Wednesday? In bed with Bob and Carol and Ted and Alice?'

'No. We're, er – going to a barbecue at the Rugby Club.'

'The *what* club?!'

'The Rugby Club.'

'Rugby!'

'But Saturday's all right.'

'Oh, good,' said Terry. ' 'cos Sunday night I've got choir practice.'

'No – *Saturday*. Alan and Brenda asked Thelma and me to bring you over to have supper at their house.'

'Who's Alan and Brenda?'

'You won't know him. Alan Boyle. He's from down south. Came up here about three years ago. We're – business associates. Quite good friends, too. I've told him about you. And Brenda was at the Grammar with Thelma. They'd both like to meet you.'

'Thanks – but I don't want to meet them. I'd rather get in touch with some of the lads and have a *real* Saturday night out.'

'Terry, you won't *find* any of the lads. Not on a Saturday. I told you. Times have changed. They'll all be out with their wives – or girl-friends, at some steak-house or *trattoria*. Or else they'll be having friends round for barbecued chicken or take-away Chinese and *Match of the Day*.'

'God save us . . . ' Terry seemed to shrivel at the prospect.

'It's all very much of a ritual, you see. If you don't grab this invitation, you'll never be a part of it. You'll become a man alone – walking the deserted streets of the Elm Lodge Housing Estate. Cut off from the sounds of laughter and merriment that float from warmly-lit windows.'

'I quite fancy that,' said Terry. 'I've got the mac for a start. And sod the Elm Lodge Housing Estate. I know what goes on behind *those* warmly-lit windows.'

Mrs Collier brought Bob a cup of tea. 'Would you like a rock-cake with it, pet?'

'No, thanks. Me Mam'll have supper waiting.'

'That never bothers Terry,' said Mrs Collier. She went back to the kitchen.

'What goes on?' asked Bob.

'Where?'

'Behind those warmly-lit windows.'

Terry glanced to see if his mother was out of earshot. 'Wife-swapping, witchcraft, suburban sex orgies, bondage, mass flagellation.'

'Really?' Bob looked interested.

'Well-known fact,' said Terry. He threw a copy of *Penthouse* to Bob. 'They've got pictures of it too.'

'Oh . . . ' Bob thumbed through the magazine with studied indifference.

'Yes,' said Terry. 'There was a bishop on *World at One* talking about the moral decay infecting the roots of our society.'

Bob turned the magazine sideways. 'Look,' he said. 'I'm only asking you out to supper. With Thelma there, you're hardly likely to be caught in a downward spiral of decay and depravity. It'll just be a pleasant meal of some kind and a game of Scrabble.'

'I hope not.'

'Well perhaps not Scrabble. You'd only come up with rude words.'

'Yoo-hoo? Anybody home?'

It was Audrey at the kitchen window. Mrs Collier let her in. She came through into the parlour.

'Hallo, Bob. How's Thelma?'

'Fine, thanks, Aud.'

'You must both come round for a meal, soon. How about the beginning of next week?'

'Tuesday's out,' said Terry. 'That's water-polo night.'

'Pardon?' said Audrey.

'And Wednesday, he's potholing with Accles and Pollock.'

Audrey eyed her brother with distaste. 'You know who you remind me of, don't you?'

'Don't tell me. Andy Capp.'

'I was going to say Old Man Steptoe.'

Terry wrinkled up his nose and stuck out his jaw in a passable imitation of Wilfred Brambell.

'He reminds *me* of Ironside,' said Bob. 'He's never out of that chair.'

'My sister's never invited *me* to her house for dinner. For babysitting and mowing the lawn, yes. But never a social occasion. Never dinner,' said Terry.

'So what did you have while Mam and Dad were away,' demanded Audrey. 'Scotch mist?'

'I'm talking about a gay *soirée* with the silver plate out,' said Terry. 'I don't count marmite sandwiches for high tea or Bournvita and biscuits.'

'You cheeky beggar! You had meat four times!'

'Only if you count two lots of Danish chopped ham.'

'Ungrateful as well as being difficult.' Audrey turned back to Bob. 'What *can* you do with him?'

Bob nodded understandingly.

'Terry,' said Audrey. 'It's impossible to fit you in. Match you up – pair you off. Especially when you go around like . . . that.' She picked at his vest.

'He's an untouchable,' said Bob.

'He's un-get-nearable,' said Audrey.

'Go on, go on. Have your little joke. Have your laugh at my expense,' sneered Terry.

'We can't invite him to any of *our* suburban sex-orgies,

can we, Audrey?'

'No.'

'And we can't invite him to any of our wife-swapping 'cos he hasn't got a wife to *swap*.'

'He hasn't even got a clean pair of Y-fronts,' said Audrey.

'He has now,' said Mrs Collier, from the kitchen. 'I put them all in the bag-wash this afternoon.'

Terry looked pityingly at Bob and his sister. 'You should have married each other. You'd have made a good pair. So superficial. So concerned with appearances. With status. But a man like me – who's travelled, can hold his own anywhere. Talk about anything – from gliding in the Dolomites to the metamorphosis of a frog.'

'Meta-what?' said Audrey.

'Biology.' Terry smiled. 'There's more to life than knowing how to make peas stay on your knife.'

'Okay,' said Bob. 'Come with us to Alan's place on Saturday and dazzle us with your scholarship and poise.'

'Bob – you're not taking him to someone's house, are you?'

'Only to a friend, Aud.'

'Even so. D'you think that's wise?'

'Shove off, puddin' face. Haddaway home and start slicing the pork luncheon meat.'

Audrey glared at Terry.

'Take no notice of her, Bob. You're on.'

'Good. I'll call for you seven thirty sharp. You'll enjoy it. His wife's a great cook, and we might play a few games after.'

'Just so long as it's not Monopoly,' said Terry. 'I went off that after a few nights locked up in Hughie McLaren's caravan.'

Terry turned his back on ITV's *World of Sport* and was ready when Bob called. Even Thelma, who was waiting in the car, was forced to admit that he looked quite presentable. Her only worry was that Terry seemed somewhat subdued. She hoped it didn't mean he was saving his energy for an excess of outrageous behaviour later on.

Alan, a pleasant-looking young man in his late twenties, met them at the door.

'Thelma, Bob, nice to see you.'

'Little early, I'm afraid,' said Bob.

'Not at all, come in, come in.'

Thelma and Alan exchanged kisses on the cheek as Bob ushered Terry in.

'Alan, I'd like you to meet Terry Collier. Terry – this is Alan Boyle.'

'How do you do,' said Terry.

'Hello, how nice to meet you.' Alan shook Terry's hand warmly then turned to Thelma. 'Brenda's still upstairs. Why don't you pop up?'

'Okay.' Thelma gave Bob a cautionary glance which indicated he was to keep a tight rein on Terry, and pattered off upstairs.

As Alan took their coats and hung them up in the hall, Terry took a look at his surroundings. Alan and Brenda lived in a nice modern house. It was the kind where the builder had run out of bricks early on and had had to finish off the outside with planks. That was probably the reason why there wasn't enough wood left to finish the stairs.

'Oh, I brought you this.' Bob produced a bottle of red wine and handed it to Alan.

'Oh, you shouldn't have.'

'Well – thought it might come in handy.'

'Let's go in and have a drink,' said Alan. 'Might as well get a head start on the girls.'

There was, in fact, no 'in' to go into, as the hall was an extension of the living–dining-room, the sole separation being a square pier of brick that also served to hold up the ceiling. Not only were the stairs unfinished, the plasterers had also forgotten to do one wall. It reminded Terry of their outside loo – except Alan's wall wasn't painted.

'What would you like to drink? Beer, whisky, gin,

sherry – sweet, medium or dry, rum, vodka? You name it.'

'Vodka and coke, Alan, please,' said Bob.

Terry shot him a look. Flash bastard . . .

'Terry?'

'I'll stick to beer – that's unless you've got any methylated spirits.'

'I beg your pardon?'

'A joke,' said Bob. He gave Terry a warning glance.

'Ah . . . beer coming up. Ice and lemon, Bob?'

'If it's no trouble.'

'Bob tells me you're from the South,' said Terry. 'London?'

'Just outside, actually. Teddington. On the river.'

'Alan's a Chelsea supporter,' said Bob.

'Oh, is he . . . '

'Yes.' Alan handed Terry his beer.

'Cheers – I mean, thank you.'

Alan grinned. 'Used to have a season ticket.'

'I hate Chelsea,' said Terry. 'They stand for everything I hate in football. With their showbiz supporters. They come out looking more like the Young Generation than a football team.'

Alan turned to Bob. 'I'll just go and get some ice.'

'He said icily . . . ' Terry sipped his beer.

Alan went through a real door into the kitchen.

'Why are you being so aggressive?!' hissed Bob. 'You're hardly across his doorstep, drinking his beer, and you're attacking his *football* team. That's not a very nice thing to do. How would *you* like it if someone attacked *our* football team?'

'Chelsea deserve it.'

'That's not the *point,*' continued Bob in the same urgent tone. 'We're not talking about the merits of Chelsea Football Club. We're talking about manners. Live and let live. Cool it.'

'Aye, okay, sorry . . . '

Alan returned with a small bucket of ice cubes. He topped up Bob's drink with a slice of lemon, poured himself a stiff whisky and raised his glass to the two lads.

'Your very good health.'

'And yours,' said Bob.

Terry had already drunk half his can of Long Life. 'Cheers, er, listen, Alan. I didn't mean to offend you like. I don't really hate *Chelsea* – '

Bob winced.

'I mean, on its own like. I hate Arsenal, Spurs, West Ham – I hate *all* the London clubs. It's because I really hate Londoners, you see.'

Bob coughed.

'Present company excepted, like.'

'That's all right, Terry. It doesn't bother me. I don't really think of myself as a Londoner anyway, and certainly not now.' Alan called up the stairs. 'Come on girls.' He walked over to a record player set into a shelf unit that lined one wall, put on Beethoven's Second Symphony and turned the sound down.

'Nice gramophone you've got there,' said Terry, hoping to gee Alan up.

'Stereo,' said Bob.

'Quadrophonic, actually.' Alan adjusted the the torque balance and got the stylus tracking perfectly. 'Are you interested in classical music?'

'Can't stand it.'

Bob coughed again. 'Alan has a fantastic collection of classical music. Especially Beethoven.'

'Oh, he's all right,' said Terry. 'I don't mind Beethoven. It's the others I can't stand.'

'What *are* you interested in?' Alan stopped to adjust the tonal balance.

'Me? Oh, a whole range of leisure activities.'

'Jigsaws, for one,' said Bob.

'*And* a lot more besides,' riposted Terry. 'That's one of the things you got in the Army. Bags of sport. Football, cricket, swimming, water-skiing – '

Thelma and Brenda came round the brick pier.

'Hallo, Bob.'

'Brenda . . . ' They touched cheeks and kissed the air. 'This is Terry,' said Bob.

'Hallo, Terry.'

Terry stared at Brenda in surprise. Bob had said she'd been to Heaton Grammar with Thelma. What he'd ommitted to say was she'd also been in their class at Park Road Juniors. By God. It was Brenda Ruddock. Form 4-B. Bye, but she'd grown into a bonny girl, though. Face was a bit hard, mind . . .

'Hallo, Brenda. Didn't expect to see you again.' Terry shook the limp, outstretched hand. It was like a glove full of cotton wool.

'Me neither,' said Brenda with a noticeable lack of warmth.

Terry turned to Alan. 'The three of us all used to be in the same class, you know.'

'Oh, really?' Alan raised an eyebrow. 'I knew that Thelma and Brenda had been at grammar school together.'

'Oh, I mean before that, like,' said Terry. He took another look at Brenda. 'Bye, she hasn't half changed. Used to be very pretty, y'know.'

Bob sucked in his breath sharply.

'Toothache?' asked Terry.

'Er, no, no.'

'Good.' Terry turned back to Alan and Brenda. 'What I meant was, she's changed from being pretty, to being even prettier.'

Brenda smiled. 'Isn't that nice, Alan?'

'Yes. Sherry for you two'?

'Please,' said Thelma.

As Alan returned with the drinks, Terry said, 'Bob tells me you work with him. Are you an ex-sparky as well?'

Alan smiled. 'No. I'm involved on the planning side. Architecture. That sort of thing.'

'Bob's hoping to do business with Alan's firm, aren't you Bob?' It was Brenda's turn to smile.

'Eventually,' said Bob, seeing his chances getting slimmer every second.

'And what are you doing these days?' Brenda asked Terry.

'Oh, looking around,' said Terry. 'Don't have to rush back to work. I'm looking round for a good business investment.'

'Ah, good idea.' Brenda smiled. 'I heard you'd been looking at a car-wash in Berwick.'

Terry gave Bob a hard-eyed stare.

'Well, well, well,' said Bob with a large overdose of jollity. 'After all these years. Isn't it nice – all of us together again?'

'Bob,' said Thelma. 'We saw Alan and Brenda last Tuesday.'

'No, I mean with Terry,' explained Bob. 'I mean the three of us.'

'Yes,' said Terry. 'It's half the back row of 4-B, Park Road Juniors.'

Brenda smiled faintly. 'I'd like to think we've all come a long way since then.'

'*You* certainly have,' said Terry genially. 'When I first knew you, you were living over your Dad's chip shop in Dog Lead Lane.'

'Alan, we're all standing around with empty glasses.'

Alan began to collect them. 'I never knew your father had a chip shop. How amusing.'

'It was a good one,' said Terry. 'And not just chips. Served fish as well – in lashings of batter.'

'I'll just check the oven.' Brenda gave Terry a glassy stare like a deep-frozen cod and went into the kitchen.

Alan handed round the refills.

'What are we having,' asked Terry. 'Rock salmon and chips?'

'I really don't know,' said Alan. 'I just look after the drinks department.'

'She was brought up on it, y'know,' confided Terry. 'I'm surprised she hasn't got spots with all that vinegar drying out her blood.'

Bob wondered if he could get his foot high enough to kick Terry's jaw.

Brenda came to the kitchen door. 'Could you come and give me a hand, Alan?'

'Of course, darling.' Alan took her glass of sherry with him.

As the kitchen door closed, Thelma turned angrily on Terry. '*You'll* never win any prizes for tact, will you?'

'What have I done?'

'Terry,' said Bob. 'There are some things Brenda doesn't like to be reminded about – and certainly not in front of Alan. You know she was always a bit, well – '

'Stuck up?'

'If you like.'

'Don't know why. When she sat next to me, her hair used to reek of fried batter.'

'Well, don't mention that, for God's sake!' said Thelma. 'When people grow up, and educate themselves, earn a bit of money and get a nice home, there's nothing wrong in wanting to forget certain things.'

'Like their working-class roots?'

'I mean unhappy memories. Unpleasant things.'

'There's nothing wrong in living over a chip shop,' said Terry. 'Even one in Dog Lead Lane.'

'And there's nothing wrong in someone, who lived over a chip shop, trying to batter themselves – I mean *better* themselves,' said Bob.

'Exactly,' said Thelma. 'Don't try and drag us all back down to *your* level.'

'So leave off. Okay?'

'In other words, I'm not to reminisce,' said Terry.

'If you must go down Memory Lane, just steer clear of Dog Lead Lane and her Dad's fish and chip shop.'

Terry looked at them both. 'Okay.'

'Promise?' asked Bob.

'My lips are sealed,' said Terry. 'Even though someone has obviously blabbed about Berwick.'

'Terry, I swear to you, Thelma and I have never said a thing,' said Bob.

Thelma didn't say anything.

Alan opened the kitchen door and Brenda wheeled out a trolley laden with a large dish of fondue, asparagus, salad, several cheeses, dessert and chilled wine.

Alan stood behind the chair at the head of the table. 'Would you like to sit down? Your names are on the place cards.'

Thelma sat on Alan's right, Bob on his left. Brenda took the chair next to Bob, and nearest the kitchen. Terry sat opposite her, next to Thelma.

'Oohh, Brenda,' cooed Thelma, unfolding her serviette. 'That asparagus looks gorgeous!'

Bob tucked his serviette between two waistcoat buttons. 'I'm so hungry, I could eat a horse between two bread vans.'

'Bob!' Thelma eyed him.

Bob winked at Terry. Terry, who didn't have a waistcoat, thought of tucking his serviette into his collar for a giggle, but decided to leave it on his lap.

'Red, white or fizzy rosé?'

'I think Thelma prefers white, Alan.'

'White all right for you, Terry?'

Terry nodded, and held out his empty beer glass.

'Do we have a fondue set on *our* wedding present list, Bob?'

'We do now.'

'Alan's mother bought this for us at Harrods,' said Brenda. 'She has an account there, hasn't she Alan?'

Alan smiled. 'I know they keep writing to ask her to pay it.'

'I love these table-mats,' cooed Thelma. 'Are they new?'

'No. I just haven't had them out before. They were a present from my Aunt.'

'Not your Auntie Elsie?' said Terry.

Brenda frowned. 'My Aunt *who*?'

'Your Auntie Elsie, a canny old soul. Used to be a cleaner at the brewery.'

Brenda's face paled under the layer of pancake make-up. Bob choked on his asparagus, and Thelma wished Terry could choke on his. Fatally. Especially as he was eating the wrong end.

Alan proved to have an engaging fund of anecdotes which probably came from listening to the John Dunn Show while he was at the office. The food was excellent, and Terry didn't drop another brick right through the meal.

'What do you think of the coffee?' asked Brenda. 'I had it specially blended.'

'Delicious,' said Bob.

'I'd love some more,' said Thelma.

'Half Moka and half Blue Mountain.'

'Beats the hell out of the Co-op's own label instant,' said Terry.

Brenda favoured Terry with a brittle smile. 'Would any of you like anything more to eat?'

There was a chorus of appreciative refusals.

'I must say, Brenda, you're a fantastic cook,' said Bob. 'With food like that, you'd make a fortune if you opened a restaurant.'

'You could coin it with a fish'n chip shop too,' said Terry innocently. 'The experience you've got.'

Bob felt the air chill about him.

'Fortunately,' said Brenda, 'with the salary Alan earns, and the prospects he's got, money isn't one of our problems.'

Alan gave Terry a knowing look.

Bob lit an Embassy Slim Panatella and waved the smoke away. 'Well, it makes you think. I mean, here we all are enjoying a sophisticated dinner party with our cigars and brandy, our Tia Maria and our wafer thin mints – and the last time the three of us sat down together at table was to eat school lunch.'

'Aye,' said Terry. 'This is a lot better than cold ham, pease pudding and mashed potatoes.'

'That was Thursdays,' said Bob. 'We had fishcakes on Friday.'

'And always burnt.' Thelma shuddered.

'Like the custard,' said Terry.

Thelma thought back. 'Mondays was cheese and potato pie.'

'And meat on Tuesdays,' added Terry.

Bob smiled at Alan. 'Stewed – so you couldn't tell what kind.'

'But while we were there, the dairy changed over from horses to electric milk floats,' said Terry.

'What did we have Wednesdays?' asked Thelma.

Nobody seemed able to remember.

Terry began to tick the days off on his fingers. 'Monday, cheese, Tuesday, stew, Wednesdays . . . '

'I know,' said Bob. 'Wednesdays was asparagus, cheese fondue, gooseberry fool and wafer-thin mints.'

Even Brenda laughed at that. Bob caught Thelma's loaded look.

'Ah, well,' he said. 'So much for Park Road Juniors . . . '

'Yes,' said Brenda. 'Alan, of course, went to a public school.'

'A very minor one,' said Alan modestly.

'It was still founded in 1776.'

'True, yes.' Alan looked at the others. 'You can imagine how draughty it was.'

'I seem to remember you saying it was one of the leading public schools,' insisted Brenda.

'In terms of draughtiness, yes,' said Alan. 'It was a leading, draughty, *minor* public school – and not very interesting, really.'

'I suppose it's the draught that gives you all a stiff upper lip,' said Terry. He lifted his glass of brandy. 'To our schooldays – and the best years of our lives.'

'I'm glad you think so,' said Brenda. She left her glass pointedly on the table.

'Oh, come on, now. They were smashing.' Thelma reached across the table and took hold of Bob's hand. 'That's where I met you, wasn't it?'

'Can I ever forget?'

'What was Bob like at school?' asked Alan.

Bob puffed up his chest. 'Top of woodwork, inkwell monitor, and secretary of the Lonnie Donnegan Fan Club.'

'While I,' said Terry, 'was founder member and

President of the Deirdre Birchwood Fan Club.'

'How funny,' said Brenda. 'I always thought Bob was President of that.'

'Not the Fan Club,' explained Terry. 'You must be thinking of the Preservation Society.'

Thelma took her hand away from Bob's.

'Who was Deirdre Birchwood?' asked Alan.

'A very common girl,' said Thelma.

'But very nice,' said Terry. 'With the most enormous – '

' – ly well-developed personality,' said Bob.

'And we worshipped every ounce.'

'You may have,' said Thelma. 'Bob had better things to do.'

'Yes,' said Terry. 'Like filling inkwells.' He turned to Alan. 'She was in the year ahead of us, and very advanced for her age. All those questions about sex your parents, teachers and the Scoutmaster would never answer – Deirdre would – *and* throw in a practical demonstration.'

Bob looked hurt. '*I* never got one.'

'I should hope not,' said Thelma. 'But then you didn't associate with girls like that.'

'No,' said Bob.

'Pity,' said Alan. 'She sounds fun. How about some more brandy?'

Brenda took a long look at them all and smiled. 'What funny memories you have. Don't tell me you've forgotten the school greenhouse.'

Thelma frowned. 'Greenhouse?'

'Yes. I *clearly* remember Bob and Deirdre volunteering several times to spray the plants in the school greenhouse.'

'Right,' said Terry.

Brenda smiled at him. 'Bob was still in short trousers at the time. I never forget seeing one afternoon in class, this enormous green caterpillar crawl out of his trouser leg. To this day, I've always wondered how it got there.'

'You're lucky you didn't catch greenfly,' said Terry.

Bob was looking distinctly uncomfortable.

'You told me you'd never had anything to do with that girl,' said Thelma accusingly.

'Well, I may have briefly,' said Bob. 'I just forget. It was all a long time ago.'

'Curious,' said Brenda. 'You seem to remember everything else so well.'

'Yes, well, let's forget about the past,' said Thelma. 'Who cares what happened at Park Road. We're all different people now.'

'My sentiments exactly. More coffee?'

Terry sighed. 'Never mind, Bob. I forgive you. I only wish I knew where Deirdre Birchwood was now.'

'Oh, I think Bob knows her address,' said Brenda, as she poured Thelma a fresh cup of coffee.

Bob went a bright pink. 'I beg your pardon?'

'Didn't you used to have an emerald green Ford Escort?' Brenda passed Thelma her cup.

'Eighteen months ago, yes.'

'With a long whip aerial.'

'Yes.'

'There you are, Alan,' said Brenda. 'It *was* Bob we saw parked on Blaydon Moor that night we came back late.'

Bob went an even brighter shade of pink.

'I'm sure there's a perfectly reasonable explanation,' said Thelma. The look she gave Bob indicated that she expected to hear about it on the way home.

'There is,' said Bob. 'There must be hundreds of green Ford Escorts.'

Brenda gave him an old-fashioned look. 'With racing stripes and an aerofoil on the boot?'

Terry burst out laughing. 'You never put a bloody *aerofoil* on the boot of an *Escort*!?'

'It was already on when I bought it secondhand,' protested Bob.

'Mind you,' added Terry. 'If Deirdre Birchwood was sprawled all over the front seat, you'd need *something* to keep the back end down.'

'Don't be disgusting,' said Thelma.

'If it had been like that, I'd have remembered. I may have bumped into her in the street sometime.'

Terry grinned. 'If you had, you'd still have the marks to prove it.'

'In any case,' said Bob to Thelma. 'We weren't engaged at the time, so it's nothing to get upset about.'

'Exactly,' said Alan. 'What *does* it matter now? I'm sure we've all got skeletons in the cupboard.' He looked at Brenda. 'Even *you*, darling.'

'I can't think of any you haven't been made aware of tonight.' Brenda smiled sweetly at Thelma. 'Fortunately, we didn't all behave like Deirdre Birchwood, did we?'

'No,' said Terry. 'But you still showed me all you'd got in the boiler room.'

'How *dare* you!!' Brenda exploded.

Alan started to laugh.

'Go on,' said Terry. 'I took your knickers home to prove it.'

'That's true,' said Bob. 'They had your name sewn in the waistband.'

Terry grinned. 'Kept them under me pillow for a week.'

'Alan!!' raged Brenda. 'Would you please *say* something!?'

Alan raised his glass. 'To our schooldays,' he said, repeating Terry's toast. 'The best years of our lives.'

'For people like Terry, perhaps,' said Brenda spitefully. 'I imagine the reason he likes to wallow in his grubby version of the past is because he has precious little to look forward to in the future – beyond the pub, the betting shop and the billiard hall.'

'They've pulled down the billiard hall and put up a sauna,' said Terry.

Brenda gave him a hate-filled look. 'Most of us have gone on to educate ourselves, to improve our lives, to develop as people. But you – all you can do is drag people down. You're an unwanted embarrassment to your family and friends.'

'This is more like it,' said Alan to Thelma. 'You can't beat a good argument. Have a brandy.'

'Now wait a minute,' protested Bob. 'He doesn't embarrass me. Mind you. I'm not saying he isn't coarse. I'm not saying he isn't vulgar – '

'Hang on,' said Terry. 'Who's side are you on?'

'Oh, shut up!' said Brenda.

'Okay, he might be crude and a bit rough at the edges – '

'A bit?'

'And he might have eaten the wrong end of his asparagus – '

'Did I?'

'But I'll tell you one thing,' continued Bob. 'He's down to earth and honest – and that's more than I can say of you.'

'Thank you,' said Brenda. 'I can see *you* haven't changed that much either. 'She turned to Thelma. 'Quite like the old days, isn't it? With the two of them together.'

If Brenda was hoping for support from Thelma, she certainly didn't get it.

'Bob's right. Terry may not be perfect, but at least he's not a hypocrite. Which is more than I can say for some people.'

Brenda gave Thelma the look of a woman betrayed. *Et tu Brute*. 'Well! I never thought I'd see the day when you'd side with – Terry Collier.'

'I like a lively discussion,' said Alan to Bob. 'Have another brandy.'

Thelma faced up to Brenda. 'Terry's honest. That's a quality most of us seem to have lost since Park Road Juniors. Terry wouldn't deny living above a chip shop.'

Terry looked at Alan. 'It's just that I haven't lived over a chip shop.'

'What exactly are you trying to infer?' asked Brenda. 'That I'm a snob?'

'I'm not trying to infer it. I'm telling you,' replied Thelma. 'You're a snob. You always have been.'

'What a bitchy thing to say!'

'It's still true. Your trouble is you won't admit it.'

Alan looked at Terry. 'Nothing like a frank exchange of views to make a dinner party go well. Have some more brandy.'

Brenda pointed to Terry. 'If I was such a *snob*, as you say, would I invite a person like *this* into my house for dinner?'

Thelma's mouth flattened into that thin line that meant trouble. 'I'll tell you why you asked Terry to dinner. It's because the only way you can measure how far you've come from Number 23 Dog Lead Lane is to parade your possessions in front of an audience. I've seen you do it over and over again. You need to have people feeling your furniture and cooing over your curtains and envying your bloody Knightsbridge fondue set!'

'I do nothing of the sort!'

'You *love* it,' said Thelma. 'You'd wet your knickers–if you wore any.'

Terry was sorry they weren't invited to stay on and play Scrabble, but he was pleased to see that Brenda hadn't forgotten any of the rude words he'd taught her back in the boiler room at Park Road Juniors.

When Bob next came round to Terry's house, he found him buried in the armchair once again, shoeless and unshaven. The floor around him was littered with newspapers, magazines and dirty teacups. Terry was reading a copy of *Photoplay*.

Bob looked him over from head to foot. 'Saturday night must have been a mirage. I thought I saw you washed and shaved and in a suit, going out to dinner with beautiful people.' Bob sat down. 'You didn't get into the drug scene in the Army, did you? I mean, like the American G.I.s in Vietnam?'

'Of course I didn't.'

'Well, you're exhibiting all the signs. You stay in all day, dozing and nodding. You're as thin as a rake, you've lost all pride in your appearance. Yes, that could explain everything. You're suffering from withdrawal symptoms . . .'

'I'm suffering from exposure to the scampi belt,' growled Terry.

'Yes, Saturday was quite a night. I'm sorry if they upset you.'

'*He* didn't upset me,' said Terry. 'He's quite a canny lad, that Alan. And *she* didn't upset me either.' He gave a dry laugh. 'I got no more than I expected from *her*.'

'I only wish you'd kept her knickers,' said Bob. 'I'd enjoy sending those back.'

Terry suddenly became serious. 'Bob, look, I know what this could mean to you, like – as far as, well – work is concerned. What I mean to say is – like, thanks for sticking up for me.'

'That's all right, kidda. Any time.'

'Because I buggered it all up to start with. But I just can't help it. When I meet these phoney buggers who start trying to bullshit me, I tend to start saying things that are a bit, well – '

'Crude. Yes, I know.'

Terry looked annoyed. 'I was going to say *forthright*. That's the word *I* would have chosen.'

'That's what I meant,' said Bob. 'Forthright. Blunt. Down-to-earth.'

'Well, I appreciated it. And especially coming from Thelma. I mean you know, Thelma and I . . . that is, me and Thelma . . . well, we've never been, like, you know – '

'Go on,' said Bob.

'Well, the point is, I thought she was bloody marvellous,' said Terry. 'And I think you're a lucky lad, and you did the right thing there, and I hope you'll be happy, and – '

'And what?'

'Is she *very* upset about the other night?'

Bob smiled. 'Not really. She didn't get on with Brenda all that well. She was just being nice because of the situation with Alan's firm.'

'And now I've gone and knackered that.'

'Oh, things are still okay with Alan,' said Bob. 'In any case, I don't think I want to get into having to do business that way. You end up having to be nice to all the wrong people.'

Terry grinned. 'It's going to leave a hole in your social calendar. Still, I suppose you could move Frank and Christine up from Tuesday, or Michael and Linda back from Friday.'

'Or we could keep it as a free evening for you and me,' said Bob.

The offer caused Terry to leap out of his armchair. 'You mean just the two of us?'

Bob stuck out his hand. 'Yes. Boy's night out.'

'You're on,' said Terry. They shook hands warmly. 'There's just one thing I have to know.'

'What's that?'

'What you were doing with Deirdre Birchwood at half-past one on Blaydon Moor, her last-known address, and how that caterpillar got into your trousers in the greenhouse.'

'That's three things,' said Bob.

'You can give them to me in any order. Where are you going?'

Bob backed towards the kitchen door. 'Tell you on Saturday,' he said. 'Thelma's asked me the same questions, and I still haven't worked out what I'm going to tell *her*.'

'I don't care what you're going to tell her, just tell me the *truth*,' pleaded Terry. 'You can trust me.'

'Oh, no, I can't,' said Bob. 'Not now the three of us are going to be friends.'

7

The Old Magic

Terry didn't see Bob on the Saturday as planned. Instead, he went down with a heavy bout of totally unplanned flu.

Bob heard the news from Audrey and went round to see him as soon as he had finished papering the back bedroom of his new house. He found Terry lying in bed in a dressing-gown, with a hot-water bottle stuffed down the front to keep his chest warm. The bedside table was chock-a-block with medicines, and there were pin-up magazines strewn all over the eiderdown.

'Not before time,' scowled Terry as Bob entered.

'Hello, Sunshine. Feeling better?'

'Where the hell have *you* been? Not a word, not a letter – '

'What for?'

'Or a card – or even a *phone* call.'

'You're not *on* the telephone.'

'That's no bloody excuse,' growled Terry. 'She is next door. Any form of communication would have sufficed. A message in a bottle, a carrier-pigeon – even smoke signals from your roof.'

'Mate, I've been up to my *ears*. What with work and getting the house together, and the wedding and – '

Terry interrupted him with a wave. 'Those are all things you put before my health, are they?'

'I just couldn't afford the risk of infection,' said Bob. 'Everyone's going down with this Chilean flu. I can't spare the *time* to be sick.'

Terry eyed him pityingly. 'I've not got the *plague*, you know. We haven't had to paint a yellow cross on our front door. You're not going to break out in boils, or go down with writhing contortions and have your hair fall out.'

'In other words,' said Bob. 'You've had a fairly trivial illness.'

'I didn't mean I hadn't suffered.' Terry coughed weakly and tapped his chest. 'I've coughed so much I think I've ruptured my lungs.'

Bob pulled the hot-water bottle out from inside Terry's dressing-gown. 'All you've got is the noise of the water sloshing about in this.' He tested it for heat. 'You need some more hot water, anyway.'

'I need sympathy, companionship and friendly faces. That's what *I* need.' Terry pulled the bedclothes up around his chin.

'Chilean flu . . . fascinating, isn't it,' mused Bob. 'I mean, that a virus can travel that far.'

'Marvellous,' said Terry. 'When I had a temperature of one hundred and three, when I hovered on the verge of delirium, just a few millimetres of mercury away from death's door, that was the one thing that consoled me – *knowing* that I had such a fascinating virus.'

'Well, you're not alone, according to last night's news. It's reaching epidemic proportions.'

'What a month,' moaned Terry. 'Out of the Forces with nothing to come home to. No bright job prospects, me old mates all gone to seed, *you* getting married – and now some bug transports itself all the way from the Andes and zeroes in on me.'

'And a few thousand others,' said Bob.

'It's the curse of the Incas.' Terry blew his nose. 'They've got me at last.'

'They've also got half our firm as well. That's why I've been so tied up.'

'I bet I was the first,' said Terry. 'I bet I was the trail-blazer.'

Bob picked up one of Terry's lurid sex magazines. On the cover was a drawing of a flight of stairs, with a school-mistress in glasses about to do herself an injury with the knob on the end of the bannisters. Bob looked at the listed contents.

'No wonder you were on the edge of delirium. What's this – "Reader's Advice Forum – a frank exchange of personal and private fears" – what personal and private fears do you have, Mr Collier? I mean, apart from baldness and relegation.'

'Loss of friends. Desertion in time of need,' sighed Terry.

'That's nothing compared to this poor fella,' said Bob, reading the magazine. 'Dear, oh, dear – have you seen this letter?'

'What page?'

'Seventeen.'

'Oh – signed "Anguished, Market Harborough"?'

'Yes.' Bob looked puzzled. 'Where *do* you buy a set of stocks, nowadays?'

'Mail order, I suppose. You know those letters stagger me. Okay, I've been away five years but, well – I never realised bondage was *that* popular.'

'Not round here,' said Bob. 'And certainly not on the Elm Lodge Housing Estate.'

'Don't be too sure.' Terry snatched the magazine back. 'Look at the addresses on all these letters. They're not from Copenhagen, or Hamburg. They're from places like Evesham, Tunbridge Wells, Peterborough. We joked about Doncaster's Latin Quarter – hell's teeth, even Harrogate's in here – and you'll never believe what she wants! What's happening to this country? If this mag's a fair sample, then every Saturday, half the nation's to be found behind locked doors, strapped in leather underwear and beating themselves to death with riding-crops. Not to mention all the skin-divers wrestling about in black rubber ten miles from the nearest water!' Terry tossed the magazine onto the bed disgustedly.

'Well,' said Bob. 'Not everyone wants to watch Match of the Day.'

'Healthy people do.' Terry folded his arms. 'Nothing wrong with people who watch sport.'

'True,' said Bob. 'But I was thinking of giving it a miss *this* Saturday. That was if someone was well enough. I was thinking of giving that someone a little treat.'

'I'm not letting any bugger whip me,' growled Terry.

'Do you *mind*? *Healthy* people don't spend time reading about what the other half's up to. I don't even *buy* this rubbish.'

'No,' said Terry. 'You get your cheap thrills reading *Practical Householder* in the lavatory. Anyway, what was going to happen on Saturday if I was well enough – which I doubt I will be?'

'I was going to take you to a new place that's just opened off the North Road past Gosforth. They've got great steaks there. Thought we'd have dinner – split a bottle or two of wine . . .'

'Why?'

'Because it's probably the last night I'll have free before I get married. You know, for the two of us to have a chat.'

'Why don't we go down the boozer?'

'Because I'd like to have a drink and a meal in more pleasant surroundings,' said Bob. 'I'd like a quiet, reflective, civilised evening – and the pleasure of your company.'

'Ah, I see. It's the guilt, is it? After leaving me here to rot.'

'Listen,' said Bob. 'If you don't *want* to have a meal with me. If you're unable to accept this last gesture of friendship from your closest mate . . .'

'Oh, all right,' said Terry wearily. 'If you're going to put it *that* way.'

'What way?'

'You know what way. When you put that voice on.'

'What voice?'

'Your Anna-Neagle-making-a-charity-appeal voice.'

'If by that you mean my voice conveys a certain amount of emotion,' said Bob, 'then you may very well be right. I don't deny it. This week marks the end of an era for me, and this meal was supposed to – well, commemorate it.'

'Sounds more like a memorial service. What do we have to wear – black tie and poppies?'

'It *is* "In Memoriam" in a way . . . '

'And where's the sweetheart of the forces in all this?'

'Thelma doesn't completely rule my leisure time,' said Bob stiffly. 'I don't have to ask her permission to go *out*. I don't have to beg for a 24-hour pass. And anyway, she's already booked to go out on her own.'

'How brave of you,' said Terry.

'She's having a hen party,' explained Bob. 'She went to meet her sister today. She's come over from Canada for the wedding.'

'Oh, yes, I'd forgotten about her. Did we ever meet?'

'Don't think so. She's about five years younger than we are – that's like a whole generation at school. She went to stay with relatives in Canada straight after she got her O-levels.'

'What does she look like?' asked Terry.

'Can't really remember. It's only been in my later, more mature years that I've started looking at schoolgirls again.'

'You want to watch it,' said Terry. 'You'll end up writing to these magazines.' He got out of bed, re-knotted the cord of his dressing-gown and paraded in front of the mirror. 'Aye, I reckon I might just be all right there – at the wedding. What with her being a bridesmaid, like, and me the best man. That's one of the best man's perks, isn't it? I mean that's the unwritten law. The best man pays for the taxis, reads out the funny telegrams and has the bridesmaid.'

Bob suddenly looked uncomfortable. 'Er, Terry . . . '

'Aye, she won't stand a chance.'

'The thing is . . . '

Terry's attention was still riveted on his mirror-image. 'Might even end up with a slice of the business.'

'Listen,' said Bob. 'I wouldn't jump to any conclusions if I were you.'

'I'm not, I'm not.'

'Good, because there's something important that I

have to tell you about the – well, the wedding. I mean, I don't think you should just take things for granted . . . '

Terry saw that Bob was full of misgivings, and thought he knew the reason why. His flippant mood faded.

'Got it – of course. Why didn't you say? *That's* why you wanted us to have a meal. A *reflective* evening. Just the *two* of us.'

'Good,' said Bob. 'You had me worried.'

'No, I understand. I understand.' Terry patted Bob on the shoulder.

Bob sighed with relief. 'Thank goodness you're taking it like that. I didn't know how to tell you.'

Terry held up a hand. 'Say no more. You've had second thoughts. I knew you'd come to your senses sooner or later.'

Bob stood up angrily. 'You never give up, do you?!' I haven't had second thoughts. I'm talking about the bridesmaids and the best man.'

'I see. You mean you're upset about the idea of me and Thelma's young sister? About what I said about marrying her and ending up with a slice of the business.'

'Of course I don't mean that,' said Bob. 'I don't care if you seduce Thelma's sister – just so long as your enjoyment doesn't spoil my wedding, I'm happy. I'm not concerned about your sexual activities – it's your *status*.'

'Status?'

'Well, what I mean is your *lack* of it.'

'In what way?'

'Well – as best man.'

'Yes . . . ' It was clear Terry had absolutely no idea what Bob was getting at.

'The best man – at my wedding – *my* best man, if you like – ' Bob took a deep breath. 'Is not *you*.'

The puzzled look on Terry's face locked solid.

'I mean, it's you in principle,' continued Bob. 'You being my – best friend, and all that. I mean, everyone will know that it's you in *principle*. It just won't be you in *fact*.'

Terry found a small, strangled replica of his own voice.

'I'm not your best man. Is that what you're trying to tell me?'

Bob felt the best defence was offence. 'Mate. *I* didn't know you were going to turn up out of the blue like that. I mean, after five years of total silence. And anyway,' he concluded lamely, 'I'd already asked Frank Clarke.'

'Frank Clarke?!' Terry's voice was fully restored and heavy with contempt. 'Frank *Clarke*?!!'

'Yes,' said Bob. 'Frank Clarke. He was – '

'You don't have to explain,' said Terry. 'You thought I'd let you down. You thought my earthy working-class ways might be a little too rough at the edges for your new middle-class in-laws with their caravans in the Lake District and their Masonic handshakes. How could someone like *me* officiate at your wedding. Someone who might turn up in overalls and clogs and toast the health of the bridesmaids in anti-freeze.'

'Oh, come on, Terry,' said Bob. 'You weren't *here*, mate! I had to make the arrangements. If I hadn't asked Frank, you'd have been my first choice. Number One.'

'I see. Only now I'm wearing the number twelve shirt. I'm sitting on the substitute's bench. I suppose if Frank Clarke makes a lousy speech, I'll be called on for the last ten minutes.'

'Terry,' pleaded Bob. 'Be reasonable. Not one single letter all the time you were away. You'd become just a fond memory. Just a photo on the mantelpiece. An I.O.U. in a chest of drawers. Five years is a long time. You can forget someone completely in five years.'

'You didn't forget the I.O.U in the chest of drawers,' said Terry. 'What was that for?'

'Eleven pounds eight and six lost at five card brag on a coach trip to Morecambe, September 1967. That's eleven pounds forty-two and a half in decimals. I'll let you off the half.'

'You'll get your money, you'll get the money.' Terry rubbed his right thigh. 'I've been away, you know.'

'Exactly,' said Bob. 'That's why you're not best man.'

The road-house restaurant was impressive. The usual, flash, instant steak-house décor, with plenty of dark rosewood plastic laminate and deep-buttoned leather-grained PVC, rough white plasterwork arches and alcoves, dim lights, menus as big as tea-trays and red tablecloths.

Waiters in black tie and tails glided between the tables to the sound of piped music. Terry took a look at his menu and saw that the management had added the cost of the dress hire to each item. He thought of asking how much discount they could get by being served by a waiter in his underpants, but let it pass. After all, it *was* Bob who was picking up the bill.

As the two lads perused the appetising list of dishes, a paunchy waiter hovered by Terry's elbow with his pencil poised over a pad. He had a swarthy complexion. Terry adopted an aggressive Imperialist manner.

'Prawn cocktail, fillet, well done, plenty of chips, onion rings, tomatoes, grilled mushrooms and sprouts.' Terry tapped the glassful of bread sticks. 'And bring us some real bread. We want to be able to eat it, not build a log cabin.'

'Certainly sir . . .'

Bob became almost subservient in his effort to compensate for Terry's arrogance. 'Do you think the, er – melon is – ?'

'Delicious, sir.'

'Fine. Okay, I'll have that, and, er – '

'I can recommend the Steak Diane.'

Bob wasn't quite sure what that was. 'Oh, good. Yes, er – could I have that medium rare?'

The waiter wrote that down. 'And what vegetables would you like with that, broccoli, green beans?'

'Er, none thank you – just a mixed salad with French dressing. Oh, and no, er, potatoes by the way.'

'Have them,' said Terry. 'You're paying for them anyway. You can give them to me.'

Bob and the waiter pretended not to hear.

'Would you like your wine opened now, sir?'

'Yes, please.' Bob obediently went through the wine-tasting ritual and pronounced it acceptable. The waiter poured out two full glasses and withdrew.

'Don't know why you bother to go through all that palaver,' said Terry. 'They're not going to take it back once they've opened it.'

'*I've* sent bottles back,' replied Bob. 'Well, once anyway. It was undrinkable.'

'Yeah? Ten to one they gave it to some other poor bugger in a carafe – or poured it all over your coq-au-vin.'

'Wine-tasting is an established procedure. It's a fine art.'

'I know all about that,' said Terry. 'It's simple. If you can pour it, you can drink it.'

Bob unfolded his serviette delicately. 'Behave yourself – and stop giving that waiter a hard time. Just relax and enjoy the food.'

'What's all this mixed salad bit? Don't they make good chips?'

'I like to watch the carbohydrates,' said Bob.

'Well, cheers.' Terry lifted his wineglass and took in his surroundings. 'I must say this is very nice indeed, Robert.'

Bob clinked glasses with Terry. 'I'm glad you were able to make such a miracle recovery in the last few hours.'

'Ahh . . . that's the thing about these foreign diseases. They're unpredictable.'

'You're right. It's amazing. When I wanted you to help me lay the stair carpet in the new house this afternoon, you'd lost the use of both legs, and your eyesight was failing.'

'I was feeling dizzy,' said Terry. 'I'd been in bed all week, remember? And I was also suffering from shock.'

'Oh, don't say you're going to go on about not being best man.'

'Calm down, don't worry. There's no hard feelings, like. But I can't pretend it didn't hurt, Bob. I mean, who's been closer to you over the years? Not even your mother, never mind about Frank Clarke. You didn't ask *him* around to help you lay the stair carpet.' Terry sighed. 'D'you know how long ago we met? When you first went out into the world. Your first day at Park Road Infants.'

'I know, I remember,' said Bob. 'Even though we were only five. The teacher said – "There's your seat, here are your crayons, playtime's at ten o'clock, if you want to be excused, put your hand up, and don't talk to Terry Collier".'

'Miss Hindmarsh . . . I loved her.' A wistful look came into Terry's eyes. 'But she rejected me.'

'Even at five years old, you were trouble.'

'A misunderstanding. All a misunderstanding.'

'I think it's amazing how people's character shows at such an early age,' said Bob. 'You haven't changed one little bit.'

'I was your first friend,' said Terry vehemently. 'I was the first person to steal your tricycle pump. The first person to split open your head with a brick. Frank Clarke can't claim things like that, can he? He won't have any of that to put in his speech at the wedding. What colourful anecdotes can *he* recall from the past?'

'Most of them aren't repeatable,' said Bob. 'Not as part of a speech at a wedding. And stop going on about Frank Clarke. He's best man and that's that.'

Terry leaned across the table. 'Frank Clarke never sacrificed five years of his life for anybody.'

'Oh, dear,' groaned Bob. 'We're not back to that are we?'

'Years of sweat and toil – and *pain*.' Terry rubbed his right thigh.

'Ah, yes, how *could* I forget? The famous "war wound". I'm still waiting to see that – and to hear how it happened,' said Bob.

'It's covered by the Official Secrets Act.'

'Oh. I told Audrey the needle must have slipped the night you were getting your left buttock tattooed.'

'The waiter never *did* bring that bread.' said Terry. He treated Bob to a look of contempt and got to his feet with difficulty. 'I've a good mind to get the police to check his passport.'

Terry limped across the restaurant and picked up a basket of bread from a side table. The waiter brought their hors d'oeuvres and another basketful of bread.

'Is your friend all right, sir?'

'Yes,' said Bob. 'He was cursed by the Incas. Whenever there's a full moon, he loses the use of his right leg.'

As Terry was about to return to their table, two well-dressed girls entered the restaurant. One was fair, the other dark-haired, and slightly slimmer, but it was all there to see. None of your Saturday night slags. This was a right pair of ravers.

Terry's eyes met theirs as they walked past and were shown to their table. He hurried back to Bob with the basket of bread and sat down in a high state of excitement. There was a good view of the girls from their table.

'Hey, did you see those two?!'

'I saw you give them what you think is your "winning" look,' said Bob.

'Pulled a good few with that.'

'And lost a hell of a lot more.'

'They've got it all there, though, haven't they?'

'They certainly cured your limp,' said Bob. 'Or was it a case of – "Take up thy bread and walk"?'

'Very funny. I don't have pain *all* the time, you know. It's spasmodic. Unpredictable.'

'Like your flu from Chile.'

Terry looked at Bob reproachfully, then jerked his head towards the girls. 'What d'you think they're doing on their own in a place like this?'

Bob calmly sprinkled powdered ginger on his melon. 'They're probably just two nice girls having dinner together. It does happen, you know. Even before Women's Lib started, it *was* possible to see unescorted females in public places.'

'Aye, but not spare on a Saturday night,' leered Terry. 'They must be on the game.'

Bob put down his forkful of melon. 'God, what bigoted sexual attitudes you have. Women without handbags are depraved, Negroes are more virile, divorcees are desperate for it. A few years ago, any fella that played tennis was a poof in *your* book!'

'A few years ago we wouldn't have let the minutes tick by like this,' said Terry. 'Shall we ask them over?'

'No, we will not ask them over.'

'Just to share a table,' insisted Terry. 'We can all go Dutch.'

'Terry,' said Bob firmly. 'I haven't come out with you to start pulling birds. Those days are over. That's what this meal is supposed to commemorate.'

'Commiserate, you mean.'

'It's the end of an era,' said Bob gravely.

'Aye,' sighed Terry. 'I suppose it is. But when you think how it was a few years back . . .' He studied the two girls and was favoured by a lingering return glance. 'Those two wouldn't have stood a chance, would they?'

'Not then – no.'

'I mean, we had it all going for us. Admit it now. We didn't half put it about.'

'True. True . . . '

'We were deadly.'

'No woman was safe.'

'Wallop. No messing.'

'We made a great team.'

'The terrible twins.'

'The dynamic duo.'

'Twin strikers.'

'Down the right wing and into the penalty area.'

'Deadly.'

'What was our best season?' asked Bob.

Terry thought for a moment. '1966. Yes . . . a vintage year. Definitely.'

'A very good year for blue-eyed girls.'

'Blue-eyed, green-eyed, cross-eyed. We swept all

before us.'

'A string of victories.'

'We were the champions,' sang Terry. 'Champions of the Roxy Ballroom and the Marimba Coff-ee Bar . . . '

The waiter appeared from behind Terry and topped up their wine glasses. 'Is everything satisfactory, sir?'

'I think we may need another bottle of wine,' said Bob.

'Very good, sir.' The waiter gave Terry a dark look and left.

'Looks like a pregnant penguin,' muttered Terry loudly.

Bob tried to cover the remark with a fit of middle-class coughing. There was no reaction from the waiter. Terry finished off his prawn cocktail in silence.

The waiter brought their steaks.

'Did you really have a string of victories?'

'How d'you mean?' Terry began to tuck into a plate of food that would have fed an Indian village for a month.

'Well, we took a hell of a lot of girls *out* that year. What I'm asking is did you have many, complete, total, knock-out, all-the-way victories?'

'Well,' said Terry, his mouth full. 'If you put it like that.'

'I am putting it like that. I want an honest answer.'

Terry laid down his knife and fork. 'Complete victories?'

'Knock-outs,' insisted Bob.

'All the way, like?'

'*All* the way.'

There was a long silence as Terry sorted out fact from fantasy.

'In all honesty, now,' said Bob, warningly.

'No.'

'I thought as much.' Bob looked at him sympathetically.

'How about you?'

'Well,' said Bob. 'I once got to extra time with Dorothy Harmison, but . . . '

'You never cracked the defence.'

Bob shook his head, and tossed his mixed salad. 'I was just thinking.'

'What?'

'A *whole* season. We must have been the only pair of 'twin' strikers that never scored.'

It was a sombre thought. They chewed their way through the rest of the meal in silence.

By the end of the second bottle of wine, and the beginning of the brandy, their spirits were restored to the point where they could contemplate their lack of success more philosophically. The waiter brought more coffee, and Bob selected two monstrous cigars. They lit up and sat back like two film producers.

Bob raised his brandy glass. 'To the end of an era.'

'Aye . . . '

'Today is the first day of the rest of my life.'

'Aye. That's one way of looking at it.' Terry puffed on his cigar. 'They were grand days, though but.'

'The best is yet to come.'

'Aye. They were great times . . . '

'There'll be better times ahead.'

'Aye, well – for some of us maybe . . . '

Bob waved his cigar expansively. 'Just think what we were like then. Now, we're mature, *civilised*. A few years ago, we didn't know "owt" from "nowt". Football and females – that was all that mattered.'

'Well, let's face it,' said Terry. 'Things haven't changed all that much. I mean, sex and soccer – that's what life's about.'

'There are *some* people who don't like sex.'

'Aye, well it takes all sorts . . . '

Bob leaned forward confidentially. 'Thelma reckons the height of ecstasy for me would be to make love to her in E-Block during the second leg of a European Cup Tie.'

Terry sniffed. 'By the time *our* team gets into Europe, making love in public will be legal.' He nodded towards the two girls they'd fancied earlier. 'And there's your last chance to make love in private before it becomes *illegal*.'

Bob took a long look at the two girls and got a long look back. He turned to Terry with a hint of desperation.

'I don't *want* to! How many times do I have to tell you? I'm into a whole different scene now. It's Bob and Thelma now. Not Bob and Terry. I wish you'd realise that. It's Bob and Thelma and their friend, Terry. You'll find some girl of your own soon, and then you'll find out how good this – this new era is. We'll do things together, of course – but with our *partners*. Our partners in life. Thelma is *my* partner . . . '. Bob began to run out of conviction. 'I have new words in my vocabulary now. Words like – marriage, trust, fidelity, understanding – '

'And mortgage, and gardening, and H.P., and mother-in-law,' added Terry.

Bob ignored the interruption. 'Other words I've forgotten. Words like – tail, spare, score, crumpet. They belong to the *old* days.'

'The good old days.'

'And the old ways. That are gone forever,' said Bob with renewed firmness. He took a sip of his brandy and studied the two girls again. 'You know – I really think we *could* pull those two over there.'

Terry was taken totally by surprise. 'But I thought you just – ?'

'I know that,' said Bob. 'But I bet we could. I mean, what are they doing here alone in a place like this? They must be on the game.'

Terry laid a restraining hand on Bob's arm. 'Bob, Bob – we're into another era now. You must have told me that at least ten times tonight.'

'I know,' said Bob, taking another look at the girls. 'But they're *spare*, and we're on. No doubt about it. You can tell by the way they've been lamping us.' Bob rubbed his hands. 'The old era might as well go out with a bang.'

'Well, if nothing else, I'm glad to see your vocabulary's coming back.'

'I fancy the dark one,' said Bob. 'Is it all right if I have the dark one?'

'Bob, listen – don't let's do anything you're going to regret later on. I mean, you're the one who has all the agonies of conscience.'

'Listen, it's just to see if the old techniques are still there. The old magic. Don't worry.' Bob signalled to the waiter. 'Just watch this.'

The waiter arrived. 'Can I help you, sir?'

'Yes,' said Bob. 'I wonder if you would be so kind as to give a message to those two young ladies.' Bob waved his cigar in their direction, and the waiter took a discreet look. 'Say we are sure we've met them previously, and if they don't think we are being too forward, perhaps they would like to join us for coffee and liqueurs.'

Terry listened spellbound, then goggled as Bob suavely pressed a folded pound note into the waiter's palm.

The waiter departed on his errand.

'By the cringe, that was good! A few years ago we'd have stopped by their table on the way to the bog and said "D'you fancy a jar?"'

Bob took a man-of-the-world puff on his cigar. 'And a few years ago, it would have been a few jars – then nothing.'

Terry took a covert glance at the girls and the waiter. The blonde girl looked straight into his eyes and smiled. 'They've got the message, they've got the message!!'

'Down, boy,' murmured Bob calmly. 'Keep it down. Hold it back . . . '

Terry felt a surge of almost uncontrollable excitement. It was like nipping off to the local kino during night manoeuvres on Lüneburg Heath – or getting your hands on a blank travel warrant.

'I didn't lead you on, you know. This was *your* idea.'

Bob gave Terry a smooth smile. 'Don't worry, I take full responsibility. Just let me handle it.'

Terry shored himself up with the last of his brandy. 'Okay, but if they turn out to be American oil-heiresses that want to whip us off to the States and set us up in Palm Springs or Hawaii – with bank accounts and swimming pools and yachts, well – don't say I didn't warn you.'

The two girls got up from their table.

'They're coming over – they're coming over!' gasped Terry.

'And this is the night when the twin strikers find their feet.'

Terry was stunned. 'I didn't think we'd do it.'

'I *knew* we could,' said Bob. 'The old magic's still there. Come on, up on your feet.'

The two lads stood up as the girls reached the table.

'Hello,' said Bob warmly. 'How do you do? And how nice of you to accept our invitation. This is Terry, and I'm Bob. We felt sure we'd met you somewhere before, but just couldn't remember your names.'

'I'm Norma,' said the blonde, 'And this is Susan.'

They all shook hands as the waiter produced two chairs for the girls. Bob ordered some more coffee and a round of liqueur brandy, then edged his chair a little closer to Susan's.

'Never been to Hawaii, have you – or Palm Springs?' asked Terry.

'We're trying to work out where we might have seen you,' explained Bob, waving away a cloud of cigar smoke.

Susan looked at Norma, then said, 'It could have been Park Road Secondary Modern.'

'Park Road?!' Terry looked at Bob with surprise.

'Yes,' said Susan. 'You were at school there.'

'And were you – ?'

'Oh, you wouldn't have known *us*,' said Susan. 'You were seniors. We were just juniors.'

'Yes,' said Norma. 'You would never have looked at us. Not you two.'

'Oh, really?' asked Bob.

'Not with all the girls you had around you *then*,' said Susan.

'Yes, of course.' Terry moved his chair a little closer to Susan.

'You were just distant objects of desire. Weren't they,

Norma?'

Norma nodded. 'Figures to idolise.'

'To worship from afar.'

'A schoolgirl's playground fantasy.'

'Glimpsed through the railings of the Junior School.'

'So near, and yet so far . . .'

This was all heady stuff for the lads. Mind-blowing material. Terry looked across at Bob.

'How could we have missed two beautiful girls like these?'

Bob shrugged. 'Fate. The same fate that has thrown us together tonight. Que sera, sera, as Doris Day said.'

'And in such a beautiful way,' said Terry. 'One of my favourite singers.'

Bob slid his arm along the back of Susan's chair. Terry gave Norma a nod and a wink.

'I hope you don't think we're the kind of girls that let men just pick us up,' said Susan.

'Oh, no, no, no, no, of course not,' chorused the lads.

'But we just had to take this once-in-a-lifetime opportunity of meeting you, didn't we, Norma?'

'Yes. I mean you two were legends in your own lifetime – at Park Road, that is.'

'Well, Terry – I hope we're not going to disappoint these young ladies. It's not easy being a living legend.'

'No,' said Terry, a little overawed.

'We'll just have to make sure the reality measures up to the myth,' said Bob in his wink-wink-nudge-nudge voice.

'Actually,' said Norma, 'I think you've lost weight since those days, Bob – er, may I call you that?'

'Please – Norma. Be my guest.'

'He watched his carbohydrates,' said Terry, wondering if the girls might be interested to learn about his gliding holiday in the Dolomites.

'But you haven't changed a bit,' said Susan.

Terry grinned. They were away here. No doubt about it. 'Would you girls like another drink?'

'I'm afraid the bar's closed,' said Bob. 'What a shame.

Still never mind.'

Terry looked around him. 'Are you sure?'

'Yes,' said Bob pointedly. 'It *IS*. But we can always go on for a drink somewhere *else*.'

'Oh, yes, I see. Yes, of course. What a pity. Yes, the bar's closed. Still we can always go on somewhere else, can't we, Bob?'

'Yes.' Bob looked at the girls. 'Is that okay with you?'

'I don't mind,' replied Norma.

'Where were you thinking of going?' asked Susan.

'Good question.' Bob flicked a nervous glance at Terry. 'I suppose we could all go back to *my* place.'

'Bob's got this house,' explained Terry. 'Which he uses when he's in England.'

'Yes, we *could* always go back there. I mean it would be quite a *good* place to go back to, actually.'

'Yes, I think they'd like that, Bob.'

'Yes, it's not a bad place.'

'Brand new,' said Terry.

'We could play some records. Have a few drinks.'

'Do you girls like drinking – I mean, *dancing*?' asked Terry.

'Love it,' said Norma. 'But what about the neighbours?'

'Oh, that's all right,' said Bob. 'No one's moved in on either side of us yet.'

'Us?' queried Susan.

'Ah – Terry and me. I mean Terry and *I*, we er –'

'Share the house,' said Terry.

'Ahh . . .'

'We could have a house-party,' suggested Bob.

'How about it, Norma?' Terry chanced his arm along the back of her chair.

Norma exchanged a long look with Susan. 'Well . . .' she said. I wouldn't want either of you to feel ashamed about anything in the morning.'

'We wouldn't, we wouldn't, would we, Terry?'

'No, no.'

'What would any of us have to be ashamed about?'

asked Bob. 'I mean, with the kind of feelings we four share?'

Norma looked at them both. 'Just so long as you're quite sure. I don't want you to do anything you might regret.'

Bob laid his hand tenderly on Norma's. 'The only regret *I* have is that we didn't meet years ago.'

'Right,' said Terry. 'My sentiments exactly. How about it, Susan?'

Susan shook her head. 'I'd like to but – I don't think it'd be a very good idea.'

Bob gripped her hand. 'Oh, but *Susan*, please – why?'

Susan looked him straight in the eye. 'Because you're due to marry my sister next week.'

As the girls got up and left, Bob just sat there with his mouth open. Terry thought Bob should offer to pay their bill, but since the news was bound to get around, there seemed no point in adding bribery to the charge of corruption.

Terry didn't hear from Bob for the next few days. Or from Thelma either, for that matter. He was just beginning to think Bob had jumped off the Tyne Bridge when he heard he'd been hiding in bed since that fateful Saturday. Pretending to be ill.

Just like Ferris to take the coward's way out, thought Terry. He borrowed a bunch of grapes from the sideboard and stole past his mother with them concealed between the pages of the latest copy of *Penthouse*.

Bob was propped up on a pile of pillows, with a thermometer in his mouth and an ice-bag on his head. Thelma's framed photograph was at his bedside.

'About bloody time too, Collier.'

Terry shut the bedroom door. 'Well, I couldn't risk catching it again, could I?'

'I could have died – for all you cared,' said Bob miserably.

'Don't give me that death's door bit,' said Terry. The only door of death you could have walked through was round at Thelma's house. As long as you stay here in bed, you're bomb-proof.'

'I've been delirious.'

'Haddaway,' growled Terry. 'Your Mam said your temperature never even reached a hundred and one.'

'It's this thermometer.' Bob took it out of his mouth. 'The glass is too thick.'

Terry opened his copy of *Penthouse* and tossed the grapes to Bob. 'Has Thelma been round?'

'No, thank God. She's in bed with flu as well. That's why she wasn't out with Susan and Norma the other night. Four of the other girls went down with it too.'

'You're sure it's not *because* of the other night?'

'No,' said Bob. 'Young Susan came round to see me. She's promised they won't let on.'

'Oh . . . '

'Well, don't sound so sorry,' said Bob. 'She's saved my marriage.'

'*I* tried,' said Terry. 'If you remember, I tried to hold you back. I don't know what came over you.'

'Must have been this bug that got into my system. Must have been partly delirious. I mean, it's obvious I wasn't behaving normally. Anyway, I told her that it was a joke. That we knew all along who they were.'

'Ahh . . . ' Terry tossed the copy of *Penthouse* onto the bed.

'This month's?'

'Yes, but you'd better not open it. I don't want to revive the symptoms.'

Bob took the ice-bag from his brow and laid it over the bare breasts of the girl on the cover. His face became serious. 'There's something I wanted to ask you.'

Terry sat down. 'Ask away, little pale face.'

'I've had second thoughts.'

'Good lad. She's a bonny girl, that Susan.'

'*Not* about my bride,' said Bob. 'About you.'

'About me?'

'About what you said.'

'About what?'

'About us having been through everything together. Even Chilean flu.' Bob wiped his nose. 'No, what you said the other night is perfectly true. How *can* I get married and not have you as best man? My best friend in the whole world.'

Terry looked wary at this sudden excess of sentiment. 'True, but – what are you leading up to?'

'I want you to be my best man. At my wedding. When I marry Thelma.'

'But what about Frank Clarke?'

'Oh, sod him. I can square it with Frank. The point is, will you do it?'

Terry looked a little overwhelmed. 'Bob – I – I don't know what to say?'

'Words can't really express what I feel, Terry. Let's just say it means a lot to me.'

Terry hesitated a moment, then gripped Bob's hand. 'Yes, of course I will, mate. My privilege.'

Bob's mother came into the room. 'I'm back love – oh, hello, Terry.'

'Hello, Mam.'

'Should you be here? I'd hate you to catch anything.'

'Oh, I'm prepared to risk that.' Terry winked at Bob. 'For a friend.'

'Everyone's going down with it,' said Mrs Ferris. 'And poor Frank Clarke's developed complications. He'll have to miss the wedding.'

'Oh, *really*?' Terry turned back to the bed, snatched his copy of *Penthouse* from Bob's grasp and walked to the door. 'I wouldn't worry. I'm sure Bob'll be able to find a replacement.'

Terry slammed the door behind him.

'Did I say something wrong?' asked Mrs Ferris.

Bob groaned and put the ice-bag back on his head.

8

Count Down

Ever since their first day at Park Road Infants, the two lads had taken it in turn not to be on talking terms with the other. After Bob's unbroken run of major rifts, it was only fair that Terry should be suitably outraged about the reasons for Frank Clarke's relegation and the way Bob had misrepresented his own substitution as best man.

It was not a thing that could be lightly forgiven.

Bob, who was on the mend, estimated that Terry would make this a two-day event. Bob gave him an extra day to start worrying that he might not be asked for a second time, then got out of his sickbed and took Terry down to the Black Horse.

After two large Bells and four pints each of Newcastle Brown, it was all over bar the shouting.

On the morning after the eternal flame of friendship had been rekindled, they attended a marriage guidance counsel-meeting at Mrs Chambers' house.

Thelma, young sister Susan, Bob and Terry sat quietly with coffee cups perched on their knees while Mrs Chambers did the talking. She was a neat, decisive woman who loved the sound of her own voice.

'Quite frankly, I'm not sure that church is going to be big enough, we've had so many "yesses" – I mean we invited one hundred and fifty, because you've got to, haven't you, but we banked on several not being able to come, in fact, I was hoping some in particular would say "no", especially all that clan of your father's from Stoke-on-Trent.' She paused for breath.

'The Lawsons are travelling all the way from Exeter,' said Thelma.

'Oh, I don't mind the Lawsons. No. She's a nice little

body. And he's not so much trouble since his asthma cleared up. But that lot from Stoke . . . '

'Are they your cousins that won the pools?' asked Bob.

'Money doesn't buy breeding, Bob. They don't know how to live in a decent house. The first thing they did when they moved in was to fill up the bath with coal. I wouldn't care, but they were fitted with oil-fired central heating!'

Terry began to laugh, and drew a look from Mrs Chambers that indicated this was not a subject for merriment.

'I really don't know who we can put them next to, at all . . . ' She looked around the little gathering and her eyes fell once more on Terry. 'Mmm . . . I wonder.'

'Thanks very much,' muttered Terry.

'No, of course, you'll be sitting at the top table, won't you? As best man.'

Susan linked arms with Terry. 'Yes. Taking care of the bridesmaid. You *will* take care of me, won't you, Terry?'

'Oh, aye,' beamed Terry. 'Don't worry about that.'

Bob could see that Terry was well on his way to becoming totally infatuated.

'We should have used a bigger church,' said Thelma. 'We should have gone to St Andrews.'

Mrs Chambers bristled. 'Over my dead body. Your father's lot might be pressed beef, but no daughter of mine is getting married in any other church than the C of E.'

'I don't see what difference it makes,' said Bob mildly, then seeing he had incurred a glance of displeasure, added, 'I mean, there are – many roads to God.'

'There may be many roads to God, Robert, but I've always thought of the Church of England as the M.1.'

'In that case,' said Terry. 'L-drivers, pedestrians, and people in invalid carriages would never get to heaven.'

Mrs Chambers carefully avoided looking at him. 'Is he being rude?' she enquired of Bob.

'Oh, come on, Mum,' said Susan. 'That was rather witty.'

'But it fell on stony ground.' Terry winked at Susan,

and wondered if there was any rule which said the best man couldn't have the bridesmaid *before* the wedding.

'I hope his best man's speech is going to be wittier than that.' Mrs Chamber's voice seemed to indicate she'd already given up hope on that score.

'Speech? I'm not making any speech.'

Mrs Chambers continued to address her replies via Bob. 'What does he mean? Of course he is. It's expected – however badly he does it.'

Bob translated for her. 'You *have* to make a speech, Terry. And you have to toast the bridesmaids' health and read out the telegrams.'

'Oh, I don't mind that bit. I just don't want to make a speech.'

Susan squeezed his arm. 'Oh, but you must, Terry. It'll be the highlight of the day.'

There is no doubt about it, thought Terry. Canada had done a lot for this girl. She'd developed a remarkable depth of perception. As well as having a great body.

'Well – if you put it like that,' he said modestly. 'I just didn't want to make a mess of things.'

'You won't, I promise you,' said Susan. 'You'll make a very *good* speaker.'

'Will I?'

'Of course you will.'

Terry gazed into her eyes and was lost.

'Hey, you two,' said Bob. 'Thelma and I are the ones that are getting married.'

'Yes,' said Mrs Chambers. 'There's so much to be done. I just don't know how I'm going to get through it all. The dressmaker's due in ten minutes. The caterer's coming at twelve, and – oh, we must go down to the hire shop and see about the pages' outfits.'

Bob paled. 'Pages?!'

'Thelma's two little nephews. Dean and Kirk. They're going to be in Royal Stewart tartan with silk ruffles.'

'Isn't that a bit Presbyterian?' asked Terry.

Mrs Chambers turned to Bob. 'Is that boy being rude again?'

'Mum,' said Thelma. I am a *bit* worried about those two. Young Dean – I mean, he can be such a . . . ' She searched for a suitable euphemism.

'Little bastard?' suggested Bob.

'Well, he can behave very badly.'

'Can you wonder at it?' asked Mrs Chambers. '*She* just lets him run riot.'

'Well, I don't want him running riot at *my* wedding.'

Bob tapped the pages of a booklet he'd been looking at. 'According to what it says here, that will be Terry's responsibility. Listen – "In case of any disturbance, the best man will do what he can to pour oil on troubled waters, pacifying the parties concerned by persuasion, politeness and tact".'

'Sound's great,' said Terry. 'But what does it mean in practice?'

Bob smiled. 'It means if young Dean gives you a hard time, you put your boot right up his kilt.'

'Robert! *Really*!' huffed Mrs Chambers. 'I don't know where you get these coarse expressions from.' She glanced at Terry. 'I can only hope you'll keep better company after you're married.'

Susan consoled Terry with another squeeze of the arm. There was a ring at the front door.

'That must be the dressmaker, Mum.' She got up to answer the door.

Mrs Chambers leapt up after her. 'Oh, goodness me, she's early! Come on girls. Clear up these coffee things and get the boys out of the way. There's such a lot to do.'

Thelma and her mother bustled round the room tidying away all traces of human occupation.

'Come on, you two boys, you can't sit here all morning day-dreaming. You've got to get your suits, haven't you?'

Bob and Terry got to their feet obediently.

'Yes,' said Bob.

'And see the taxi-people.'

'Bob's got it all in hand, Mum,' said Thelma. 'Calm down.'

'And don't forget the flowers for the church. What did we decide?'

Bob ticked them off on his fingers. 'Church flowers, bride's bouquet, bridesmaids' bouquets, buttonholes. Flowers at the reception are being provided by the hotel.'

'Good,' said Mrs Chambers. 'And you've got to ring the Vicar to check the cost of the choir, the bell-ringers and the use of his organ.' She frowned. 'Oh, dear, who left this apron here? Should be in the kitchen, and *you* should be upstairs.' She shepherded Thelma from the room.

'By the cringe!' growled Terry. 'Do you *have* to take all this? Yes, m'am, no, m'am, three bags full, m'am. Haven't you got *any* say?'

'What can I do?' asked Bob. 'You saw what happened about the pages. I've been against them all along. Even Thelma didn't want them.'

'Well, put your foot down. Draw the line somewhere. Be firm with them.'

'Like you were with Susan, I suppose. She soon talked *you* into making a speech.'

'That's different,' said Terry. 'I didn't want to offend *her*.'

'Well, I don't want to offend Thelma.'

'But you can *afford* to offend her. For Christ's sake, Bob. She's going to be your wife!'

'Listen,' wheedled Bob. 'It's their big day. Just go along with it. You know how women feel about weddings.'

'I know, but it's getting a bit heavy, isn't it? I'm surprised the service isn't in Durham Cathedral with the massed pipes of the Scots Guards. I'm surprised they're not cancelling *World of Sport* and televising your wedding instead.'

Bob waved his little booklet. 'According to this, you're supposed to sustain me all through this week with advice and comfort.'

'I'll give you some advice. Call it off.'

'It's gone too far for that,' said Bob. 'We've had to pay the caterers in advance.'

Terry grabbed the booklet and sat down on the sofa. Bob slumped down beside him and watched as Terry flipped through the pages.

'Just what are the rest of my functions, then? . . . "Get you to the church on time . . . stand by your side throughout the service" . . . ' Terry's mouth dropped open. ' – "Settle the account in the vestry"?'

'Only if the bridegroom has forgotten to do it,' said Bob. 'But you do have to tip the verger.'

'What old Breakey? Does he get tipped at every wedding? Bye, he must be cracking it there. What with christenings and funerals, he must take home more than an archbishop!'

'I wish you'd take your duties more seriously,' said Bob.

'I wish your future mother-in-law would take *me* more seriously,' said Terry. 'And stop using you as an interpreter.'

Bob tapped the booklet. 'It says in there that the best man is the hub around which a well-run wedding revolves. It says I should choose someone who is gay but reliable.'

Terry laid a limp hand on Bob's knee. 'I won't let you down, sailor.'

'Gerroff! Terry – couldn't you, just *once* in your life, just for this week – couldn't you try to be polite, helpful and agreeable? I know you've just come out of the Army, but please – let's keep your barrack-room vulgarity out of the service.'

Terry gave him a hurt look and went back to the booklet. ' – "The ushers are in charge of the congregation" – who have you got for ushers?'

'A cousin of Thelma's – who you don't know, Podge Rowley and John Gibson.'

'Not *Big* John?'

'Yes.'

'I only hope he's off the bottle on the day,' muttered

Terry. 'I don't want *him* drunk in charge of a pew.'

'Don't worry, he's just on cider, these days.'

Terry slipped the booklet into a pocket. 'I'll keep this till I'm word perfect. What's this other one?'

Terry picked it up before Bob could grab it.

'It's nothing,' said Bob. 'Thelma's mother gave it to us. It's just the Medical Council thingy . . . '

Terry grinned. 'You've gone all red. Where are the dirty bits?' As if in reply to his question, the booklet fell open at page twenty-eight. Terry read the first words that caught his eye. ' – "And so to bed, and the great adventure of sleeping together for the rest of your lives" – God preserve us, there can't be much adventure left by the time you reach sixty. What else? – "Will I make a good lover?" – "Will I satisfy her?" – "Will it hurt?" – "What will she think of my body?" – does she know about your knobbly knees?'

'Of course.' Bob looked hugely embarrassed. 'I don't need to know that stuff. It's the other articles – on useful shopping, things for the home, that sort of thing.'

'Aye, I can see that,' said Terry. 'They've got a funny sense of priorities. There are three pages on sexual problems and eight on floor coverings. Mind you, it could be useful if you're going to have it away on the carpet.'

'I wouldn't know,' said Bob. 'There's not much in there that I didn't already know. It was for Thelma really.'

'It also says – "Try to make sure the bedroom is warm and that your bed doesn't creak" – ' Terry laughed. 'And it also says – "But there's nothing wrong with the sitting-room for a change of scene" – !'

Terry threw the booklet aside and embraced Bob with mock passion. They tumbled back onto the sofa as Bob struggled to get free.

'Gerroff, you great pillock!'

'Don't fight it, darling, kiss me! The washing-up can wait!'

'But the wedding can't,' said Mrs Chambers.

Still entangled together, Bob and Terry looked over

the back of the sofa and saw Thelma's mother standing by the sitting-room door.

'I thought you two boys were going to see about your morning suits.'

Bob and Terry got up meekly and left the house.

Mrs Chambers went back upstairs to the bedroom where Thelma was being pinned into her wedding dress.

'Was that Bob who just went out?'

'Yes,' said Mrs Chambers. 'And if you ask me, the sooner you marry that boy the better.'

The two lads got themselves kitted out in morning suits and stood in front of the mirror. Bob had been loving every minute of it, but Terry had maintained a surly attitude from the moment they had walked into the shop.

To make matters worse, Terry had got the distinct impression that the assistant had lingered overlong while taking his inside leg measurement.

'Let's see you with your top hat on,' said Bob. He put the topper on Terry's head.

The hat, which was several sizes too big, slid down and folded over Terry's ears, then stopped on a level with his eyebrows. Bob collapsed with laughter.

'Very funny,' snarled Terry. He ripped the hat from his head.

'Careful!' said Bob.

'I look bloody ridiculous.'

'Only with it on. It doesn't matter. You don't have to wear them anyway. You just carry them. Look – like this.' Bob tucked the topper under his arm. 'You put your gloves and your prayerbook inside.'

'There'll be room for a quart of brown ale as well, in that one.'

'Do you have any grey gloves?'

'I've got a pair of wollen mittens at home.'

'I mean proper ones. Thin, grey suede ones. You'd better get a pair here.'

Terry exploded. 'What a bloody *farce*!! I'll look like the MC on Olde Tyme Music Hall.'

'And remember you'll have a carnation in your buttonhole. That's another of your functions – to hand round the carnations.'

'And what do I do with the ones that are left over?' demanded Terry. 'Stick them behind my ear? I don't know – thin grey suede gloves, top hats . . . I'll never be able to hold my head up in the Black Horse again.'

Bob began to take off his morning suit. 'Listen, we might as well do things properly. St Marks is mainly blue serge suits and sprigs of heather. Our wedding will bring a touch of class. Bring a whiff of Belgravia to Station Road.'

'There's nothing wrong with honest-to-goodness, no-nonsense, salt-of-the-earth blue serge,' growled Terry. 'All this is just another concession to your lower-middle-trying-hard-to-be-upper-class mother-in-law.'

'It's nothing to do with her. *I* suggested morning suits.'

'Don't give me that,' sneered Terry. 'Never in a million bloody years. It was *HER*. And it wasn't a suggestion, it was a Royal Command. And that's what *this* is – a bloody Royal Command Performance!'

'You know your trouble? Shall I tell you what your trouble is?'

'All right,' said Terry. 'Go ahead. Tell me.'

'You're an inverted snob.'

'Bollocks.'

'All we're doing,' said Bob, 'is hiring a suit of clothes. Clothes that are appropriate for the occasion.'

'*And* top hats.'

'Your Uncle Wilf wouldn't have gone down the Deep Six at Ashington without his safety helmet, would he? It's part of the *outfit*. Hell's bells, we'll only have the clothes on for about five hours.'

'It's a betrayal of everything I stand for,' said Terry bitterly.

'Terry – all we're doing is putting on morning coats and striped trousers. We're not taking over Lloyd's – or the Stock Exchange. We haven't got a marquee the size of Billy Smart's circus on the lawn at Chatsworth with a thousand guests dancing to the music of Edmundo Ros.'

Terry shook his head. 'Bob, you're still trying to be something you're not. Tossing away good money for the sake of your social aspirations. When there's getting on for a million unemployed in this country.'

'Not when the figures are adjusted to take account of school leavers and seasonal trends,' said Bob.

'Well, *however* many there are, there are still too many, and *I'm* one of them.'

'Terry. *I'm* paying for the hire of the suits.'

'I don't give a damn who's paying for them – as long as it's not me. But that's not the point. It's a matter of principle.' Terry paused gravely. 'The principle of what we're fighting for. Equality of opportunity, a decent wage for a job well done, a fair crack of the whip, a fair slice of the cake –'

'And four weeks paid holiday a year.'

Terry ignored the interruption. 'A chance to hold your head up high, to bring your kids up decent. Take away a man's work and you take away his pride.'

'Get away,' jeered Bob. 'You were watching that documentary on the BBC last night.'

'Pardon?'

'Come on – after the nine o'clock news. I was watching it too.'

'So what? I'm *interested* in the issues of the day. Social inequality. Injustice. I'm interested in the rationalisation of industry, the redeployment of the labour force –'

'You crafty bugger – that's exactly what the bloke said last night! I suppose you know you missed *I was a Teen-age Werewolf* on the other side?'

'I've seen it four times,' said Terry. He waved away Bob's laughter. 'What do *you* know? How can *you* understand? Marrying into the Tory Party. You'll be chairman of the Junior Chamber of Commerce next.'

'It's a bit late for you to develop a social conscience, isn't it? After all these years of being a "Don't Know".'

'What d'you mean a "Don't Know"? I've *always* been

a solid supporter of the Left. Committed to the crusade against the unacceptable face of capitalism.'

'Get out of it,' jeered Bob. 'You've always been a "Don't Know". So have your family. Nobody in your family's known for generations. They probably decided between the Roundheads and Cavaliers on the toss of a coin.'

'Fascist . . . '

The assistant returned to the fitting room. 'How does everything fit?'

'Fine,' said Bob.

'The hat's too big,' said Terry.

The assistant laid Bob's suit over his arm. 'One doesn't wear the hat, sir. You just carry it under the arm – so. With your gloves and prayerbook inside.'

'You see?' said Bob. 'I told you.'

'Have you got one that's waterproof?' asked Terry. 'I may feel like drinking champagne out of it.'

Bob coughed. 'I'll, er, come out with you and settle up.' He left with the assistant.

Terry turned back to the mirror and stared morosely at the capitalist version of himself. A middle-aged man came out of one of the changing cubicles and stood in front of the mirror. He was also dressed in a morning suit.

They stood awkwardly side by side for a moment.

'D'you feel as daft as I do?' asked the man. He pulled his waistcoat down in an effort to make it fit better.

'It's all a load of old cobblers,' muttered Terry.

'It's the women,' said the man. 'They're the ones who like this.'

'Aye. Some of them more than others.'

'Are you the groom?'

Terry shook his head. 'The best man. It's his in-laws that are at the back of all this.' He flipped the lapel of his morning suit. 'Snobs. Jumped up from nowhere to a posh semi with a monkey puzzle tree.'

'Oh, aye . . . '

'Terry, if you'll get that lot off, we can have them packed and get out of here.'

Terry and the man turned to see Bob at the door.

'Hallo, Bob,' said the man.

'Hello, George. They've got you on the trot too, have they?'

'They have that,' said the man who was George.

Bob walked over to them. 'Terry, I'd like you to meet Thelma's Dad – Mr Chambers – Terry Collier, my best man.'

Terry shook hands dumbly with Mr Chambers.

'Pleased to meet you, lad. Our Susan's told me a lot about you.'

'I, er – well, er –'

'That's all right, lad,' said Mr Chambers with a wink. 'I never liked that bloody tree meself.'

The two lads took Mr Chambers down to the Black Horse where they parked their cardboard attaché cases from the dress hire firm under the table, and got Tom to pull up three pints of Export.

Mr Chambers took a couple of inches off the top of his pint, wiped his lips, and said, 'Yes, well, I'm very comfortable now. Done well in building. Did all right in the post-war boom, survived the sticky patch after, then picked up these other firms, structural steelwork – and the electrical side of things.' He grinned. 'Started out as a bricky, y'know. Yes, I've been very lucky, but I'm still a bricky at heart. It's Thelma's mother who's always had the grand ideas. One of her sisters did very well for herself.' He winked. 'Yes, it was always "luncheon" in our house – even if I only wanted bread and cheese and a pickled onion. But I went along with it, to please her like. We take the *Daily Telegraph*, but it's only to impress the newsagent. Yes . . . she's very fond of putting on airs and graces. Daft, I call it, but it's quite harmless – mostly . . .'

'I didn't mean any offence back there, like,' said Terry awkwardly.

'None taken, lad.'

'Oh, God, what have you said now?'

'Nothing, Bob,' said Mr Chambers.

'I was just a bit upset about having to get all tarted up,' explained Terry.

'Me too.'

'Terry, I keep telling you. It's just a uniform. A suit for the occasion. Like when you go riding, you wear jodhpurs – or if you play cricket, you wear a white shirt and flannels.'

Mr Chambers nudged Terry. 'I think Bob's really lapping this up on the quiet.'

'I just have a sense of occasion, that's all.'

'Well, I know one thing,' said Terry. 'I'll be taking the long way round to the church on Saturday.'

'Why?' asked Bob.

'Because I'm not running the gauntlet of the High Street. D'you think I'd be able to get past The Ship, The Cross Keys, The Stick and Bottle, the Institute – the Billiard Hall, and the RAOC Club without someone spotting me?'

'Yes,' said Mr Chambers. 'I'll be taking some stick from my father. That's if he turns up, like. No love lost between him and the wife.'

'Well, it's Terry's job as best man to keep the peace.'

'He might have to, if my old man gets at the bottle. He's a canny old soul, like. Ex-pitman. Chews shag tobacco and never takes his hat off at table.

Terry looked at Bob. 'This wedding mightn't be so bad after all.' He turned to Mr Chambers. 'My grandad was a pitman, and so was my Uncle Wilf. They were both on the hunger march from Jarrow.'

'But they both dropped out at Durham,' added Bob.

'He was never a well man, my grandad.'

'He was never a sober one. He and your Uncle Wilf dropped out as soon as the pubs opened.'

'They were marching for the right to work,' said Terry stoutly.

'Listen,' said Bob. 'I don't know about your grandad, but your Uncle Wilf has spent his life *avoiding* work. He lives here *because* of the high unemployment. He's the only man the Labour Exchange have ever thought of giving a clock and a long service medal to.'

Mr Chambers laughed.

Terry looked pained. 'He couldn't work. He had black lung.'

'If he did, which I doubt,' said Bob. 'He got it through drinking too much stout.'

'All *I* know,' replied Terry soberly, 'is that if my grandad saw me poncing around in this Ascot get-up, he'd turn in his grave.'

'You mean turn in his urn. He was cremated.'

'Bollocks to you, Ferris.'

'How about a whisky?' suggested Mr Chambers. 'I can't take too much beer, meself.'

Terry started to get up. 'A large one?'

Mr Chambers pulled him back down. 'Put your money away, lad. This wedding's costing me so much, a few whiskies aren't going to make much difference. Not that I begrudge Bob and Thelma, mind. I'd just rather have spent the money on – well, something useful for the house.'

Mr Chambers called for three large Johnny Walkers.

'Just don't make waves. That's my attitude,' said Bob. 'In a week's time it will all be over. The speeches, the confetti, the champagne buffet. They'll just be a memory, and we can become two ordinary married people.'

'Well, speaking frankly,' said Terry, 'I don't think young people should get married these days. I think the answer is living together. People should just live together. That's what should happen now.'

'According to my Sunday papers, it's happening already,' said Mr Chambers.

'Yes,' said Terry. 'Marriage is an out-dated institution. I know. I've tried it. Living together – that's the answer.'

'You can't live together up here,' protested Bob. 'It may be all right in London, or Paris, or West Hartlepool, but it's certainly *not* all right on the Elm Lodge Housing Estate.'

'Why?'

'Because you can't. That's why. They've got Resident's Associations and car rally clubs and baby sitting rotas. They wouldn't accept it as – living together. They'd call it "living in sin" or "co-habiting" –'

'And you're the man who called *me* a sexual bigot,' said Terry.

'But you'd be a threat to the stability of the social group,' continued Bob. 'They wouldn't invite you to their Guy Fawkes parties.'

Terry groaned and held his head.

'And besides which,' said Mr Chambers. 'You might not get a mortgage.'

'More of your middle-class hang-ups,' said Terry. 'Why should you worry about what other people think? The one thing that's struck me since I've come back from abroad is that you're so – provincial.'

'But I *am* provincial,' said Bob. 'I live in "the provinces". That explains my provincial attitude. What attitude would you like me to adopt – an Albanian attitude – a Peruvian one? Perhaps I should adopt a Zulu attitude? Then I could have five wives and a goat and live in a mud hut on the Municipal Bowling Green.'

'They'd never allow it,' said Mr Chambers. 'It's taken thirty years to get that turf right.'

'Excuses, excuses,' said Terry. 'All excuses for your small-town mentality.'

Bob went a bright pink. 'Well, your free-wheeling, non-conformist attitude hasn't got *you* very far! I think you should wait till you've got something behind you before you start to criticise other people.'

Terry opened his mouth to reply but Bob steamed on angrily.

'And before you drag up the last five dreary years again, I mean something *more* substantial than a broken marriage, a doubtful war-wound and a tattoo on your left buttock!'

It was Terry's turn to go bright pink. He tapped his chest. 'I had years taken out of my life. By someone not a million miles from here. You and your fancy friends have had five years' start on me. That's quite a handicap. I haven't even been back five *weeks*!'

'Now, now, lads, come on now . . . '. Mr Chambers pushed them gently back into their seats. 'This wedding's causing enough rows as it is. Me and the wife have nearly had a divorce over it, the people who didn't get invitations aren't speaking to me, half the one's who did are grumbling 'cos they've got to fork out for a wedding present, and now you two are at it hammer and tongs.' He shook his head. 'I should have loaned you a ladder, Bob. You and Thelma could have eloped and saved us all a lot of time and trouble – and money. That I'd have been happy to put in the bank for you.'

Mr Chambers took a thoughtful sip of whisky. 'You don't fancy that, do you? There's a nice light-weight aluminium ladder in the yard. It'd do the trick nicely.'

'I'd like to help out, George, but it's too late now.'

'It's never too late,' said Terry sourly.

Bob ignored him. 'All the invitations have gone out, and you've paid for the catering in advance.'

'Aye, I know, lad. Mind you it's not the money. It's all this fuss and palaver. The whole thing has got out of hand. We started out with a simple wedding, and we've ended up with a Royal Garden Party.'

'Well, I think you should draw the line somewhere,' said Terry. 'I was saying the same thing to Bob this morning. You've got to put your foot down.'

Mr Chambers looked at the two of them. 'I think you've got a point there. The time's come to make a stand. Get things in proportion.'

'But what can we do?' asked Bob.

'Well, first,' said Mr Chambers, 'we'll have a few more pick-me-ups – just to confirm our convictions as it were, then we'll strike a blow for men's lib.'

'How?' asked Terry.

'Well, we can't burn our bras,' replied Mr Chambers, 'but we can at least take these bloody things back –' He kicked his dress hire case out from under the table and across the floor.

'As a token of solidarity,' said Terry. He put his foot behind his own case and sent it slithering across the floor to collide with Mr Chambers' case.

'One for all and all for one,' said Bob. As he stood up and kicked his case, Mrs Chambers put her head round the door of the snug.

'I thought we'd find you in here,' she said.

Thelma and Susan followed her in.

'Bob!' said Thelma. 'How on earth did you put your foot through that case?'

'Er, I, er – tripped.' Bob hopped about trying to shake the case off his foot.

'I don't wonder at it,' said Mrs Chambers. 'Fancy leaving them all over the place like this.' She set the other two cases the right way up and fastened her eye on Mr Chambers. 'What exactly is going on here?'

'We're just toasting the health of the bride and groom.' Mr Chambers finished his drink.

Bob extricated his foot from the case. 'Is everything all right?' he asked Thelma.

'It is now.' She raised a fourth cardboard suitcase. 'You forgot to pick up the page boys' outfits.'

'I didn't know we had to do that,' said Bob.

'No, it was Dad,' said Susan.

'Typical,' said Mrs Chambers. 'Shouldn't you be at the florist's?'

'On our way,' said Bob.

'And have you been in touch with the taxi people?'

'All under control.'

'They've been drinking,' pronounced Mrs Chambers. 'That's what they've been doing. Sitting here wasting time. You ought to be ashamed of yourselves.'

Mr Chambers drained the last of Bob's whisky and stood up. 'Mary,' he said firmly. 'Bob and I have had enough.'

'You certainly have for one day,' said Mrs Chambers. She took him by the arm. 'You can come down to the florist's with me, and Bob can look after the rest.' She steered her husband towards the door.

Mr Chambers looked back over his shoulder at the two lads.

'I'll leave you to tell them about the suits, Bob.' He disappeared.

'Suits?' asked Thelma. 'Is there anything wrong with them?'

'Er, no,' said Bob. 'Absolutely perfect.'

Susan flashed her baby-blue eyes at Terry. 'I bet you look smashing in yours. Will you put it on for me when you get back to the house?'

'His top hat's too big,' said Bob.

'Ohh . . . ' Susan looked concerned.

'But it'll be okay,' said Terry. 'I don't have to wear it. I just carry it under my arm to keep my gloves and prayer-book in.'

Due to the excess of revolutionary fervour, Bob didn't get around to checking the car bookings till the day after. He was on the phone when Terry arrived at his house.

'That's right . . . one Rolls, the Austin Princess for the bridesmaids, the Granada automatic for the parents, and two Zephyrs to ferry the guests . . . yes . . . thank you.' Bob replaced the receiver.

'You look cheesed off.'

'I am,' admitted Bob. 'You were right. It's all too much. We shouldn't have chickened out yesterday.' He sat down. 'Have I missed anything?'

Terry fished a list out of his top pocket.

'Car?'

'Hired.'

'Photographer?'

'Contacted.'

'Flowers?'

'Arranged.'

'Bellringers?'

'Rung.'

'Hymns?'

'Booked.'

'That's about it then – until Saturday.' Terry put the

list away.

'What happens then?'

'You get married! Twit . . . '

'Oh, yes, I do, don't I?' Bob sighed wearily. 'Compared to this, that should be a piece of cake.'

'Cake!' exclaimed Terry. He whipped out his list again.

'Baked,' said Bob. 'Arrives on Friday.'

'You still have to pay for the choir and the organist, and I have to tip the verger.'

'What does a choir cost these days?'

Terry shrugged. 'Depends. If it's the Vienna State, or the Huddersfield Choral Society, probably more than you can afford. On the other hand, the St Mark's syncopating six *may* accept Green Shield Stamps. Let's see what the book says.'

Terry pulled out his now heavily thumbed copy of 'Wedding Drill'. ' . . . choirs . . . here we are, Boys – 40p, Men and Women – 70p.'

'It only used to be a shilling when I was in the choir,' said Bob. 'I had a fine little voice.'

'I'll make a note of that for my best man's speech,' said Terry. 'It's got something about speeches in here.' He referred once more to the booklet. '– "It is a good idea for the best man to relate some anecdotes about the groom's childhood" –'

'Well, don't mention Deirdre Birchwood. I've got enough problems without *her* name cropping up.'

'But since it has,' said Terry. 'I'd like to remind you that I'm still waiting for a detailed explanation of what you two were doing on Blaydon Moor.'

'So is Thelma. I'll tell you after the wedding.'

'Why not now?'

'Because it will be safer then,' said Bob enigmatically.

The two lads jumped up guiltily as Mrs Ferris showed Thelma into the room.

'Hallo, Terry.' Thelma favoured him with an almost real kiss on the cheek. 'How's it all going?' The question was directed at Bob.

'Oh, fine, love. Just fine.' Bob gave her a little hug.

'Everything's under control. Terry's been a fantastic help. Exciting, isn't it?'

'Do you really think so?' Thelma flopped down into an armchair. She looked exhausted and unutterably depressed. 'It's driving me out of my mind. No, I mean it. My hairdresser's just gone on holiday, so it means getting it done by Denny, but he's never *done* mine before, the dressmaker can't guarantee Susan's alterations in time, Mother's sending me up the wall, and that little bugger Dean has just set fire to his kilt.'

Thelma's face crumpled. She began to cry.

Bob rushed over and put a consoling arm around her. 'Hey, hey, hey, come on, love! What's wrong? There's no need to get upset. It'll be all right on the night – on the *day*, I mean.'

Thelma wiped her eyes and blew her nose. 'Why didn't you just ask me to come away with you? Why didn't we decide just to *live* together? That's what we should have done. Marriage is an out-dated institution. I mean, that's what everyone says nowadays, isn't it?' Thelma began to cry again.

Bob looked helplessly at Terry. 'Well, don't just stand there. You're the best man. You've read the booklet. During moments of crisis, you're supposed to sustain me with comfort and advice.'

As Thelma continued to sob, Terry thumbed through the booklet then threw it away in disgust.

'I'll go and get that ladder,' he said.

9

Boy's Night In

On the night before the wedding, Bob composed himself in front of the living-room mirror and ran through his wedding speech for the umpteenth time.

It was still a desperately under-rehearsed and wooden performance. His brain cells seemed to be glued together, and he had become heartily sick of his own voice.

' . . . my wife and I . . . I'll have to get used to saying that – pause for laugh – my wife and I would like to thank you all for coming today, and especially Mr and Mrs Chambers for putting on this marvellous do – pause for applause – and to Thelma's Uncle Norman for his kind words. I don't know how to follow a funny speech like that, so I won't try – pause for laugh – blast!' Bob's memory failed him.

He leafed through his notes in an effort to find the next words. The original neat lines of handwriting had been savaged with scrawled insertions of mordant wit, last-minute grammatical revisions and corrected spelling.

'Ah, here we are . . . ' Bob cleared his throat and held his chin up. 'We would both like to thank you for all the wonderful presents – pause for smile – It's a good job Thelma and I both like toast, because we now have a toast rack for every day of the week – pause for laugh, should get a good one there . . . '

Bob held up his hand to quiet his imaginary audience. 'No, but seriously, we have had some marvellous presents, haven't we darling?' As he turned to the chair that was standing in for Thelma, the front door bell rang.

So as not to interrupt the flow, Bob continued to deliver his speech all the way to the front door, welcomed Terry with a nod, and ushered him into the living-room.

Terry put down a zipped travelling bag.

'My Uncle Norman has known Thelma since she was so high,' said Bob, shutting the living-room door. 'And I myself have known her since she was not so much higher – pause, bet we won't get a laugh – in fact, since Park Road Junior School, Form 4-B, one fateful autumn day when her desk was moved next to mine . . . '

Terry began to say something but Bob signalled him to be quiet.

'So you can see that our romance has hardly been a whirlwind affair. No, it has been a . . . ' Bob snapped his fingers as he tried to recall the lines.

Terry came to his rescue. 'A rather long, drawn-out, boring affair, of no interest to anyone but yourselves.'

Bob referred to his notes. 'An affair, which has, in the words of the song – "grown better every day, stronger in every way" – pause for applause.'

'God preserve us.' Terry clapped wearily.

'Listen to this bit. I like this bit,' said Bob. 'It's a good job Thelma and I like toast, as we now have a toast rack for every day of the week.'

Terry sat down and looked at him with a face of stone.

'That should get a laugh, shouldn't it? At the wedding?'

Terry sucked in his breath sharply and shook his head. 'Bob, don't ever try and be funny. You know how terrible you are at telling jokes.'

Bob checked his watch. 'The service is at three in the afternoon. That gives you at least . . . nineteen hours and fourteen minutes for your last words of insult, derision and contempt.'

Terry laughed. 'I've got no intention of stopping just because you're getting married, mate! As far as *I'm* concerned, I've got a lifetime's work ahead of me.'

Bob smiled. 'You can say what you like tonight. Nothing's going to get up my nose. I'm above it all, on a different plane. Serene.'

'You've been watching those Yoga classes on television again,' said Terry accusingly. 'I've warned you about that. Could do yourself an injury.'

'I don't need Yoga. It's all a question of mind over matter. I've achieved serenity through concentration and discipline – plus four sleeping pills and six tranquillisers.'

'You what?' Terry jumped to his feet. 'You'll sleep through the whole honeymoon, you great pillock!'

'Plus three travel sickness pills and an Iron Jelloid,' beamed Bob. 'They're just starting to work.'

'Why an Iron Jelloid?'

'That was a mistake. Wrong bottle. I hope it doesn't clash.'

'Your system'll never stand the shock. You'll be a drug addict by the time you get there.' Terry shook his head. 'Poor Thelma. She thinks she's married to a nice young man with management prospects. What a shock *she's* going to get tomorrow night. She'll be eagerly laid out on the bed in her nylon nightie and you'll be writhing around on the floor going through the shakes of cold turkey and screaming for your Iron Jelloids.'

Terry's dire predictions had absolutely no effect on Bob. 'Sleeping pills haven't made me tired at all, but I do feel tranquil. Calm, relaxed and incredibly tranquil . . .'

'Yes? Well, I've lost the ring.'

Bob's Buddha-like mask slipped. 'You what? You idiot!! I knew this would happen, I knew it!'

Terry held up the wedding ring. 'Calm down, calm down. Just testing your discipline and control. So much for *your* serenity. I'd go to the chemist's and ask for your money back.'

Bob heaved a huge sigh of relief. 'You shouldn't joke about things like that. In my state that could be dangerous. God knows, what you've done to my metabolism. I'd better take another pill.'

Terry laid a restraining hand on Bob's arm. 'There's only one sure way of unwinding, and that's to get a few bevvies under your belt. Come on, get your coat on. All the lads are waiting for us down at the Black Horse.'

'All *what* lads?'

'Frank, Tony, Blakey, Jack, Big Dave. All the lads.'

'Terry, I told you yesterday. I am not going out to-night. That Saturday we went out was *my* celebration. I asked you round here tonight to keep me company.'

'Just you and me?'

'Yes, just the two of us.'

'But this is a little surprise,' said Terry. 'I arranged it behind your back. As a little surprise, like.'

'That's very nice of you,' replied Bob. 'But I can't come. I'm staying *in* tonight.'

'Why?'

'I want to finish my packing.'

'Oh, come on, Bob – for God's sake! It's your *STAG* night.'

'But I don't want a stag night,' said Bob steadfastly. 'Not in the old-fashioned sense of the word, anyway.'

'And just what *is* the old-fashioned sense?'

'Oh, you know,' smiled Bob. 'It's so – pathetic. All that last-minute, desperate drunkeness.'

'And what's wrong with that?' demanded Terry. All that "last-minute, desperate drunkenness" is what a stag party's about! That's a *proper* stag party. A great roaring piss and punch-up. Not the two of us stuck in front of the Epilogue with two cups of cocoa.'

'Terry, I am not going near a pub.' Bob sat down firmly and folded his feet up under him.

Terry looked at him. 'My God, what are things coming to? Do you mean to tell me you're just going to sit there in the Lotus position with your socks tucked under your armpits?'

'Yes. I am.'

'But, Bob . . . ' Terry sat down opposite him in despair. 'You're letting the *side* down.'

'Times have changed,' said Bob. 'People don't have night-before rave-ups any more.'

'They *do*!' said Terry emphatically. '*I* did. And the night before I got demobbed from the Army, there was a quart of beer on the table for every month I'd served. Ninety-six pints between seven of us.' Terry grinned.

'Bye, there was some desperate drunkenness that night.'

'But I'm not getting demobbed,' said Bob. 'I'm joining up.'

'Aye – with a monstrous regiment of women. You should feel ashamed at breaking a tradition like this. It's the drunken do the night before that gives the wedding some bite. Some *drama*. Because no one knows if the groom is going to make it.'

'Well, I have every intention of making it,' said Bob. 'That's why I'm staying here and staying sober.'

'Listen, we can't just sit here ticking off the hours to blast-off. It'll be agony.'

'Terry,' said Bob patiently. 'I'm getting married, not going into lunar orbit. I don't feel any agony. All that is going to happen is that at three o'clock tomorrow afternoon, I'm going to get *married*. I'm going to arrive at the church looking good, and refreshed, and a credit to my bride, and a splendid advertisement for that nice Jewish man who hired me the morning suit. If I go out with you and the lads, the chances are I'll wake up in a police station or a casualty ward – or bound and gagged on a North Sea oil rig.'

'But Bob – what are the lads going to think?'

'They can think what they like.'

'I'll never be able to look them straight in the face again.'

'That's your problem. You arranged it.'

Terry made a last desperate effort of persuasion. 'Bob – *please*. Think of the great stag parties of the past. Think of the lads whose memory you're betraying. Think of Bob Shearer who was sick in the vestry, of Tony Charles who went to the wrong church, of John Webb, the kiss of life and the stomach pump – of Maurice, who no one found till a week later. Did they all booze in vain?'

Bob shrugged. 'More fool them.'

'Fools? These men are living legends.'

'Terry, your personal Hall of Fame is peopled solely by the great drinkers of our time – with Big Dave as the all-time great.'

'The first man to break the four-second pint,' said Terry reverently.

'Anyone who can sink twice the number of jars of the average man passes into legend - beyond the criticism of ordinary mortals. And when he dies, he no doubt staggers off to that Great Brewery in the sky.'

'While you, of course, will end up in the Heavenly Tea Rooms. Ah, well . . . ' Terry sat down and pretended to give up. 'What a disappointment.'

'It shouldn't be,' said Bob. 'You knew what *my* plans were, and besides, alcohol on top of these tranquilisers could be dangerous.'

'There are times, Bob, when you *have* to live a little dangerously. You can't go through life worrying about how you're going to feel tomorrow.'

'But I'm not worrying. I haven't got a worry in the world. I'm perfectly calm, relaxed and serene.'

Terry pursued his original thesis. 'I mean, if you did that, you'd never drink in case you got a sore head, you'd never eat in case you got a sore stomach, and you'd never make love in case you got a – sore back. You must live for today, the moment - keep something spontaneous about life. A sense of adventure, excitement. Agreed?'

'Absolutely.' Bob got to his feet.

Terry leapt up to face him. 'So what do we do?'

'Well, first,' said Bob, 'we'll put the kettle on to make the cocoa, and then we can have a game of Ludo.'

At 11.30 p.m. Terry gazed disconsolately at the remains of their game of Ludo that had been abandoned after extra time. There was an inch of cocoa left in the bottom of his mug. It was cold, but he drank it anyway. The lads would be tottering home from the Black Horse by now.

Bob pushed open the living-room door with his foot, and staggered in with two large suitcases, a pair of skis and a red anorak. He dumped them down by the sofa and sat down with a sigh of satisfaction.

'There. All packed. All done. No last-minute panic.

No last-minute rush.'

'You'd make someone a wonderful road manager,' said Terry sourly.

Bob favoured him with another tranquil smile. He was still sky-high and climbing. 'I just feel easier in my own mind – knowing I'm all done. All packed.'

'Should we get off to the church, now?' suggested Terry. 'To avoid a last-minute panic. Make sure we've got a good pew. I mean we've still got fifteen hours left, but the church *is* a good three-quarters of a mile away.'

Bob began to check his wallet. 'Passport, tickets, traveller's cheques, five pounds in kroner, five pounds in sterling. Yes, that should see us through . . . ' He looked up. 'What have you been doing?'

'Who, me? Oh, I've been sitting here beside myself with excitement waiting for the epilogue and the late-night weather forecast.'

'Would you like some more cocoa?'

'I'll cocoa you,' growled Terry. He slumped back into the armchair and crossed his arms.

Bob tossed a colour brochure into his lap. 'I thought you might like to look at our honeymoon holiday hotel.'

Terry dropped it onto the floor beside him. 'I think I'd rather play solo Ludo.'

Bob sat down again. 'Thelma and I have always wanted to go skiing – and Norway's so handy from here. Yes, this time tomorrow, we'll be in our centrally-heated double-glazed chalet with every modern comfort.'

'Aye, and by this time the day after, you'll be in your centrally-heated, double-glazed plaster cast.'

'Oh, I think I'll manage all right,' said Bob. 'Thelma and I have been doing the exercises.'

'Ahh, been at it already, have you?'

'The *skiing* exercises. For balance, poise and suppleness.'

'It'll end in tears, this honeymoon,' muttered Terry. He searched for something that would burst the balloon of euphoria with which Bob had surrounded himself. 'Yes, as soon as your poise and suppleness goes. Soon as you lose your balance, your honeymoon will be over. Just try making love in traction in twin hospital beds.'

Bob smiled. 'We'll just hold hands till we get better.' He reached down and retrieved the colour brochure. 'Here's the hotel – isn't it great?' He held up a double-page spread for Terry to see.

Terry refused to look.

'Yes, the dining-room boasts an international cuisine. There's a sauna bath, beauty parlour, and in the Troll bar, our guests from many lands can relax with an après-ski cocktail.'

'I suppose you know they have mixed toilets in Scandinavia,' said Terry. 'And showers.'

'Rubbish. Each chalet has its own private bathroom. We're completely self-contained.' He continued to read from the brochure. 'And for late-night revellers, the Viking Discotheque offers dancing till dawn to the latest in-sounds.'

'Not for limbless ex-skiers, it doesn't,' said Terry. 'You *do* know you are *bound* to break something, don't you? I mean, I know you fancy yourself as Robert Redford in *Downhill Racer*, but he's been at it since he was a kid.'

'I used to rollerskate.'

'A leg or a collarbone. It's usually one of those two, the first time out. Plus the frostbite, of course.'

'*I'm* not going to get frostbite.'

'You're in Norway, aren't you? Knee-deep in snow, aren't you? That's the kind of place you catch frostbite. Attacks the extremities. The appendages. Your fingers and toes – and all the dangly bits. Hardly the kind of thing you want to catch on your honeymoon.'

'For God's sake,' said Bob with a laugh. 'I'm going on a skiing holiday, not a polar expedition. To *Norway*. The Land of the Midnight Sun.'

'That sun is as warm as a frozen cod ball, mate. That brochure only talks about the centrally-heated *indoors*. It gives no clue to the hazards without. It avoids mention of the bottomless crevasses in the glaciers, the avalanches, and the packs of man-eating wolves.'

'Where do you get all this rubbish from? Biggles in the Antarctic?'

'Bob, there are no wolves at the South Pole. That only shows how little you know about what you're letting yourself in for. Why take unnecessary risks? You're going to spend most of your time giggling under the sheets, so why not spend your honeymoon somewhere safe – like Edinburgh? You're not going to get eaten by wolves in Princes Street.'

'Terry, I don't propose to get eaten by wolves anywhere.'

It was no good. Bob was fireproof on Level Seven. All on one Iron Jelloid.

Terry tried his last card. 'Well, don't blame me if you are. But, if you're lucky, and just *break* something, just remember that while you're in the Troll Bar with your plaster foot propped up on the counter, your Thelma will be out on the slopes trapped in the arms of a six-foot, nut-brown, Nordic ski-instructor.'

'I don't have any doubts about Thelma,' said Bob.

'Listen,' said Terry. 'You can't expect her to sit by your wheelchair all day. Not after what it's cost to rent two pairs of skis. She's going to be out there, mate – where it's all happening. The only time you're going to see her is when it's time to change your bandages.'

'Even so,' said Bob, quite unruffled, 'she's not going to start flashing it to every Tom, Dick and Sven the moment my back is broken – I mean, *turned*. What kind of a girl d'you think I'm marrying?'

'A very sweet, lovable, *loyal* person,' replied Terry. 'But that's got nothing to do with it. This is just something that happens to nice English girls when they get overseas. It's something to do with the air. Happens all the time, to all sorts of girls – even staunch Methodists. Even to my cousin Olive who was a Brown Owl and a sub-postmistress and who is now married to a Maltese chippy.'

'Thelma is an assistant librarian . . . ' Bob's tranquility

seemed to be vaguely troubled.

'Ah, now your intellectuals are *very* vulnerable,' said Terry. 'It was all in that *News of the World* exposé on English girls abroad.'

'You mean "Ecstasy – for export only"?'

'That's right. Once they bridge that short strip of channel, they drop everything – reserve, manners, morals – knickers.'

'But that article was all about the way they behave in the Mediterranean. There was no mention of *Norway*. It's too cold to go around dropping your knickers up there.'

'Norway's full of Norsemen,' insisted Terry. Everyone knows they like nothing better than to rape and pillage and carry off women – they don't spend *all* their time down at the factory tinning sardines.'

Bob's happiness was now distinctly clouded. 'I know that's all codswallop, but what *would* I do if I broke a leg?'

'There's only one thing you *can* do, Robert.'

'What's that?'

'Break Thelma's leg.'

Terry picked up his travel bag and went upstairs.

Undermined by Terry's predictions of disaster, Bob lay in bed and stared morosely at the white ceiling. In his mind's eye, it became a snowy slope across which Thelma tumbled in the embrace of a six-foot, nut-brown ski-instructor. Delilah . . .

Terry returned from the bathroom in his pyjamas. He put away his towel and toothbrush and looked down at Bob.

'I thought you'd be asleep by now.'

'Those pills don't seem to be working. I've never been so awake in my life.'

'Mmm, that's the trouble with those things. They can have a delayed action effect with some people. You're obviously one of them.'

'How do you know? asked Bob.

'It's a well-known medical fact. Hard luck too, 'cos there's nothing you can do about it. You'll just flake out when you're least expecting it.'

'You're supposed to offer me advice and comfort,' said Bob.

'Well, let's hope it doesn't hit you at ten past three tomorrow afternoon. "Do you take this woman to be your lawful wedded – zzzzz. Wake up, Mr Ferris" – I'd better arrange for a stretcher.'

'Maybe if I were to read for a bit,' suggested Bob. 'I could always go over my speech again.'

Terry sat on the bed. 'We should never have played Ludo. All that tension and excitement . . . '

Bob rifled through his notes. 'I'm not too sure about the toast-rack bit. Maybe I should take that out. Don't want to be too controver –'

'What's the matter?' demanded Terry.

'I thought I felt a yawn coming on. That's a good sign, isn't it?'

'Just close your eyes and go to sleep.'

'Well, if you'd get into bed, we could turn the light out,' said Bob.

Terry looked unhappy. 'Do I *have* to sleep with you? Why aren't I in the spare?'

'Because our Beattie's in the spare and she's got the door locked.'

Beattie was Bob's mother's elder sister.

'Well move over, then, and give me some room.' Terry got cautiously into bed. 'Shift your feet.'

'I've moved them.'

Terry lit a cigarette and wriggled down under the sheets on the extreme edge of the mattress. 'I'm not sure Thelma would approve of this.'

'She'll never believe what we did this evening,' said Bob happily.

'I can hardly believe it myself.'

'Terry.'

'Yes?'

'I don't think that was a yawn. I think it was just wind.'

'God save us . . . '

Bob switched out the light. They lay there for a while in silence. Terry stubbed out his cigarette and began to doze off.

'Perhaps I ought to take another pill.'

'Close your eyes. Just close your eyes, have a little fantasy and you'll soon be away.'

'I'll try. Goodnight.'

'G'night.' Terry turned on his side and buried his face in the pillow.

There was another short silence.

'I've had my fantasy,' said Bob.

'Yeah . . . ? What happened?'

'We won.'

Terry lifted his head. 'Won what?'

'Cup and League double. Four one at Wembley against Arsenal.'

'Good.' Terry fell back on the pillow.

'I'm still wide awake though.'

'Give yourself a chance. Go into Europe.'

There was another silence. Almost a full five minutes this time, then Bob sucked in his breath sharply.

'We're losing. Playing away to A.C. Milan.'

'Bring on a substitute,' murmured Terry sleepily. 'Pick yourself. That's what I always do. Score a goal a minute from the end.'

'We'd still only draw.'

'Oh, for God's sake!' Terry turned round irritably. 'Try something else. Have a go at one of the dancers on *Top of the Pops*.'

There was another and more prolonged bout of silence. Terry turned onto his side again and tried to sleep.

'I think I've got one.'

'Then keep it to yourself . . . '

'I've had this one before, but I never tire of it.'

'I'm tired of it already . . . '

'I'm on this white stallion, in a white T-shirt and white Levis on this long curving beach of white sand. Barbados, probably – or Montego Bay. Drinking rum. Tinkling the ice cubes round in this tall glass. And there's this girl coming out of the sea towards me –'

'Don't tell me,' said Terry. 'She's selling deckchair tickets . . . '

'No. Her long hair is streaming in the breeze. I can see the firm swell of her breasts, her flat, boyish stomach. She's naked except for a wide belt around her hips. And there's this big knife hung on the belt. She has long, beautiful thighs –'

Terry rolled onto his back. 'Long beautiful *bronzed* thighs . . . '

'That's right. I dismount and walk to the water's edge. The blue Caribbean laps the frayed bottoms of my sun-bleached Levis.'

'Go on.' Terry was now wide awake.

'We kiss, then fall to our knees and roll over in the white foam of the breakers, our wet bodies locked together in a passionate embrace.'

'That's not one of yours,' jeered Terry. 'You lifted that out of *Doctor No* and *From Here to Eternity*.'

'I put in the bit about the white stallion,' protested Bob. '*And* the frayed Levis.'

'Who's the girl – Ursula Andress ?'

'No, Thelma.'

Terry sat bolt upright in bed, leaned across Bob and switched on the bedside light. 'Why *Thelma* ? Why not a film star, or Miss Guyana, or – or anybody ?'

'Because I happen to love Thelma. Because I'm marrying her tomorrow.'

'I know *that*,' said Terry indignantly. 'But you can have your fantasies, can't you ? I mean, just because you love someone, they don't have automatic access to your *fantasies*. They don't own the sole rights. I never wasted one on *my* wife-to-be, *or* after! I mean, she was there in bed with me when I went to sleep, and she was there when I woke up, but in between she never got a look in.'

'What sort of fantasies *do* you have now ?' asked Bob.

'Well, I've allowed myself to be unduly influenced while judging the Miss World Contest. I've been on night manoeuvres with a platoon of Israeli girl soldiers, I've been a ski-instructor –'

'Watch it.'

'And I've been the new biology master at an exclusive girl's boarding school . . . ' Terry paused reflectively. 'Been having that one more and more lately . . . '

'Yes,' said Bob. 'Schoolgirls are beginning to worry me. I've even started to watch *Top of the Form* instead of *Top of the Pops*.'

'Mind you, I always like to balance things up with something nice and healthy – like winning the Cheltenham Gold Cup, or the Round Britain Milk Race.'

'Aye, well . . . goodnight.' Bob switched off the light.

'Forget about the fantasies,' said Terry. 'Just count sheep, or something.' He turned over onto his side, closed his eyes, and took Bob's place in the foaming surf. He drew the big knife from its scabbard and sliced the wide leather belt from Miss Senegal's dusky hips. There was no point in wasting a fantasy like this on Thelma Chambers.

Bob stared silently into the darkness until half-past three then switched on the bedside lamp and got quietly out of bed. Terry snored away happily. Bob put on his morning suit and top hat and stood in front of the mirror for a full-dress inspection. He checked the right and left profile, looked over his shoulder at his back view, then walked round to Terry's side of the bed and prodded him gently.

Terry slowly opened one eye, caught sight of the tall, dark form leaning over him and jerked back in fright.

'Jesus Christ!!'

'It's only me.'

'God, you didn't half give me a fright. I thought it was the bloody undertaker!'

'I'm sorry. Did I wake you?'

'Of course you bloody did! What the hell are you all dressed up for?'

'I can't sleep.'

'Is that what you woke me up to tell me?'

'I haven't slept a wink all night.'

'But what have you got your *clothes* on for?'

'I was having a dress rehearsal.'

Terry grabbed his wristwatch and saw the time. 'At *four* o'clock in the morning?' he screamed.

'Ssshh!! You'll wake everybody. I didn't want to leave it till the last minute.'

'Oh, Bob, for goodness sake, take off that stupid hat and come back to bed.'

'It's no good,' said Bob. 'I can't sleep.' He sat down at his writing desk, took out his wedding speech and rummaged through a drawer till he found a fountain pen.

Terry eyed him irritably. 'What the hell are you going to do *now*?!'

'SSShhhhh. Keep your voice down.'

'What are you *doing*?' hissed Terry.

'I'm rewriting my wedding speech,' whispered Bob.

'Can't you do that downstairs? Then at least I could have the light out.'

'I can't. If I disturb the cat, she'll start miaowing.'

'Sod the cat. Chuck her out.'

'Can't. There's too many Toms around.'

Bob tried the pen, found it was dry and found a bottle of ink. He began to refill the pen.

'Do you *have* to have all the lights on? Can't you use a torch – or your luminous rabbit?'

'What?'

As Bob turned to look at Terry, he jerked the bottle of ink over with the fountain pen. The ink flooded across the flap of the desk and poured onto Bob's striped trousers.

He leapt up with a cry of alarm. 'Oh, my God! Now look what you've made me do!'

Terry sat up in bed. 'Me? What have *I* done? I've just been lying here.'

'*Talking!*' said Bob angrily. 'Look at me!' He pulled out his trousers to display his ink-spattered crotch. 'What am I going to do?'

'Don't ask me.' Terry propped himself calmly up on the pillow to get a better view of Bob's discomfiture.

'But I *am* asking you. That's why you're here. As best man, you're supposed to handle taxis, telegrams and emergencies.'

'And the bridesmaids,' said Terry.

Bob flexed his knees experimentally. 'It's gone right through! The ink's gone right through!'

'Have you got any grey paint?'

'Why?'

'Well, you could try painting back the stripes.'

'Oh, Terry, don't muck about. What are we going to do?'

'*We?*' Terry got out of bed. 'I know what *I'm* going to do, white man – and that's have a drink.'

Terry borrowed a nearly three-quarters full bottle of Scotch from the Ferris' drinks cupboard and drove down to the all-night launderette with Bob.

Bob dumped his ink-stained trousers into one of the big Bendix machines, started the washing cycle and sat down to watch the process through the circular loading window.

Terry found two plastic beakers and sat down beside Bob. 'I knew I'd get you out in the end. The lure of the bright lights was too much for you. Here –'

Bob took the beaker and Terry topped it up with whisky.

'Why is it all foamy?'

'They use them to put the detergent in the machines.'

'Yukkkk. . . '

'Best I could find. The coffee machine's empty. Drink up – a bit of detergent'll give you inner cleanliness. Cheers.'

'Cheers . . . and thanks, Terry. Thanks for keeping me company and everything.'

'A pleasure, mate.'

'I'll put all this in my speech. At least it's bound to get a laugh.'

'What a night.' Terry shook his head in disbelief. 'Still, we're out on the town now, aren't we? Best launderette in the district. We can have a couple here, then go down to that new one in the High Street. You get fifteen minutes of steam pressing for 20p. We'll have a quick snifter there while you put the creases back in, then if there's any left in the bottle, we can have a couple of Irish coffees at that stall down by the Fish Market.'

'I feel a bit strange,' said Bob. 'Dizzy.'

'That's from watching your trousers go round and round. Face the other way.'

'I shouldn't have had that whisky on top of those pills.'

'You're right. You should have had the whisky *instead* of those pills.'

'I feel terrible.'

'So do I.'

'But today is the most important day of my life.'

'Yes,' said Terry. 'I only hope your trousers dry in time.' He filled up both beakers with whisky.

'Did *you* have a stag party the night before you got married?'

'A classic,' replied Terry. He was now beginning to glow a little as the water of life seeped into his system. 'In the true tradition which seems to matter so little to you. The record of that night is now enshrined in the history of the regiment. It was held in the Corporal's Mess. There was my lot, some Gunners, and a few Jocks from the Gordons. I had fourteen lagers, and a bottle of Schnapps before I lost count – and beat up a Bombardier. It was the talk of B.A.O.R.'

'The drink made you mellow, did it?'

'Taffy Lewis broke a fire hydrant, and Les Shillingford broke his arm falling off the roof.'

'What was he doing on the roof?'

'Looking for his motor-bike.'

'Of course. What else? Silly of me to ask.'

'We put a plank over from the roof of the garage and drove it up there. He tried to drive it down again but someone pulled the plank away.'

'Ahh . . .'

'Then all the lads grabbed me, pulled me trousers down and boot-polished me all over. Six hours before I was due in church. I had more shine on my bollocks than on my best boots.'

'My God,' gasped Bob. 'Did you get it off in time?'

'In time,' said Terry. 'But not in time for the wedding. Almost spoilt my honeymoon . . .'

As Terry drank a toast to the memory of that night, Bob slowly keeled over onto the line of seats.

'Bob –?' Terry put down the bottle of whisky and shook him. 'Bob!'

Bob slid onto the floor and the whisky in his beaker spilled over his face and shirt. Terry knelt down beside him and patted his face anxiously.

'Come on, mate, wake up, wake up. You're getting married today.'

As he continued to pat Bob's face, Terry became aware of a large pair of boots on the floor behind Bob's head. They turned out to belong to an even larger police constable.

'Ahh – good evening, officer.'

'*Someone's* been having a good evening by the look of it. Painting the town a little too red.' P.C. Plod inhaled the aroma of the whisky evaporating from Bob's face, and eyed the almost empty bottle of Scotch on the seat beside Terry.

'We haven't drunk all that,' explained Terry. 'It was nearly half-empty when we drove down – I mean, *walked* down here.'

'Oh, aye . . . What are you doing here, anyway?'

Terry nodded towards the foam-lined porthole of the washing machine. 'We're just waiting for his trousers.'

P.C. Plod went down on one knee and shook Bob. 'Come on, lad, pull yourself together.'

Bob didn't stir. He just lay there with a dreamy smile on his face.

'How much has this lad had to drink?'

'Hardly any. He's hardly touched a drop.'

'He's out cold.' Plod got his hands under Bob's arms. 'Help me get him up off the floor.'

Terry took hold of Bob's legs. 'He's not like this because of the drink, you know. It's the *drugs*.'

As soon as he'd said it, Terry *knew* it was the wrong thing to say.

The police cell was a clean, white-tiled affair with two hard, uncomfortable bunks. Central heating replaced blankets. Terry sat with his feet up and his back against the wall and watched dawn break through the bars.

Bob snored peacefully through the pre-dawn chorus with an expression of total serenity on his lovable chump chops. His eyes fluttered open at about a quarter to nine and focused slowly on Terry.

'Bye, that was a fantastic sleep.' He stretched and yawned a yawn like the Channel Tunnel. 'Has me Mam been in with the tea, yet?'

'No,' said Terry. 'Not yet.'

Bob rubbed the sleep from his eyes and stared at the bare light bulb in the ceiling. He frowned. 'Where's the lampshade gone?'

Terry watched as the alarm signals began to buzz through to Bob's brain. He jerked upright and felt the white-tiled wall. 'Where's my bedroom gone?'

'Relax,' said Terry. 'Don't panic. There's nothing to worry about.'

'Where are we?' squeaked Bob.

'We're in a cell.'

'What d'you mean – "we're in a cell"? What cell? Why?'

'We were arrested and are being held under the Emergency Powers Act, pending investigations.'

Bob stood up and rattled the door. 'Terry, for God's sake! You've got to get me out of here!'

'Relax,' said Terry. 'We're not in Death Row, you know.'

Bob tried to control his hysteria. 'But why are we here? What happened?'

'Sit down. Sit down and calm down. Everything's all right.'

Bob sat down.

'Do you remember the launderette?'

'Just.'

'Good. Well, you crashed out there just as your pants went into the rinse cycle. Your system collapsed under a mixture of Scotch, tranquilisers, sleeping pills and detergents. I was trying to pick you up off the floor when the Law came in.'

A look of alarm crossed Bob's face. 'Thank God I didn't have any of those pills on me. You didn't say anything about me taking them, did you?'

'Of course I didn't say anything,' said Terry.

'So what are they going to charge us with?'

Terry shrugged. 'Vagrancy. Disorderly conduct. Drunk in charge of a spin dryer. We'll probably be fined three packets of Daz and be ordered to have our Y-fronts endorsed.'

Bob looked at his watch. 'Terry, look at the time! Have you seen what time it is?'

'Bob, don't *panic*. I've already told them you're getting married today. They'll probably give you a motorcycle escort to the church. A motorcade with flashing blue lights and sirens.'

'I hope not. Thelma's mother would have a heart attack. She nearly fainted when a policeman checked my road tax once.'

The door to the cell opened and the Station Sergeant entered.

'Ahh, he's alive then, is he?'

'Just,' said Terry.

Bob coloured rapidly. He always did when in close proximity to the Law. 'I'm sorry, sir. I didn't mean to cause any trouble.'

'That's all right, lad. Go on, get yourselves home. We're not going to press charges this time.' The sergeant winked at Terry.

'Oh, thank you, sir,' said Bob, with what Terry thought

was an excess of subservience.

The sergeant walked with them to the front door of the Police Station.

'I don't know,' he said. 'You lads will never learn. If you're going to have a stag party, why not have it a few days earlier, then have a *quiet* night before the wedding? It's an important day, y'know.'

'I know, sir,' said Bob.

'The most important day of your life.'

'Yes, sir.'

'You don't want to turn up feeling terrible – like *I* did.'

'No, sir,' said Bob. 'I'll remember next time.'

The Sergeant gave him an old-fashioned look, then picked up a carrier bag from the station desk. 'I think these are yours.'

'Oh, God, of course! My trousers.'

'We dried them on the boiler,' said the Sergeant.

Bob took the carrier bag and pulled out a mis-shapen, shrivelled pair of morning suit trousers that might just have fitted Wee Georgie Wood. He stared at them in horror.

Terry grinned broadly. 'Now *that*'ll get a laugh at the wedding,' he said.

10

The End of an Era

When the verger of St Mark's arrived at the church on the Saturday morning, the first thing he did was to pin up a new, and strongly worded notice forbidding the throwing of confetti or rice within the precincts of the church.

He would have liked to add 'under pain of excommunication' but doubted his chances of getting that particular threat endorsed by the United Council of Churches.

Bob retrieved his car and a £2 parking ticket from outside the launderette, and rushed off with Terry to get a fresh pair of trousers from the dress hire firm.

Thelma was up in her bedroom busy making last-minute alterations to Susan's bridesmaid's dress. Susan stood there patiently as the pins were put into the various tucks, and kept one ear open in case Ed Stewart mentioned Thelma's name in his list of wedding requests.

Mrs Chambers came in with a tray of tea and toast.

'I thought you were going to lie in.'

'Heavens Mam, I couldn't sleep a wink.'

'Neither could I,' said Susan. 'Ow! Watch those pins!'

'Well, I never closed my eyes once. And your father's been up since six.' Mrs Chambers put sugar in the teas.

'What on earth has he been doing?' asked Susan.

'He's weeded the lawn and given the car a six-thousand-mile service. Not that it needed one, mind. It's only just come back from the garage.'

'Well, I'm determined to get this dress right,' said Thelma. 'That girl's got no idea how to make dresses. Turn round this way again – and hold your tum in.'

'It *is* in,' said Susan.

'Don't let your tea get cold, you two.' Mrs Chambers started on hers. 'I'm hoping this'll settle my stomach. It keeps turning over. Your father never touched his breakfast. He looked terrible – all dark shadows.'

'That's probably axle grease,' said Susan.

'Never seen him look so peaky.'

'It's just nerves, Mam' Thelma got up off her knees and took the pins out of her mouth. 'It's the excitement. Everyone'll be in a state today. I bet it's just the same at Bob's house.'

'I expect you're right, dear. Here, have a bit of this toast with your tea . . . ' Mrs Chambers' face began to crumple. 'It'll be the last cup I'll ever bring you –'

She fled from the room in a flood of tears.

'Poor Mam,' said Susan. She picked up her cup of tea.

'Yes,' said Thelma. 'Mind you don't spill anything on that dress.'

There was a similar low-key drama being played out in Bob's mother's kitchen. Surrounded by plates of cakes, scones, sandwiches and piles of paper napkins, Mrs Ferris sat dabbing her eyes with the end of her pinafore.

Bob's Aunt Beattie, a small energetic drop-out from a geriatric ward, bustled in with a sheaf of greetings telegrams.

'Oh, dear, what's wrong now?' she demanded of her sister-in-law.

Mrs Ferris sniffed and searched for her hankie. 'I've just taken him a pot of tea. I was just thinking – it'll be the last one I'll ever make for him . . . '

'Damn good job, too,' said Beattie. 'About time he learned to fend for himself.'

Mrs Ferris found her hankie and blew into it with a noise like a coaster's foghorn. 'Do you think I've made enough to eat?'

'Alice, they'll have eaten at the reception. There's only our lot coming back. There's enough here to feed the five thousand.'

'Well, there's Annie and Tot, Tom and Lil, Auntie Mary, Helen, Con and Les and all their youngsters. I did the jelly trifle for them. Then there's Wilf and Eileen –

and Great Aunt Olive, if she's up to it.'

'Right, you go on counting, I'm going to pop next door and get her cups what she's loaning us.'

'You're a tower of strength, our Beattie.'

'Haddaway with yer.'

'I don't know how you can do it. I can hardly stand on my own two legs.'

'Ah, well, that'll be the excitement, pet. I expect the lads are starting to feel it now.'

If they were, it didn't show on their faces. Bob and Terry sat in the front room in their dressing gowns, and stared blankly at the wavering but everlasting glow of the Berry's Magicoal fire.

Around them, on every horizontal surface, were spread more plates of cakes, pies and sandwiches, and the serried ranks of bottles made the bay window look like an off-licence.

'What time is it?' enquired Terry.

'Twenty past ten.'

'Don't have to leave here for another four hours, then.'

'Really?' Bob appeared to be sinking into a state of total inertia.

Terry eyed him. 'Isn't it time you started getting excited? Pacing the floor. Biting your nails. Wondering if she's going to turn up.'

Bob just managed a slight shrug of the shoulders. 'I don't care about it anymore. I suppose it's all those tranquilisers I took. I just feel – above it all.'

'You're usually hopeless in a crisis.'

'I know. But I feel calm and relaxed today.' Bob yawned. 'I even feel a bit bored.'

'Well, your mother's worried sick. When she brought our tea up this morning, she thought we'd eloped.'

Bob turned his head towards Terry. 'I hope you didn't say anything about –'

'I told her we'd been for a run round the park. What time is it now?'

'Twenty-*one* minutes past. Where's your watch?'

'I left it upstairs.' Terry picked up the newspaper. 'Is this all there is to read?'

'There's the church magazine in the hall.'

Terry sat forward in the armchair. 'Isn't there something we can be doing? Packing, or anything?'

'I did that all last night.'

'Well, how about unpacking to scc if you've forgotten something?'

'I did that last night while you were asleep.'

'There must be *something* we can do,' said Terry impatiently.

'You could always rehearse your speech,' suggested Bob. 'Or polish the ring.'

Terry stood up. 'How about a walk – or a game of snooker?'

Bob shook his head. 'I'm quite happy just sitting here contemplating the endless days of future happiness and nights of nuptial bliss.'

'God preserve us . . . ' Terry sat down again disgustedly.

'You could use the bathroom first, if you like. You can have your bath, then me Mam, then Aunt Beattie, then me. Or alternatively, *I* could go first and you could go last. I don't mind which. Or Mam and Aunt Beattie could go first, and then you and I could have our baths last – in whichever order you like. It's up to *you* really.'

'At least we've created *some* excitement,' said Terry sourly. 'I never knew it could be such fun working out bath rotas.'

Over at the Chambers' house, Thelma was having her hair combed out by Denny. Susan's hair was still in rollers.

Mrs Chambers went all round the house looking for her husband and finally found him out in the driveway underneath the family car.

'Excuse me, boys.' Aunt Beattie bustled into the front room with another tray of food.

'Please,' said Terry. 'Disturb us. We're just sitting here hoping that someone will get in our way.'

'Mrs Redhead from the corner has just brought round these lovely drop scones. Isn't that kind? You can tell they're made from real butter.'

Beattie looked around the room. 'I don't know where the hell I'm going to put them.'

Bob's mother came in with the lads' morning suits on coat hangers. 'I pressed these other trousers you got. In fact I pressed both suits again.'

'Don't press them any more, Mam,' said Bob. 'You'll burn a hole in them.'

'And I've run your bath. Water's hot. Away you go upstairs and don't forget to wash round it after.'

'Oh, Mam, there's hours to go yet.'

'I know,' said Mrs Ferris. 'But we've all got to use that bathroom.'

'I'll go up,' said Beattie. 'That'll be me out of the way.' She put the tray of drop scones on Bob's lap.

'Just stop panicking, Mam. Calm down. Go and iron your hat.'

Mrs. Ferris gave her ungrateful son a sharp look and followed Beattie out of the room.

'She'll be off to the hairdresser's soon. We'll get a bit of peace then.'

'*I* don't mind,' said Terry. 'I welcome these interruptions. Adds to the growing sense of excitement.'

'D'you want one of Mrs Redhead's drop scones?'

'Not really.'

'Mmmm, they *are* made with real butter.'

'What time is it now?'

'Eleven twenty. The car's calling for us at two twenty sharp.'

Terry consulted the newspaper. 'Do we have to leave that early? The 2.30 at Chepstow's on the box.'

'I'm not being late for a horse-race.'

'If you'd put your wedding back half an hour, we could have seen the 2.45 at Haydock Park. I've got a two-way bet on that one.'

'Never mind the 2.45 at Haydock Park,' said Bob. 'On a Saturday at this time of year, St Marks has couples under starter's orders every half-hour right through to 4.30 p.m. If you don't time it exactly right, you could end up with the wrong bride.'

'We're missing a fantastic Grandstand,' muttered Terry. 'Racing, a rerun of the Bugner-Frazier fight, League Cup Match with Warrington versus St Helen's, Mick McManus versus that 24-stone ex-Guardsman . . .'

'How selfish and inconsiderate of me to get married on a Saturday.'

Terry folded the sports pages away with a sigh. 'I expect you had your reasons.' He looked around at the roomful of food. 'What's that book behind you?'

'Teach Yourself Norwegian.'

'You what?' laughed Terry.

'Since I'm spending my *honeymoon* in Norway, it's as well to know a few useful phrases.'

'Like – "Help, help, I have broken my leg" – and – "My wife has run off with a randy ski-instructor".'

'Are you sure you won't have a drop scone?'

'No thanks.'

'*Nei takk.*'

'Beg pardon?'

'*Nei Takk*. That's Norwegian for "No thank you".'

'You'd do well to teach Thelma that one. Might come in handy during her après-ski lessons out on the slopes.'

In spite of the warning notice pinned to the board inside the porch of St Mark's, it had been snowing miniature pink and white rose petals all morning. By twelve o'clock, the desecration of the paths and surrounding grass was virtually complete, and the verger was considering the use of a flame-thrower.

Thelma and Susan now had their hair arranged in exuberant masses of backcombing, curls and ringlets, like two lady dancers from a formation foxtrot team.

Susan helped Thelma into her wedding dress. 'Are you feeling all right?' She began to zip up the back of the dress.

'Why – don't I look all right? I haven't got that rash coming back have I?'

'What rash?'

'On my back.'

'No.'

'I get it in times of stress. Like when Bob broke off our engagement for the first time – or when Dad fell through the greenhouse roof. And when Terry Collier came home again.'

'You're just as bad as Mam, the way you go on about that poor lad. Especially seeing you went out with him.'

'That was years ago, before I knew better.'

'Still . . . Turn around. You look smashing.'

Thelma helped Susan into her dress. 'When I went out with Terry Collier, I was going through the stage all young girls go through at one time or another – I still think these sleeves are too long.'

'They're just right. What stage?'

'When they want to be mistreated by someone coarse, and rough – and vulgar.'

'Yes, I know what you mean,' sighed Susan. 'I can hardly wait.'

Thelma zipped Susan into her dress. They both looked pretty sensational. They admired themselves in the mirror.

'Wasn't Bob coarse and vulgar once upon a time? After all, he and Terry did grow up together.'

'Oh, he was never ever anywhere near as bad,' said Thelma. 'And thank goodness, while Terry was away, Bob had the chance to develop as a person. The chance to mature, to become well groomed. Ambitious.'

'Ah, but is he as much fun as he used to be?'

'Just because Bob's placid and kind doesn't mean he hasn't got a passionate nature. You should've seen him on our under-30's Travel Club Holiday to Greece last year. After two rounds of Zorba's dance and half a bottle of *ouzo*, he was – well, quite – *untamed* is the only way I can describe it.'

'Always happens in the Aegean. You should have gone back there for your honeymoon. At least you wouldn't run the risk of frostbite on your first night.'

'Susan, Bob is not exactly a sexual novice, you know. He and Terry didn't spend their formative years playing ping pong in the Youth Club. Bob and I have known each other – very well, for a number of years, and I can assure you his performance is quite independent of the temperature of his surroundings. There'll be no problems in *that* department.'

'Well, don't tell Mam,' said Susan. 'Your white dress cost her sixty pounds.'

The two lads began to don their morning suits. Terry buttoned up his shirt and suddenly looked serious.

'Robert, is there anything you'd like to ask me? Any advice that I can offer at a time like this?'

'I don't get you.'

'Well, I *am* more experienced than you in these matters. I've travelled extensively, under more – rigorous conditions, and I *am* a married man.'

'Put your trousers on. I can't take you seriously with those legs.'

Terry reached for his striped trousers. 'Nothing wrong with my legs. They might have graced the turf at Wembley, had not fate struck me a cruel blow while in the service of my country.'

'Yes, yes, yes, we all know about that. I must say the wound's healed over miraculously. How about showing me that famous tattoo?'

'After you're married, Robert. After you're settled down. Only then will I show you what you have missed.' Terry buttoned on his braces then put on his waistcoat.

'What was your honeymoon like?'

'A time of great distress, Robert.'

'Where did you go?'

'Down the Rhine on a barge. Yes, on a barge down the

Rhine. Or up the Rhine. I can't remember. It was one or the other. I *do* remember the barge was full of Germans in *lederhosen* playing accordions and slapping their thighs and the soles of their jackboots.'

'What about the castles? They look fantastic in the pictures I've seen.'

Terry shrugged. 'When you've seen one *schloss*, you've seen them all. Then *she* got laryngitis, from the fog, probably, gave it to me, it pissed down all week, we rammed a jetty on the way back and all went home by bus.'

Bob paused half-way through tying his tie and looked at Terry sympathetically. 'You really *do* feel bitter about your marriage, don't you? About everything connected with it.'

'Aye, well, it's all water under the bridge now.'

Bob put his hand on Terry's shoulder. 'It shows, you know. I mean, I'm not blind to it. And on a day like this – which is a day of, well, great *joy* for me, I'm aware of your unhappiness even more.'

'Daft bugger . . . ' muttered Terry. He turned his face away from Bob's and checked the buttons on his waistcoat several times.

'What I'm trying to say is – well, I'm sorry you got such a bad break to begin with. But it *can* work. Maybe later – with someone else. But you must believe that. Otherwise you'll always have that – that chip on your shoulder, and you'll end up – well . . . '

Terry blew his nose twice, then eventually turned round to face Bob. 'I had a letter from her this week.'

'You mean, Jutta?'

'Yes. Ironical, isn't it? This week of all weeks.'

'What did she say?'

Terry shrugged. 'Wants to see me. Wants to talk things over. Wants to come over *here* and talk things over.'

Bob beamed. 'But that's marvellous! D'you think there's any chance you two might – ?'

'No, no, no, no,' said Terry hurriedly. 'Not a chance.'

'But she still wants to see you,' persisted Bob. 'There must be something, mustn't there? I mean if she's willing to come all this *way*. Some affection, some love, some feeling. Don't you want to see her and talk things over?'

'No, I don't,' said Terry.

'You mean it's too – painful?'

'No,' said Terry. 'Too bloody expensive. I haven't sent her allowance for three months.'

'Terry! How much do you owe her?'

'More than I can afford. Anyway, why should I? I'm not working, and Germany's a hell of a sight better off than we are. I don't see why *I* should have to send *them* economic aid!'

'But she might not be coming over because of that. She really might want to try and get it together again.'

Terry began to look irritable. 'Bob, look, just because you're getting married, you don't have to try and teach the world to sing in perfect harmony. I wish you and Thelma all the best – just don't start playing Marjorie Proops with *me*.'

'Sure, sure, mate, I understand.' Bob went to pat Terry on the shoulder again but Terry side-stepped and moved away to the mirror above the fireplace. He made a show of checking his appearance.

Bob gazed at his reflected image for a moment, then went to the sideboard and pulled out an old, leather-bound photograph album. He walked over to Terry.

'Here, I want you to have this.'

Terry looked down at the album then up at Bob in surprise. 'What d'you mean?'

'I want you to have it.'

'But that's your – your most treasured possession.'

'That's why I want you to have it. It's your present for being best man.'

'But – Bob . . . it means so *much* to you.'

'Yes, but there are two lives in here, and I'm only one of them. By rights, it should belong to both of us. You've said that yourself often enough.'

'I know, but I can't take it,' protested Terry. 'Not now. Not knowing how much it means to you.'

'Look, it would have been easy to go out and buy you a

pen and pencil set, or monogrammed cuff-links. This is given – well, from the heart . . .'

Bob held the album out. Terry didn't say 'Thank you', but he took possession of it as carefully as if it were the Lindisfarne Gospels.

As Bob and Terry arrived at St Marks, the Jamaican bride and groom in the 2.30 event were neck and neck at the wych gate with the runners-up obscured by a cloud of illegal confetti.

They watched them get into the white-ribboned car, then walked to the church past the white-faced trembling verger. Someone had emptied a box of confetti over him as he lurked behind one of the gravestones.

Bob and Terry took their seats at the front of the church. Quiet, tranquil music flowed through the reeds of the organ pipes.

'They have music like this in Air Iberia jets, just before take-off,' whispered Bob.

'Sounds more like Air Vatican,' said Terry. 'What time is it?'

'A quarter to three. Where's your watch?'

'Still upstairs in your room. We could have stayed at home, had another cup of tea and watched the 2.30 at Chepstow.'

'I think those tranquilisers have worn off,' said Bob. 'I've lost that numb feeling.'

'What do you feel now?'

'I feel as if I want to go to the lavatory.'

'You can't. They don't have lavatories in churches.'

'They do. I used to go before choir practice.'

'Spare me the sordid details. You don't really want to go. That's fear. It's all in the mind.'

'No it isn't. It's all in the bladder.'

'Tension, nerves. Happened in the First World War. In the trenches. Just before they went over the top. When did you put that plaster on?'

'Just after I said goodbye to the cat.' Bob held out his bandaged finger for inspection. 'I shut her in my sock drawer six years ago. Accidentally, of course, but she's obviously nursed a grudge ever since.'

'My cousin Martin got his arm scratched by a cat. Swelled up to twice its normal size – his arm. I mean. Some cats carry very nasty infectious diseases. Just an ordinary cat this was. Much the same as yours.'

'Thank you.'

'Should have had an anti-tetanus injection on the way here,' said Terry cheerfully. 'Still, it'll be well into the bloodstream by now.'

Bob looked at his watch. 'Thelma should just be leaving.'

'Oh, good. She'll know what won the 2.30 at Chepstow.'

'I doubt it. She hates horses.'

'She what?'

'Well, race horses, anyway.'

'That's more like it. I didn't think she'd miss watching Princess Anne at Badminton, or the chance of seeing Mark fall on his jacksie.'

'Terry, keep quiet, pack it in. The place is starting to fill up. Haven't you got anything to do? Shouldn't you be in charge of the ushers or something?'

'All under control. All organised.' Terry slid forward on the seat and stuffed his hands into his pockets. 'I'm not going to leave your side, Robert.'

'Sit up, sit up.' Bob looked back over his shoulder at the arriving guests. 'Who are all that lot? I don't recognise any of them.'

'All those on this side are friends of the bride.'

'No, they're not,' said Bob. *This* side is for friends of the bridegroom. But I don't recognise any of them.'

'Maybe we've got the wrong church.'

Bob began to rise in alarm. Terry pulled him back down. 'Relax. It's the hats. That's why you can't recognise them. Look, there's your Auntie Edie from Bishop Auckland.'

'Ah, yes.' Bob gave a little wave and sat back reassured. 'She gave us a salad bowl.'

'Teak?'

'No, cut glass.'

'She's had that on her sideboard for years.'

'It's an heirloom.'

'Your Aunt Lil's just come in.' Terry waved to her.

'Table mats. With "Scenes from the Hunt". Is Thelma's mother in sight yet?'

'No, otherwise we'd have heard the fanfare. People would have been prostrating themselves in the aisles.'

'Have you got a handkerchief?'

'What for?'

'To do conjuring tricks with. That's what for. Just give it to me, my hay fever's coming on.'

'No, it isn't. It's all in the mind.'

'Yes it is, and it's all in the nose. Give me the handkerchief.'

'Hang on . . . ' Terry pulled out his handkerchief, carefully removed a ball of chewing gum from one corner and stuck it under the pew.'

'I hope that's not the lump you had on the train,' said Bob. He blew a bassoon-like blast into the handkerchief, wiped his eyes, and removed the carnation from his buttonhole. 'It must be the pollen. Take yours off, will you?'

'What's the point? The church is full of flowers, and Thelma'll soon be sticking her great bunch under your nose.'

'My eyes are streaming.'

Terry unpinned the carnation from his lapel. 'It's probably the first symptoms of cat disease. First your nose, then your eyes – the brain'll go next.'

'No, it's just some kind of allergy.'

Terry brightened with a sudden flash of inspiration. 'Maybe you're allergic to marriage! Maybe you'll spend the rest of your married life sneezing and snivelling, and the only cure will be divorce.'

Bob sneezed by way of reply. Neither of them noticed Bob's mother and Beattie arrive in the pew behind them.

'You can get a quickie divorce in Mexico,' said Terry.

'All you have to do is live there two weeks. Mind in some countries, you only have to stay the weekend. And in Guatemala, I think you only have to send a letter enclosing a five-pound postal order.'

'But surely,' said Bob. 'That only means you're divorced in Guatemala. That's not much help if you're living on the Elm Lodge Housing Estate.'

'What are they talking about?' whispered Mrs Ferris.

'Bob's thinking of getting a divorce in Guatemala,' said Beattie.

'Oh,' said Mrs Ferris. 'I thought they were going to Norway.'

'No, that's for their honeymoon.'

'Ahhh . . . '

'Unless, of course, you want to live there,' said Terry. 'But I can't see that. Not with your hay fever and your terror of spiders.'

'Are they very nasty, the spiders in Guatemala?'

'Terrifying.' Terry leaned towards Bob. 'They can devour a guinea pig in a minute.'

'Do they only eat guinea pigs?'

'No, that's what they can eat in a *minute*. Something like a fox terrier takes a bit longer.'

Beattie leaned forward between them. 'Your mother wants to know why you're talking about divorce.'

'We're not,' said Bob. 'We're talking about Guatemalan spiders.'

'Aye, and they're that big.' Terry turned round with his thumbs locked together and his fingers arched outwards.

Beattie sprang back in alarm.

'What are they saying, our Beattie?'

'That there's some kind of spider as big as this.' Beattie spread out her hands.

'Doesn't surprise me,' said Mrs Ferris.

Terry tapped Bob's knee. 'And in Colombia, beyond the far, uncharted reaches of the Amazon, lives the deadliest animal in the world . . . ' He paused for effect and lowered his voice. 'The great venomous toad, an ounce of whose poison could wipe out the entire population of West Hartlepool.'

'They've got enough trouble down there with their beer,' murmured Bob.

Terry looked over Bob's shoulder. 'And speaking of venomous toads, here's Thelma's mother.'

Bob turned to smile sycophantically at Mrs Chambers as she took her place across the aisle.

She acknowledged their joint presence with a regal nod, then cast her eyes over the rest of the wedding congregation.

'She's wearing that smile of hers.'

'What smile?' asked Bob.

'As if she's about to unveil the new wing of the abattoir. What time is it?'

'I do wish you'd stop asking. Just gone five to three. She'll be half-way between Marshall's Plastics and the pickle factory.'

'And the race at Haydock Park'll be on. Coming into the last two furlongs. Come on Credo's Daughter . . . '

'Don't you have *any* sense of decorum?' asked Bob. 'Don't you think it's about time you composed yourself for what is about to follow?'

Bob opened the Book of Common Prayer at the appropriate page. 'See that? "The Solemnisation of Matrimony". That's what's about to happen. Something solemn and profound.'

'Yes, and I've got a solemn and profound five quid on Credo's Daughter,' said Terry. 'How can I take you seriously when you're snivelling into my hankie, with your eyes streaming and a sneeze up your nose?'

'It's clearing now. Here . . . '

Terry took his handkerchief back and took another look behind him. 'Looks like a good house. They're having to pack them in at the back. I must say Thelma's lot don't look a bundle of laughs.'

'Maybe,' said Bob. 'But they gave the best presents.'

'Our Audrey's just arrived. Bye, she cut it fine.'

'A dozen fish knives and forks.'

'What a mercenary sod you are,' muttered Terry. 'You look down the rows of pews and all you see are electric kettles and pop-up toasters.'

'Pam and Ivor.'

'You what?'

'They gave us a pop-up toaster.'

Terry eyed Bob with disgust. 'I don't know why your mother's upset. She's not losing a son. She's gaining a daughter and a department store.'

Podge Rowley trundled up to the lads, resplendent in his grey frock coat and striped trousers. 'She just arrived, Bob.' He winked at Terry.

'She's early.'

'Blast,' said Terry. 'That means she'll have left before the result of the 2.30.'

Bob gripped Terry's arm. 'Terry – '

'What is it?'

'I think I've lost the use of both legs.'

'Well, you were going to lose the use of them skiing, anyway.'

'This is no joke, man. I'm paralysed from the waist down. Seriously.'

'Nerves,' said Terry. 'All in the mind.'

'No, it isn't. It's all in the knees.'

Terry got his cue from the usher by the door. 'Here we go . . . ' He stood up.

'I can't, I can't.' Bob sat rooted to the pew.

Mrs Ferris gave him a nudge in the back. 'Go on, pet. Up you get.'

Terry hauled Bob to his feet and supported him by the elbow. 'It's just like a paratrooper taking his first jump Like Alan Ladd in *The Red Beret*. This is it. "Geronimo"!'

Terry walked Bob forward to the rail. 'I dunno, Ferris. Here you are on your wedding day, and you're still leaning on me.'

The organ struck up Handel's Wedding March, and the congregation stood up and turned to catch a glimpse of the bride as she passed by.

Thelma walked up the aisle on her father's arm. She looked as every bride should look on her wedding day – radiant. Holding her long train were the two kilted page-boys, Wayne and Dean, followed by Susan and Norma, her two bridesmaids.

'Terry,' hissed Bob. 'Promise me you won't let go.'

'I'm going to have to, Bob. You'll confuse the vicar. He'll think you're marrying me.'

Thelma arrived at Bob's side and smiled at him. And at Terry. Triumphantly.

There was no doubt about it, thought Terry. He was forced to admit that Thelma had been transformed by the occasion. Happiness had made her terrifyingly – well, there was no other word for it but – *beautiful.*

Like a female Guatemalan spider about to devour a miner's whippet.

Bob and Thelma emerged from St Marks to be greeted by a brief burst of sunlight and the cheers of their friends and relatives.

The photographer got in two or three fast ones of them on the steps, then he and his assistant went to work like a Welsh shepherd and his collie, rounding them up into tidy groups and chasing the breakaways back into line for the traditional series of wedding photographs.

There was every possible permutation.

Thelma and Bob.

Thelma and Bob, Terry and Susan.

Thelma and Bob, Terry, Susan, Norma, Dean and Wayne.

Thelma, Bob, Terry and Mrs Ferris, Mr and Mrs Chambers, Susan, Norma, Wayne and Dean squinting.

Mr and Mrs Chambers on either side of Thelma.

Thelma by herself, then flanked by Susan and Norma, then with Wayne and Dean with his tongue sticking out.

Then the same picture again without Dean's tongue sticking out.

Terry, Susan and Norma, with Susan holding onto Terry's arm very tightly, and almost cheek to cheek.

Mr and Mrs Chambers, and Mrs Ferris and our Beattie, then the same again with Terry pulling his old Man Steptoe face over Mrs Chambers' shoulder.

The formal portraits completed, the photographer switched to his 35mm SLR for a series of 'action candids' with daylight flash as Bob and Thelma ran the gauntlet of confetti that lead to the gleaming silver Rolls Royce.

The verger had managed to herd most of the confetti throwers outside the wych gate, but a sudden gust of wind swept the cloud of paper petals back over the wall and into his face.

The euphoria that had been triggered off by the warm burst of sunlight was increased by the lavish reception at the County Hotel, and the champagne which, if it did not flow like water, at least flowed like Moet and Chandon and not Asti Spumante.

When speech time came round, Bob got his first laughs with 'My wife and I', and by the time he got to the toast racks, they were rolling in the aisles.

Thelma looked at him adoringly.

'A lot of people,' continued Bob, 'said it could never happen, some said it *should* never happen, and at least *one* person, not a million miles from here, said it would only happen over his dead body. Still it *has* happened, and I'm glad he felt well enough to be here to share our happiness.'

Bob bowed to Terry amid general laughter, and Terry clenched his hands together above his head like a winning prizefighter.

'Thelma and I,' said Bob, 'are just knocked out by the wonderful presents, and everybody's good wishes and kindness, and we would like to express our special thanks to Thelma's mother and father for organising this marvellous reception. Bless you both.'

There was another round of cheers and applause which pleased Mr Chambers, and which Mrs Chambers acknowledged with her abattoir-opening smile.

'And apart from worrying what Terry Collier is going

o say in his speech, Thelma and I will remember this day as the most wonderful, happiest day of our lives. Thank you all very much.'

More cheers, applause, and the drumming of spoons on tables. Bob held up his hand for silence.

'And now, it is my duty, and my *very* great pleasure to propose the health of the bridesmaids. Ladies and gentlemen – the bridesmaids . . . '

Bob lifted his glass to Susan and Norma, and there was a ragged chorus of – 'the bridesmaids' as everyone replied to the toast. Bob sat down to another round of applause.

Susan squeezed Terry's hand as he got up amid total silence and surveyed the gathering.

Mrs Chambers leant towards her husband. 'It's been perfect up to now . . . '

'Give the lad a chance,' he whispered.

'A blemish on the whole proceedings . . . '

Bob grinned nervously at Terry and gripped Thelma's hand.

Audrey averted her eyes and prepared for the worst.

'Aye, well, ladies and gentlemen,' began Terry. 'I've had lots of instructions and advice on how I should make this speech – right up to a few moments ago, when Bob passed me a note on a paper napkin saying – "Don't mention Deirdre Birchwood" – there's no need to worry, Bob, I wasn't going to.'

'I knew it,' hissed Mrs Chambers.

Thelma's lips tightened as Terry drew a ripple of laughter from the guests.

'Bob also gave me a book on etiquette – and how to behave at a wedding. I know many of you here today feel I should be given a book on how to behave *anywhere*, and I'm aware that a lot of you are expecting me to tell a few jokes, a few anecdotes about Bob's and my own, so-called, sordid past. But what would that do? Only get a few cheap laughs and some blushes.'

Everyone was now listening with rapt attention and in complete silence. Terry reached under the table and produced Bob's photograph album.

'Bob gave me another book today. This one.' Terry held it up. 'It's a photograph album, and together with his autographed picture of Rhonda Fleming, it's his most treasured possession. I know that, because over the years, I've tried to beg, borrow or batter it from him without success.

'If you flick through it, it tells you all about his past – and about mine.' Terry slowly turned over the pages. 'There's one here of his fifth birthday party. I wasn't invited to that one. They didn't think I knew how to behave. But looking at the rest, there we both are – with our first Guy Fawkes, at scouts camp, school sports, Villa Park for an away match – we even got beyond the third round that year.

'Our first day at work, cycling through the Pennines – Bob's the one with the flashy waterbottles and the five-speed gear. And a classic – Bob with the Bronze Medal from the Filey Butlins Jiving Championships. Our first trip abroad. The Costa Brava – costa fortune. Me at *my* twenty-first, with his present – a silver beer tankard. Bob, at *his* twenty-first, with my present – another silver tankard.

'But you know, this is also a summary of someone else's life. Thelma's. She doesn't feature much early on. Her first appearance is in the school sports. And very sexy she looks too, in her singlet and baton. I remember she beat me in the Mixed Relay. But there are more and more pictures of her in these last pages, and by the time you've stuck in the wedding photographs, you'll need a new album . . . '

Terry closed it and turned to face Bob and Thelma. 'Bob, I know how much this book means to you, and, therefore, how much it meant in giving it to me. And I appreciate that gesture more than I can say – but I can't accept it. I can't accept it because this book is not just about Bob and Terry, it's about Bob and Thelma – and only Bob and Thelma from now on.'

Terry held out the album. 'Bob Ferris – "This is Your Life".'

There was a moment's silence as Bob took the book, then prolonged and thunderous applause, and cheer after cheer.

Audrey, Bob, Susan, and Mrs Ferris had tears streaming down their faces. Thelma looked on the brink of tears, and her mother looked as if she had undergone an incredulous and wonderful revelation like Saul on the road to Damascus.

Susan hugged Terry delightedly as he sat down.

'Here,' said Terry.

Bob took the proffered handkerchief, blew into it loudly, wiped away the tears, and almost put his left eye out with Terry's hidden ball of gum.

In the airport departure lounge, an eager crowd of would-be invalids were clustered round Gate E, dressed in woolly ski-caps, stretch pants and après-ski boots.

Terry and Susan had come to see Bob and Thelma off. They joined the crowd by Gate E and looked awkwardly at each other.

'What time is it?' asked Terry.

'Five to. Where's your watch?'

'Still upstairs in your bedroom.'

'Expect we'll go through in a minute,' said Bob.

'Yes . . . '

Thelma took Terry's hand. 'Thanks for everything, Terry. You were an absolutely smashing best man. Much better than we ever – I mean – '

'I know,' grinned Terry.

Susan squeezed his arm. 'Mam was over the moon.'

'And thanks for making things go so smoothly, and for that lovely speech – '

'And for giving me my album back,' added Bob.

'And for coming here to see us off.' Thelma kissed Terry warmly on the mouth. 'There. It's a long time since I did that.'

Terry looked embarrassed by this unexpected emotional reconciliation. Thelma looked at Bob.

'I'm just going to buy *Nova*, or something.'

'I'll come with you,' said Susan.

They went off to the magazine stall. Bob and Terry eyed one another. Bob grinned sheepishly.

'Well, I did it.'

'Aye. Home and dry.'

'Thanks.'

'I didn't do anything special.'

Bob smiled. 'I meant, thanks for *not* doing anything – well, you know. That speech . . . '

'I tried to be rude,' said Terry. 'But somehow it came out all – ' He shrugged.

'Listen,' said Bob. 'Anytime you want to come round and look at that album . . . '

'Aye, I know. But things will change now.'

'Yes, I suppose so. Different scene.'

'Parting of the ways.'

'End of the line.'

'You've got your life to live,' said Terry. 'I've got mine.'

'Nothing will ever be quite the same.'

'No. Time to move on . . . '

As if on cue, the flight announcement came over the Tannoy. 'This is the first call for Flight BKS 423 to Oslo. Passengers should now proceed through Gate E. Flight BKS 423 to Oslo, now boarding through Gate E.'

'Here we go,' said Bob.

Thelma and Susan came hurrying back. Bob gripped Terry's hand. 'Goodbye, mate.'

Terry held onto the handshake. 'Bob – I'm sorry I gave you a hard time. About the marriage, I mean. Stirring things up. Putting you down. That was just me and my hang-ups. What I mean is – I wish you both the very best. Marriage is what life's all about. That's why I envy you your happiness.'

Bob was unprepared for such a serious parting. 'Terry – what can I say – except thank you? I just hope that one day – who knows – perhaps there'll be *four* of us.'

'Goodbye, Terry.' Thelma took Bob's arm. 'Bye, Sue . . . '

' 'Bye – have a super trip.' Susan kissed them both on the cheek.

'What day d'you get back?' asked Terry.

'Tuesday week,' said Bob.

'Hey, there's a darts match that night.'

'Who against?' asked Bob, as Thelma steered him through the departure gate.

'Podge's lot at the Stick and Bottle!'

'Great,' called Bob, as he walked backwards. 'I'll pick you up at half-past seven!'

A doubt clouded Thelma's brow. It was a small doubt, but it persisted all the way from the terminal to the aircraft and through several rounds of duty-free champagne. Terry's wiry frame still seemed to cast such a giant shadow. Perhaps, she thought, nothing had changed after all. . .

Other BBC Books from television and radio

Quiz Books

Leisure

Rock Face

RON JAMES

An introduction to rock climbing which will appeal to beginners and more advanced climbers and also to the armchair enthusiast. Ron James gives expert guidance on the best and safest techniques, and advises on choice of equipment.

90p

Mr Smith's Gardening Book

ARTHUR BILLITT AND GEOFFREY SMITH

An introduction for beginners to the basic techniques of gardening, with advice on soil preparation, lawn care and the cultivation of shrubs and trees, flowers, fruit and vegetables.

75p

Flowers for All Seasons

An introduction to creative flower arranging by Richard Jeffery. It includes a full-colour illustration of an arrangement for each month of the year, and details of how to make them.

75p

Hammer it Home

TONY WILKINS

An illustrated step-by-step guide to home decorating for beginners which explains how to make good the walls and ceilings, how to hang wallpaper and lay carpets, and how to build simple furniture.

50p

Biography

A Child in the Forest

WINIFRED FOLEY

In this charming book Winifred Foley recalls her childhood in the Forest of Dean. A miner's daughter, she was brought up in a poverty-stricken village during the Depression, and she contrasts the harsh conditions she endured with the humanity and love shown her by her family and neighbours.

£2.25

The Edwardians

PETER BRENT

The Edwardian age produced many famous people, among them household names like Baden-Powell, Rolls and Royce, Conan Doyle and Lloyd George. This book contains biographical sketches of nine prominent figures from all layers of Edwardian society.

45p

The Love School

JOHN HALE

A story based on the lives and loves of Millais, Hunt and Rossetti, founder members of the rebellious Pre-Raphaelite Brotherhood.

40p

Children's Books